The Great Brain Race

The Great Brain Race

How Global Universities Are
Reshaping the World

Ben Wildavsky

PRINCETON UNIVERSITY PRESS   *Princeton & Oxford*

Copyright © 2010 by Princeton University Press

Published by Princeton University Press, 41 William Street,
Princeton, New Jersey 08540

In the United Kingdom: Princeton University Press, 6 Oxford
Street, Woodstock, Oxfordshire OX20 1TW

press.princeton.edu

LIBRARY OF CONGRESS CATALOGING-IN-PUBLICATION DATA

Wildavsky, Ben.
The great brain race : how global universities are reshaping the world / Ben Wildavsky.
p. cm.
Includes bibliographical references and index.
ISBN 978-0-691-14689-8 (hardcover : alk. paper)
1. Education, Higher. 2. Education and globalization.
3. Universities and colleges. 4. Competition, International. I. Title.
LB2322.2.W55 2010
306.43'2–dc22   2009052993

British Library Cataloging-in-Publication Data is available

This book has been composed in Adobe Garamond and Stancia Lyrica

Printed on acid-free paper. ∞

Printed in the United States of America

1 3 5 7 9 10 8 6 4 2

Contents

Acknowledgments / ix

INTRODUCTION
What Is Global Higher Education—and Why Does It Matter? / 1

CHAPTER ONE
The Worldwide Race for Talent / 14

CHAPTER TWO
Branching Out / 42

CHAPTER THREE
Wanted: World-Class Universities / 70

CHAPTER FOUR
College Rankings Go Global / 100

CHAPTER FIVE
For-Profits on the Move / 141

CHAPTER SIX
Free Trade in Minds / 167

AFTERWORD / 194

Notes / 199

Index / 221

IN MEMORY OF MY FATHER

Acknowledgments

This book would not have been written had I not had the good fortune to join the Kauffman Foundation in the spring of 2006. Carl Schramm, the foundation's remarkable president and CEO, has demonstrated repeatedly, by his own example, his desire to make Kauffman not simply a grant-making organization but also a place of ideas. Almost from the moment I started work, Carl urged me to write a book. Once a suitable idea took form in my mind, he offered me unstinting support and remarkable flexibility during the research and writing phases. I am deeply grateful for his encouragement.

My other great debt at Kauffman is to Bob Litan. I first met Bob over the phone when I was a magazine journalist seeking an expert to discuss an international trade dispute involving, I recall, Mexican tomatoes. Years later, after he became vice president for research and policy at Kauffman, Bob played a key role in bringing me to the foundation. His never-ending enthusiasm and creative energy helped launch this project, sustain it, and bring it to completion. Among other things, he read every outline and every chapter, offering valuable suggestions and support at each point in the process. In all the roles in which I have known Bob—journalistic source, recruiter, boss, and mentor—he has served as a wise sounding board and tireless intellectual guide. I am lucky to work with him.

Many other Kauffman colleagues helped along the way. Indira Dammu was a summer intern at the foundation in 2008 and continued working as my research assistant during her senior year at Indiana University. She kept assiduous track of new developments in global higher education and wrote research memos that I drew on extensively when writing the chapters on student mobility and world-class universities. Her efforts were indispensable. Mindee Forman helped get the book to the finish line. In the final months of the project, she performed last-minute research, checked and double-checked facts and endnotes on deadline, read the entire manuscript, and offered useful editorial suggestions—all with the good cheer, efficiency, and tech-savvy for which she is well known at the foundation. Alyse Freilich, a gifted editor, read large parts of the manuscript and improved it substantially with her suggestions. I was fortunate to get feedback from many others at Kauffman during an in-house work-in-progress presentation.

Kauffman associates provided other kinds of assistance, too, whether planning logistics for my extensive travels, connecting me to overseas contacts, suggesting interview subjects closer to home, helping with book promotion, or simply providing encouragement and brainstorming help. I thank all these colleagues, including Melody Dellinger, Norma Getz, Wendy Guillies, Tim Kane, Lesa Mitchell, Glory Olson, Margo Quiriconi, E. J. Reedy, Munro Richardson, Trayce Riley, Thom Ruhe, Dane Stangler, Bob Strom, Joy Torchia, Wendy Torrance, and John Tyler.

I have also been fortunate to find a second home as a guest scholar in Governance Studies at the Brookings Institution. I am grateful to Pietro Nivola, former head of the department, for bringing me on board, to his successor, Darrell West, for keeping me, and to a fantastic group of colleagues for providing helpful feedback throughout my book project. I benefited enormously from presenting my work at an in-house Research in Progress lunch, and from ongoing conversations with Governance Studies colleagues, including Sarah Binder, Bill Galston, Jonathan Rauch, Kent Weaver, and Russ Whitehurst. I had useful discussions with others at Brookings, too, including Bill Antholis and Belle Sawhill. Brookings' crack librarians, especially Sarah Chilton and Laura Mooney, helped me in numerous ways. Koria Davis, Ellen Higgins, Christine Jacobs, and other colleagues helped organize a launch event for the book. All in all, I couldn't ask for a more stimulating and congenial work environment.

I owe further appreciation to the Shalem Center in Jerusalem. Its president, Dan Polisar, generously offered me the use of an office as I was finishing my manuscript in the summer of 2009. This enabled me to spend a glorious summer in Jerusalem with my family while also getting a significant amount of work done. My research talk at Shalem on global college rankings, organized by Amichai Magen, managing director of academic programs, helped sharpen my thinking on the subject. Dan, who is embarking on a higher education initiative of his own with the creation of Shalem College, later took the time to review my manuscript page by page. The incisive critique he offered, on points large and small, significantly improved the quality of the final product. I'm especially pleased to have forged a professional as well as a personal connection to Dan, several decades after we became friends in our teens, and fifty-some years after our fathers met as classmates at Brooklyn College.

Thanks, too, to David Brady, Mandy MacCalla, and Deborah Ventura of the Hoover Institution at Stanford University, where in June 2008 I spent an enjoyable and productive week as a visiting scholar, the most recent in a terrific series of such visits in recent years.

Many others provided indispensible assistance as I worked on this project. Jamie Merisotis of the Lumina Foundation kick-started my research by getting me invited to a Shanghai conference that influenced my thinking considerably. There I met a number of higher education scholars who became valuable intellectual guides, including Phil Altbach and Ellen Hazelkorn. Checker Finn of the Thomas B. Fordham Institute gave me terrific practical advice about my trip to India. He also put me in touch with Anil Virmani and Viren and Nishi Madan, all of whom provided gracious hospitality in Delhi and useful information about the workings of the Indian Institutes of Technology. I greatly appreciate the help of numerous other individuals not quoted directly in the final manuscript who took the time to talk to me and, in some cases, to arrange valuable reporting visits. Among them were Desh Deshpande, Ludo Van der Heyden and his colleagues at INSEAD in Fontainebleau, Nicola Owen, Dan Stoll, and the staff of Tejas Networks in Bangalore.

Kevin Carey of Education Sector gave me the opportunity to road test my thoughts on global college rankings, first in the *Washington Monthly* and then at an American Enterprise Institute conference on accountability in higher education, which will lead to an edited volume. At the *Monthly*, I appreciate the editorial guidance of Paul Glastris, Charlie Homans, and Tim Murphy (who is living proof that fact checkers are the unsung heroes of the journalism world). Adrienne Burke, executive editor of the *New York Academy of Sciences Magazine*, commissioned an essay drawn from the book and was a pleasure to work with. I also want to acknowledge the fine journalists of the *Chronicle of Higher Education* and *Inside Higher Ed*, whose coverage of the ever-changing world of global higher education was indispensable to my knowledge of the subject.

Certain debts combine the personal and the professional. I thank Eric Patashnik, whose contributions ranged from offering moral support and superb editorial advice to giving last-minute PowerPoint assistance. My regular dining companions of many years, Vin Cannato, Ira Carnahan, Noam Neusner, Matt Rees, and Tevi Troy, tolerated my occasional angst, offered some bona fide book advice, and provided welcome comic relief. Others who offered ideas and help of all kinds include Bart Aronson, Cati Bannier, Rajika Bhandari, Julian Barnes, Roger Benjamin, Ulrich Boser, Corky Bryant, Richard Colvin, Andrew Curry, Pascal Delisle, Steve Denning, Liz Farrell, Rodney Ferguson, and the entire staff of Lipman Hearne, Andy Ferguson, Bruce Friedland, Richard Garrett, Darren Gersh, Madeleine Green, Terry Hartle, and Tim McDonough of the American Council on Education (for which I consulted in 2007 on a short writing project), Art Hauptman, Rick Hess, Anne Himmelfarb, Rick Kahlenberg, Helaine Klasky, Ron Machtley and the Bryant University board of trustees, Bill Meehan, Kris Mehuron, Ken Newbaker, Lynn and Steve Olson, M. A. Pai, Tony Pals, Steve Pelletier, Rafe Sagalyn, Peter Stokes, Barry Toiv and the Association of American Universities Public Affairs Network, Dan Troy, Alex Usher, and Richard Whitmire and Robin Gradison.

I had a high opinion of Princeton University Press long before it accepted my manuscript, thanks mostly to my acquaintance with its director, Peter Dougherty. Now direct experience has more than confirmed that impression. My editor, Seth Ditchik, was a wise, unflappable, and good-humored colleague and guide throughout the editing process. His hard work improved the book enormously. Joan Gieseke was the best copyeditor I could have asked for (or should that be "for whom I could have asked"?). Jessica Pellien applied her considerable energies to publicizing the book, while Shaquona Crews ably handled serial rights and Kathleen Cioffi efficiently managed the complex business of turning a manuscript into a finished book. Pam Schnitter created the first-rate jacket design and Tobiah Waldron crafted the helpful index. I also thank the anonymous reviewers who evaluated my manuscript and made many helpful suggestions.

This book is dedicated to the memory of my father, Aaron Wildavsky, an immense and much-missed presence in my life. The son of immigrants with limited formal education, he turned into a globe-trotting academic himself. I think he would have appreciated this analysis of the increasingly global nature of the institution that made possible his life's work.

As I worked on *The Great Brain Race*, I also thought often of my late mother, Carol Wildavsky. Born in Brooklyn, she became an enthusiastic citizen of the world and would have enjoyed the far-flung reporting that went into this volume.

I have been fortunate during two-plus years of research and writing to live in a house full of activity, warmth, passionate discussion, and enduring affection (with a healthy degree of chaos mixed in as well). For this, and much else, I thank my family. My three children, Eva, Aaron, and Saul, also assisted me in a very practical way: each spent time at my downtown office helping to bring order to my scattered files. They continue to bring me joy every day.

As for my wife, Rachel, it is hard to know where to begin. She is perhaps the best editor I know. She read the manuscript in its entirety and made numerous useful editorial suggestions. She also held down the fort with characteristic good humor and efficiency during my many foreign and domestic trips. She provided a steady stream of encouragement and reassurance as I tackled what has probably been the most ambitious project of my professional life. Above all, throughout our eighteen years of marriage, Rachel has made my life better in every way.

While I appreciate the considerable help I have received, any errors of fact or interpretation—and, of course, the book's conclusions—are mine alone.

Chevy Chase, Maryland
January 2010

The Great Brain Race

Introduction

What Is Global Higher Education— and Why Does It Matter?

At first glance, the Indian Institute of Technology (IIT) in Madras seems to be an incongruous place to witness the increasingly international reach of academic life. Nestled in a national park filled with deer and magnificent banyan trees, IIT–Madras's lush campus in southeast India looks somewhat remote and sleepy. But appearances can be deceiving. The institute's director, M. S. Ananth, has just returned from Davos, where he took part in an international higher education working group headed by Yale University president Richard Levin. The university guesthouse, where monkeys sometimes invade visitors' rooms if windows are left open, is hosting a range of foreign academics, including David Mumford, a prominent Brown University mathematician. Outside the campus recruiting office are sign-up sheets for students to schedule interviews with Google, McKinsey, and the like. And along the same hallways is a poster advertising scholarships to the King Abdullah University of Science and Technology, or KAUST, a brand-new graduate school in Saudi Arabia that is hurrying to become a world-class center of learning.

That KAUST seeks to recruit IIT graduates is no surprise—these students have become a prized commodity in the new global talent market. The IITs, a network of elite engineering schools that date back to India's postcolonial days, are celebrated for educating the nation's top students, including the cofounders of such pioneering high-tech firms as Infosys and Sun Microsystems. These prestigious schools admit less than 3 percent of all applicants. Indeed, the frenzy to gain acceptance is such that some students even leave home for one or two years at the end of high school, living in hostels while they attend coaching centers to cram full-time for the insanely competitive IIT entrance exam. The quest for victory takes on all kinds of unexpected forms. At one of the cram schools that dot a street near IIT–Delhi, a pie chart in the director's office spells out the secrets of success on the admissions test. It lists such conventional striver attributes as hard work, mathematical aptitude, and analytical skills. Then, without apparent irony, it throws in this crucial quality: "killer instinct." Still, rhetorical excess notwithstanding, the demanding selection and training of IITians, as they are called, has created an elite class both in India and beyond its borders.

What's more, the porous boundaries between the IITs and their academic counterparts around the world, along with the routine recruiting of their students by universities and employers from Hong Kong to Oxford, are by no means unique. In the worlds of business and culture, the globalization trend is so well known as to be cliché. But a lesser-known phenomenon, the globalization of universities, is equally important and has perhaps even more far-reaching consequences. For a burgeoning number of universities, national boundaries have become largely irrelevant. The same Saudi university trawling for top Indian students, for example, has also sought to catapult itself into the top ranks of world scholarship by forging alliances, backed by lavish funding, with the likes of Imperial College, London, and the University of California, Berkeley. And in another demonstration of international scholarly recruiting, KAUST's first president was poached from the National University of Singapore. For the new president, this move capped a globe-trotting career that has taken him from Asia to Canada to the United States and then back to Singapore before his new Middle East posting.

Few parts of the world have been untouched by the new university globalization. Singapore, for instance, has forged a role as a regional and even global hub for higher education, attracting institutions from around the world with considerable success. By way of illustration, a visitor to the renowned global business school INSEAD arrives at the well-groomed corporate-style campus an hour outside Paris to find that a scheduled interview with the head of the MBA program will take place by video conference. The dean, Jake Cohen, is in a conference room at INSEAD's Singapore campus, where he spends a significant portion of his time. Students can begin their studies at either site—"we don't make distinctions between the two," Cohen says—and demand for the chance to earn a degree by spending time on both campuses is high.

INSEAD's students are clearly prepared to embrace a life of transcontinental travel, as are the millions of others who move from nation to nation in search of educational opportunities. However, some students in the new borderless world of higher education can find the international educations they seek much closer to home. In Abu Dhabi, the Brooklyn-born president of New York University instructs a group of young students from the United Arab Emirates in the niceties of the First Amendment. And in Doha, Qatar, female engineering students in black *abayas* emerge from a colossal campus building next to banners reading "Welcome to Aggieland" because they are earning their degrees at a branch campus run by Texas A&M University.

Even at universities where there may be neither significant mobility of students and faculty nor a satellite campus, the influence of globalization is unmistakable, first and foremost through the movement of ideas. On the massive suburban campus of Shanghai Jiao Tong University, for instance, the many volumes on the bookshelf of the director of the university's higher education department include *A University for the 21st Century*, by former University of Michigan president James Duderstadt, and, of course, Thomas Friedman's *The World Is Flat*. In other ways, too, students and faculty at research institutions everywhere are conscious that they are in an academic competition that extends well beyond the campus gates. At Shanghai Jiao Tong, which has expanded rapidly from its original western Shanghai campus as part of a government-funded effort to reach international prominence, a banner near the dormitory buildings gives students their marching orders: "Work hard. Don't waste time. Don't waste money. For the nation and for yourself."

What does all this mean? Simply put, the global academic order is transforming in far-reaching ways—and not for the first time. Scholarly mobility has a long-standing tradition, dating back some nine hundred years to a time when students from around Europe flocked to the first universities in Bologna, Paris, and Oxford. The twentieth-century version of this phenomenon emerged in the United States, which, after World War II, became an unsurpassed magnet for students and professors from around the world. U.S. research universities are lavishly funded and house a vastly disproportionate share of top-ranked departments, elite students, Nobel Prize–winning professors, and cutting-edge laboratories. Borrowing from the groundbreaking model pioneered in nineteenth-century Germany, American institutions adapted and perfected the combination of teaching and scholarship under one roof, becoming the universally acknowledged masters of the modern research university. For the past half century, American universities have been the envy of the world—and may well remain so for decades to come.

But the same forces of globalization that have shaken up almost every sector of the economy have greatly intensified competition and mobility in higher education. In the new educational marketplace, more truly worldwide than ever before, an unprecedented number of students are traveling to universities outside their home countries. The United States market share, while likely to remain formidable for years, is slowly but surely being eroded by stepped-up competition from overseas universities, not only in the West, notably Australia and Great Britain, but also in the Middle East, Southeast Asia, Japan, and China. At the same time, popular Western universities are acting more like businesses—moving closer to their customers by establishing satellite campuses in Asia and the Middle East, and teaming up with overseas universities to forge strategic alliances that offer scholarly and marketing advantages to both sides.

Amid this rush of academic activity around the world, an even more consequential shift is taking place: increasing numbers of countries have an urgent wish not simply to send students to the United States, or to host "branch campuses" on their own soil, but to build world-class universities of their own. That desire explains why nations from China, South Korea, and Saudi Arabia to Germany and France are engaged in expensive and ambitious projects to create U.S.-style research institutions designed to be competitive at the highest levels. The progress of these new and improved universities is being measured, inevitably, by a burgeoning set of national and global college scorecards modeled in whole or part on the success of the controversial *U.S. News & World Report* rankings.

My goal in these pages is to chronicle and analyze the growing globalization of higher education in all its dimensions: the ever-more-intense recruitment of students and faculty; the swift spread of branch campuses; the well-financed efforts to create world-class universities, whether by upgrading existing institutions or by building brand-new ones; the innovative efforts by online universities and other for-profit players to fill unmet needs in higher education markets around the globe; and the closely watched rankings by which everyone keeps score. These rankings are increasingly taking new forms as they are refined to capture vital elements of the university experience, notably how much students actually learn while on campus.

Along the way, I will discuss the "why" behind this far-reaching phenomenon. There is no single why, of course, but rather a constellation of reasons: the quest to build knowledge-based economies that has led so many governments to scramble to improve their higher education systems; the notion that a well-educated person today must be exposed to ideas and people without regard to national boundaries; the enormous student demand for foreign degrees; the financial attraction for many Western universities of overseas students who pay full freight; the prestige that many colleges seek in international initiatives as they begin seeing themselves as global rather than purely local players; and the practical fact that better communication and faster, cheaper transportation allow people to teach, study, collaborate, and compete across national borders as never before.

But why does any of this matter? Because, taken together, these developments reflect the rise of a new kind of free trade: free trade in minds. As students and academics become citizens of the world more than ever before, the same kind of meritocracy that emerged in the United States when elite universities began talent-based admissions, drawing students from around the nation, is now beginning to take hold on a global scale. In this worldwide marketplace, more and more people will have the chance, slowly but surely, to advance based on what they know rather than who they are. When students and researchers traverse the globe with increasing ease and in significant numbers, and when universities compete ever more fiercely for the best minds, the trend toward a world in which talent can rise and reach its greatest potential seems unmistakable. Press accounts and academic articles have described individual aspects of this phenomenon before, but too little attention has been paid to the transformative nature of campus globalization as a whole. The academic mobility made possible by our increasingly borderless academic world will, like other kinds of free trade, bring widespread economic benefits, along with valuable intellectual ferment and tremendous opportunities for individuals.

For all its potential, the worldwide expansion of higher education has been accompanied by myriad missteps and problems, which any honest account must address. To name just a few, there are the numerous examples of satellite campuses that have fallen short of expectations or been closed; quality problems rooted in the difficulty of persuading home-campus faculty to venture overseas and the related reluctance of some elite schools to dilute their valuable brands by entering into international partnerships; the threat that substandard institutions will capitalize on the thirst for foreign degrees; the financial conflicts that can occur when recruiters are paid twice—once by the overseas students that seek university places and again by the universities that seek to enroll those students; and the controversies over free speech, women's rights, gay rights, and recognition of Israel that have erupted when institutions such as Berkeley, Stanford, and New York University have created new campuses or forged academic partnerships in the Persian Gulf.

But these difficulties should be viewed as the inevitable growing pains of a movement that is sure to gain ground, with huge social consequences. A bigger obstacle is the considerable alarm and hand-wringing sometimes brought on by the increased educational competition now facing individuals, universities, and entire nations. Some governments and universities around the world have responded to the growth of cross-border higher education with outright academic protectionism. Perhaps the two biggest culprits are China and India, which are notorious for the bureaucratic barriers they erect to foreign universities wishing to open new campuses or create new partnerships. Other nations focus not on keeping foreign institutions out but on excluding foreign students, and trying to keep domestic students at home. In Malaysia, the Ministry of Higher Education has gone so far as to place a 5 percent cap on the number of foreign undergraduates who can attend the country's public universities. In a contrasting twist on impeding student mobility, the president of one IIT responded to the huge overseas demand for his high-flying students by grounding them— he banned undergraduates from taking foreign internships.

Elsewhere, notably in the United States, scholarly mobility has been slowed or halted by visa policies that are typically not protectionist in any explicit sense but nonetheless have unfortunate effects. Stepped-up security reviews in the years since the September 11 terrorist attacks, while justifiable in some cases, have had the de facto effect of keeping out students and professors who would be an asset to U.S. universities and to the nation. At the same time, the stringent limits that have been placed on visas for highly skilled workers—in the name of protecting American jobs—have created an obstacle to attracting some talented international scholars, who often attend U.S. universities in the hope of staying on to work and in some cases to become permanent residents or citizens.

More broadly, an even larger barrier to the flourishing of global higher education is psychological: it can be seen in the widespread notion that a nation whose education system is on the rise poses a threat to its economic competitors. This phenomenon is, of course, particularly noticeable in the case of the West's fear about the rise of China and other Asian nations. It has become commonplace to fret, or even panic, about the alleged threat, both educational and economic, posed by the enormous number of science and engineering PhDs produced by those nations. This mind-set isn't necessarily linked to any explicit attempts to restrict academic mobility or, for that matter, to inhibit the creation of world-class universities around the globe. It might be considered simply a spur to greater efforts in the West on the grounds that developing countries are catching up in the global brain race. Its net effect, however, is to suggest that there is something worrisome about other nations' efforts to upgrade their teaching and research capacities, that the West may lose out when others move ahead.

But the globalization of higher education should be embraced, not feared. The worldwide competition for human talent, the race to produce innovative research, the push to extend university campuses to multiple countries, and the rush to produce knowledgeable and creative graduates who can strengthen increasingly knowledge-based economies—all of these trends are hugely beneficial to the entire world. *Increasing knowledge is not a zero-sum game.* Intellectual gains by one country often benefit others. More PhD production in China, for instance, doesn't take away from America's store of learning. In fact, Chinese research may well provide the building blocks for innovation by U.S. entrepreneurs—or those from other nations. "When new knowledge is created, it's a public good and can be used by many," says RAND economist James Hosek. Just as free trade in manufacturing or call center support provides the lowest-cost goods and services, benefiting both consumers and the most efficient producers, global academic competition is making free movement of people and ideas, on the basis of merit, more and more the norm, with enormously positive consequences for individuals, for universities, and for nations.

As the world's academic landscape is reshaped, traditional patterns of mobility, knowledge transmission, and economic growth are already being upended. A case in point: Several decades ago, some observers expressed much concern about the brain drain experienced by developing countries whose most promising citizens often departed to seek better educational opportunities and better lives in the West. More recently, however, this term has been replaced by "brain circulation" or "brain gain," as many of those who had left nations such as India or China begin to return home to seize opportunities in these countries' newly booming economies (including, especially in China, their revitalized universities). What the global university movement promises to do, as nations make sizable investments in education, compete to nurture human capital, and send students and researchers back and forth to universities around the world, is to go one step further: from brain drain to brain circulation to what might be called brain growth.

This isn't to say that global competition in university education won't create some winners and losers. No doubt it will. But again, as with other kinds of free trade, the net benefits will be significant. Three of the most important higher education trends of the last half century—mass access, growing reliance on the merit principle, and significantly greater use of technology—will all be accelerated by globalization. And there is no reason to believe that gains for one academic player will inevitably mean losses for all the others. Indeed, academic free trade may be more important than any other kind. All this has one clear policy consequence: nations around the world should move quickly to lower barriers, both practical and psychological, to truly global higher education. The trend will no doubt proceed in fits and starts, and it would be a mistake to be Panglossian about its positive effects. Nevertheless, while it is easy to become inured to the rhetoric of globalization, which seems to be on the lips of every ambitious college president, the trend is real and important. Ultimately, it holds the keys to sustaining the knowledge economy and advancing global prosperity.

Drawing on extensive research, including more than one hundred interviews conducted in India, the Middle East, Western Europe, the United States, and China, the chapters that follow detail the new universe of global higher education, argue for its crucial importance, and offer informed speculation about what the future holds for the worldwide marketplace of scholars and ideas.

Chapter 1 zeros in on the rapid growth of student mobility and the intense competition it has spurred among universities eager to expand their market share by recruiting the brightest minds (as well as the tuition dollars they bring with them). It describes growing faculty mobility, too, as exemplified by the efforts of universities such as the Korean Advanced Institute of Science and Technology and Italy's private Bocconi University to expand their horizons by hiring more foreign professors. And it traces the long history of academic mobility, beginning in the Middle Ages and continuing to the present. The chapter also suggests that mobility can apply not just to physical movements but also to the movement of ideas. Thus, the growing push for internationalization among universities around the world is a result in part of a changed worldview, in which institutions have come to see that their research competitors, and their potential collaborators, are no longer just regional or national but global as well.

Chapter 2 explores the phenomenon of branch campuses, almost all established by Western universities, which have proliferated in recent years, largely in the Middle East and Asia. There are now 162 such campuses, an increase of 43 percent in the past three years. One of the most audacious efforts to create a new overseas presence is New York University's plan to create a new campus in the United Arab Emirates, in Abu Dhabi. This chapter begins by exploring the challenges facing this effort, addressing the questions critics and supporters alike are pondering: Can an elite university's quality be preserved in a remote location? Will faculty, the heart and soul of a top institution of higher learning, be willing to teach halfway around the world? And can the academic freedom and other liberties that are taken for granted on Western campuses be sustained in the vastly different social and political terrain of the Middle East? The chapter also examines Education City, a lavishly financed facility on the outskirts of Doha, Qatar, that houses branch campuses of such U.S. universities as Georgetown University's School of Foreign Service, Northwestern University's Medill School of Journalism, and Texas A&M University. Branch campuses have already faced many challenges—including expense, controversy, and closure—and they are likely to face more. But the huge student demand for Western education suggests that universities are likely to keep seeking new ways to create some version of these unconventional outposts.

The book's third chapter probes the ways in which nations are expanding and improving their own universities—and in some cases creating new institutions from scratch—in an effort to create world-class campuses that can nurture human capital and compete with the best postsecondary institutions around the world. China, perhaps the most prominent example, has pushed to increase both the quantity of students and the quality of its universities. The total number of undergraduate and graduate degrees quadrupled from 1999 to 2005, while the government spent more than 30 billion yuan ($4.4 billion at 2009 conversion rates) on a group of forty leading universities in an effort to vault them into the top tier worldwide. India, too, is trying hard to expand its high-quality but miniscule elite sector—it recently embarked on a hasty and by no means smooth initiative to significantly increase the number of IIT campuses around the country. The chapter goes on to explore Saudi Arabia's ambitious plans to turn KAUST into a top-flight research university, one that is accessible to both men and women, and examines whether such an institution can thrive in the notoriously restrictive desert kingdom. Finally, it discusses how the world-class university phenomenon has taken hold in Europe, the cradle of Western higher learning. Germany and France, for example, with universities that remain popular with foreign students but have fallen far from their glory days, are busy trying to restore their academic luster. Governments in both nations have launched pricey initiatives to improve quality at a select number of institutions, in pursuit, like their counterparts elsewhere, of research excellence, innovation, and economic success.

Global education markets, just like other markets, need information to function effectively. In the fierce race to create world-class universities, a diverse collection of college rankings has taken on that role, spreading around the globe remarkably quickly and generating considerable controversy. Chapter 4 explores the new world of global college rankings, including the granddaddy of contemporary rankings, created by *U.S. News & World Report*, which debuted in the early 1980s and quickly became far more influential than any of the piecemeal efforts of the previous century. In the intervening twenty-five years, many other nations have followed the lead of *U.S. News*. More than forty countries, from Kazakhstan and Slovakia to Peru and Italy, have now developed some sort of ranking of their national universities, whether created by journalists, universities, government agencies, or nonprofits. But the biggest players in the university rankings game are Shanghai Jiao Tong University and the British publication *Times Higher Education*, which have created widely followed worldwide rankings that have come to be the arbiters of how well universities are faring in the global pecking order. Like the *U.S. News* rankings, the new global "league tables"—a term borrowed from European sports rankings—have garnered scorn and influence in roughly equal measure. Their methodologies are often critiqued, with justification, for significant shortcomings. Nevertheless, universities and nations often cite their progress or lack thereof in these global standings, either to trumpet their successes or to justify their demands for greater resources. At the same time, change is in the air. Institutions such as the Organisation for Economic Co-operation and Development (OECD) are in the midst of developing new global assessment measures that take better account of the outcomes of higher education, in particular how much students really learn while at university. Rankings are clearly not going away, but it seems inevitable—and desirable—that they will be considerably refined and improved.

Most of the world's prominent research universities are public, with the private nonprofits that dominate the U.S. elite sector being the most prominent exceptions. Chapter 5 takes a look at a less-discussed but fast-growing and influential sector: the private, for-profit institutions, from vocational colleges to full-fledged universities, that are playing an ever-greater role in higher education. This trend has a distinctly international dimension, as the same for-profit players that have had major success in the United States begin to take advantage of huge global demand. The chapter describes the expansion plans of firms such as Baltimore-based Laureate Education, an offshoot of the firm that created Sylvan Learning, a thriving private tutoring business; the Apollo Group, parent company of the office-park-and-online giant the University of Phoenix; and Kaplan, Inc., another academic preparation powerhouse now entering the higher education field. All are vying for market share with one another, or with domestic competitors, from Latin America to Europe to Asia. The common thread behind their efforts, which often entail buying existing for-profit institutions, is focusing on segments of the population that tend to be poorly served by existing state-run universities and offering career-oriented programs that appeal to students seeking a fast track to success. In many nations there has been considerable resistance to for-profits, partly on philosophical grounds—some critics view education as a purely public good—and also because of concern that for-profits' quality is uneven and that tighter regulation is needed. But whatever form the burgeoning industry takes, and whatever regulatory frameworks are imposed on these new institutions, their growth seems assured so long as the need they fill is so great.

The sixth chapter builds on the information and analysis in previous chapters to amplify and expand the book's core argument: that higher education has become a form of international trade—and that the beneficial principles of free trade should be applied to scholarly exchange just as to other parts of the global economy. With the development of an increasingly transnational higher education market, elite students now exhibit a global brand mentality in choosing the universities at which they pursue degrees. They use rankings and other sources of information to locate the best available scholarly destinations, with little regard to national boundaries. This worldwide marketplace is made possible in turn by the development of an academic talent pool selected more and more on the basis of meritocratic principles—giving some assurance to employers and graduate schools that university admissions and degrees were granted on the basis of academic accomplishment. Thus, the national admissions tests that have become institutionalized in nations such as India and China, while spawning unfortunate test-prep mania, have also advanced students' educational opportunities both at home and overseas. But even as obstacles to mobility have been lowered—half the top physicists in the world no longer work in their home countries—many nations still resist the idea that the global movement of talent is a healthy phenomenon. The chapter details why academic protectionism, immigration barriers, and fretting about the growing prowess of overseas universities have no place in a worldwide knowledge economy. After all, ideas may be the new currency, but there is no reason to believe that gains for one nation mean losses for the rest of the world.

Finally, the afterword underscores the benefits of academic mobility for individuals and for nations. It concludes that the economic returns of higher education are so significant that nations will continue to have powerful incentives to expand their university systems and to attract talented students and faculty from near and far. Whatever shape global higher education takes—and whatever challenges and setbacks it inevitably faces along the way—it is hard to imagine that it will disappear. Just as other forms of globalization have been resisted but never reversed, once barriers of distance, money, and attitudes have been overcome in higher education, students, faculty, campuses, and ideas are sure to continue circulating at unparalleled rates. That trend will bring continued academic advances, social change, and economic progress, which universities, political leaders, and ordinary citizens around the world will have every reason to welcome.

Chapter One

The Worldwide Race for Talent

When Claire Booyjzsen finished her master's degree at the University of Witwatersrand in Johannesburg, South Africa, the world was her oyster. Intent on pursuing a PhD in chemistry, she consulted global rankings of universities to identify some of the strongest. Then she conducted more research, corresponding with professors and students to narrow down her list. She ultimately applied to eleven institutions. After the acceptance letters came in, she traveled to Coventry, England, where she is now a third-year doctoral student at the University of Warwick, an institution where one in five students comes from overseas. "It's really multicultural here," says Booyjzsen, who works as a tutor in a student dormitory. "I've met people from all over the world."[1]

A relatively young university—it was founded in 1964—Warwick has become one of Great Britain's most sought-after institutions. It is also regarded as one of the nation's most entrepreneurial universities—and one of the most international as well. Warwick has systematically recruited students around the globe. In some instances, such as Booyjzsen's, its purpose is to search for talent; her studies are supported by a graduate fellowship funded by the university. In others, the search for international intellectual ability comes with a significant financial incentive (though the two are not mutually exclusive, of course). Almost all undergraduate and professional-school students from nations outside the European Union (EU) have "full pay" status. That means they don't enjoy the huge tuition subsidies received by British and other EU students—and thus represent a significant source of tuition revenues for Warwick and other universities that face declining state funding.

Warwick has attracted its international study body, at least in part, by establishing a network of recruiting offices around the world. Headed in almost every case by Warwick alumni, these outposts can be found in Beijing, Shanghai, Hong Kong, New Delhi, Singapore, and many other cities.[2] Warwick's vice chancellor, Nigel Thrift, notes that the university now attracts students not just from major "sender" countries such as India and China but from a total of 120 nations. He downplays the budget-balancing aspect of his university's recruiting efforts, highlighting instead how the large number of overseas students exposes British students not only to intellectual firepower but also to global diversity. "It's just an enormous asset to the way the university is," Thrift says. "It makes it into kind of a little world city. I love that."[3]

As Warwick goes, so goes the world: students like Booyjzsen have plenty of company. In recent years, international student mobility has been enormous—and consequential. Nearly 3 million students now study outside their home countries, a number that has risen steeply in a short period. From 1999 to 2009 alone, the number of students studying outside their home nations increased by 57 percent, according to UNESCO (United Nations Educational, Scientific and Cultural Organization) and OECD data reported by the Institute for International Education (IIE).[4] Methods of counting foreign students are imperfect and vary from country to country, but the magnitude of the trend is indisputable. Indeed, the UNESCO/OECD figures understate the amount of foreign study because they include only students who go abroad for more than one year.

Where are all these students going? Above all, to the United States—by far the world's biggest magnet for international students. The United States began to assume that role after World War II, and consolidated it with the flood of foreign students who came in the 1970s and 1980s to study at research universities that had become the best in the world.[5] Today, the U.S. market share of those 2.9 million[6] mobile students worldwide stands at 22 percent, according to a report by the London-based Observatory on Borderless Higher Education. That puts the United States far ahead of its closest competitors, the United Kingdom and Australia, which played host, respectively, to 12 percent and 11 percent of those students.[7]

The U.S. edge among graduate students is even higher: about two-thirds of all foreign graduate students worldwide study in the United States.[8] In certain fields, more than half the PhD students at American universities come from overseas: the percentages are 65 percent in computer science, 65 percent in economics, 64 percent in engineering, 56 percent in physics, and 55 percent in mathematics,[9] to cite the best-known examples. Indeed, a recent survey found that China's Tsinghua and Peking universities surpassed Berkeley as the top sources of students who go on to earn American PhDs.[10] One professor of astronomy at a top-ranked U.S. university describes having to resort to "affirmative action for Americans" in order to ensure that his program enrolls more than a token number of native-born doctoral students.

Where do all these international students come from? Of the 572,509 foreign nationals who studied in the United States in 2004, more than half came from Asia; the top five countries of origin were India, China, South Korea, Japan, and Taiwan.[11] China and India are the top source countries among Great Britain's overseas students, making up a combined 69,000 of the 318,390 foreign students who studied in the U.K. in 2005.[12] Similarly, India and China are the largest "sender" countries to Australia, which has become a major force in global higher education. It recruits students through an organization known as IDP Education, which has a network of over seventy-five offices in twenty-nine countries that hold education fairs and the like.

France and Germany, while relatively popular, are both considered secondary higher education destinations, and tend to attract students based on their own historical and cultural ties. A large majority of the 265,000 international students enrolled in French universities in 2006 came from Algeria, Morocco, and Tunisia.[13] Germany, which enrolled nearly 190,000 foreign students in 2008, up 82 percent over the previous decade, attracts Chinese students more than any other nationality. After that, Germany is primarily a destination for Europeans from nations such as Bulgaria, Poland, and Russia.[14] It has also attracted substantial numbers of Turkish students.

A Grand Tradition

Students of global higher education are unanimous in their view that more students move to more universities around the world today than ever before in world history. "The notion that students can move great distances today, going from nation to nation with great ease, is certainly unprecedented," says higher education scholar Daniel Fallon, an emeritus professor at the University of Maryland at College Park. "Going back only two hundred years, you had to have passports and visas to go, within a country, from one town to another. What we do today is ridiculously simple compared to that."[15] Nevertheless, while academe has never before seen such widespread movement of students and professors around the world, the history of Western universities has long been marked by student migration. "In the beginning was the Road," writes French historian Joseph Bédier, describing how the flow of ideas and knowledge in the Middle Ages was made possible by the roads linking ancient cities, which had become the sites of cathedrals and thus centers of learning.[16]

The first Western universities were located in Paris and Bologna, which began to flourish during what has been called the Renaissance of the twelfth century. Early universities began as scholastic guilds, typically attached to cathedrals, and were called *studia generale*. Eventually, they came to be referred to as *universitas*.[17] And it did not take long for a version of internationalization to follow. Just as contemporary students' journeys around the world have been vastly eased by the Internet and cheap airline travel, so too did their predecessors benefit from their own periods' versions of better transportation and communication networks.

The best early evidence for quite extensive student mobility can be seen in the formation of "student nations" in the early 1220s, in which university students from different parts of Europe joined together for "mutual protection and help according to their home countries or provinces."[18] Birthplace and mother tongue determined a student's membership in a nation.[19] At the University of Paris were four such nations—the French, the Normans, the Picards, and the English.[20] Still more diverse was the University of Bologna, which was home to nineteen nations, with students hailing from such disparate areas as Hungary, Poland, Spain, and Germany.[21]

What accounted for such early significant patterns of mobility at a time when this was far from the norm? Most prosaically, of course, students in areas without universities—Scandinavia, Ireland, and Eastern Europe, for instance[22]—had no choice but to travel if they wanted to pursue higher studies. "If you were interested in anything scholarly, you took off," says Fallon. Another incentive to travel in search of learning lies in a set of privileges awarded to traveling scholars in 1158 by Frederick Barbarossa, the Holy Roman Emperor. Known as the *authentica Habita*, these rules protected individuals traveling to foreign lands to study.[23] More broadly, churches and kings across Europe provided foreign students with financial assistance—call it the earliest version of today's scholarships—in the form of outright aid or inexpensive food and lodging. There was a catch, to be sure—in return for this assistance, students were expected to work for either the state or the Church.[24]

Then, too, world events had a role to play. Just as wars and revolutions in the past century have led to mass migrations of people and scholars, so the patterns of student movement in the Middle Ages were influenced by the happenings of the day. In 1229, for instance, students in Paris, enmeshed in disputes with local citizens, rioted violently (*plus ça change*, one is tempted to observe). The result? The king of France dissolved the university for six years, resulting in what one academic termed "The Great Dispersion" of French scholars.[25] The king of England, Henry III, like university leaders today who are constantly on the lookout for fresh talent, apparently saw the French contretemps as a recruiting opportunity—he welcomed the exiles from Paris into British universities.

In a similar parallel, just as various modern nations have fretted about brain drain, tried to keep more students at home, and, in some cases, erected barriers to their free movement across borders, so too did their counterparts in the Middle Ages. By the late fourteenth century, student mobility had declined, in part because countries devoted considerable resources to promoting local or regional educational opportunities. In addition, some countries passed laws that excluded from public office any students who had attended foreign universities.[26]

Still, as the sixteenth century dawned, academic mobility was once again on the rise. This new era of movement across national boundaries and exchange of ideas is personified by the travels of Desiderius Erasmus, the Dutch Renaissance scholar and Catholic theologian. Something of an itinerant student and academic, Erasmus studied at the University of Paris and the University of Cambridge. He also spent time at universities in Italy, Germany, Belgium, and Switzerland.[27] So renowned was his contribution to international academic exchange that some 450 years after his death, the EU initiated the Erasmus program, which is intended to facilitate such exchange between students and teaching staff in European universities.

For all the circulation of students and ideas that characterized the first six centuries of Western research universities, it wasn't until the nineteenth century that foreign students began to flock in large numbers to the country that would become the birthplace of the modern research university: Germany. The nation hadn't previously been a big draw for foreign students. On the outbound side, it sent several thousand students to Bologna and Paris from the thirteenth to fifteenth centuries.[28] But Charles IV significantly stemmed the flow of German students abroad by founding the University of Prague in 1347. (The new university was also an early instrument of meritocracy: "From this time on," writes historian Helene Wieruszowski, "education became a social leveler with the slogan 'career open to merit.'") By the beginning of the fifteenth century, the University of Prague was a distinctly cosmopolitan institution, attracting some 2,000 foreign students to its community of about 4,000 scholars.[29]

German universities became particularly attractive to foreigners—not only as a study destination but also as a model for replication—with the founding of the University of Berlin (later Humboldt University) in 1820. The father of the German university is widely considered to be Prussian education reformer Wilhelm von Humboldt, who was committed to the proposition that a university should be a place that encouraged scholars to conduct research without government interference.[30] As a result of their emphasis on advancing research while also promoting technical and vocational education, the universities in Berlin and other German cities emerged as major destinations for international students by the end of the nineteenth century.[31]

The numbers are not large by today's standards, but they made up a not-insignificant share of enrollment. In 1900, for instance, 1,750 foreign students were enrolled at German universities, accounting for 7.6 percent of all tertiary enrollment in the country. A few years later, those numbers had grown considerably, with particularly heavy enrollment from Europe. In 1910, 4,646 Europeans were studying in Germany. Half were natives of Russia, while others came from Austria-Hungary, Switzerland, Bulgaria, and Romania. German universities even drew students from parts of Africa and Asia.[32]

While many of the students initially drawn to Germany were European, Americans, too, soon became a significant source of foreign enrollment. In 1911, American students made up 4.6 percent of overseas enrollment at German universities. At the most popular institution for U.S. students, the

University of Göttingen, 22 percent of the student body was American. By 1936, overall U.S. enrollment at German institutions had grown to 11.5 percent before dropping precipitously in the run-up to World War II.[33]

Other nations certainly continued to attract overseas students, particularly England and France. In 1928 French universities enrolled a record 14,368 foreign students.[34] In the United States, institutions such as the University of Virginia and Williams College were in various respects modeled on French universities.[35] And throughout the twentieth century, exchanges abounded between U.S. and French institutions—the University of Paris, for instance, prepared a special course for American students.[36]

Nevertheless, the German model was uniquely influential. When American students returned home from their studies, they attempted to replicate these German institutions, which had pioneered the combination of research excellence and teaching, not to mention such bedrock concepts as academic freedom.[37] Perhaps the best known of the institutions created as a result was the Johns Hopkins University, founded in 1876. Hopkins aimed to be the first German-style university in America; this aspiration was exemplified by the fact that many of its founding faculty members were former students at German institutions. Other influential universities, including the Massachusetts Institute of Technology (MIT) (1860), Cornell University (1868), and the University of Chicago (1890), were similarly founded on German academic ideals.

Yet if the roots of today's American research universities can be found in nineteenth and early twentieth-century German institutions, the vast influence that U.S. universities have come to occupy in the global academic enterprise traces more immediately to the period following World War II. As at the universities of Paris, Bologna, Oxford, and Cambridge over the previous eight hundred years, overseas students started flocking to U.S. universities as they began to achieve worldwide renown. Once a critical mass of foreign talent was in place in America's halls of academe, those students in turn contributed their brainpower to further advancing the United States' intellectual reputation—a virtuous cycle marked by, and powered by, mobility.

The number of foreign students attracted to the United States was relatively modest before the Second World War, but it grew quickly, rising from around 10,000 in the prewar years to some 36,000 students in 1955, of which one-third were enrolled at the graduate level. A 1957 *New York*

Times article headlined "Foreign Students Choose the U.S." cited a survey released by the National Science Foundation that said the dramatic increase could be attributed to a combination of factors: "a reflection of the prosperity and influence of the United States; of financial support extended to foreign students by educational institutions, private agencies and both the United States and foreign governments; and of the achievement by educational institutions of an internationally recognized status that had been attained earlier by European universities."[38]

As Europe was rebuilding a devastated and demoralized continent, American universities moved from strength to strength. Graduate education improved significantly as the PhD degree was introduced and the position of assistant professor was created, permitting young faculty members to conduct independent research.[39] At the same time, support from the federal government permitted universities to spend previously unimaginable sums on scientific research. By 1961, U.S. colleges and universities devoted nearly $1 billion to research, a thirtyfold increase in just two decades.[40] Subsidies from the federal government accounted for 60 percent of this amount. Private foundations and industry contributed another 5 percent, while universities themselves made up the rest.[41]

These efforts came on top of a post–World War II effort to conceive of higher education as a tool for diplomacy and international cooperation.[42] Accordingly, the nation created several programs and scholarships to facilitate and encourage international student migration between the United States and other countries. Probably the best known of these efforts is the Fulbright Program, created in 1946. Senator William Fulbright of Arkansas, the architect of the program, said it was intended to serve as a "much-needed vehicle for promoting mutual understanding between the people of the United States and the people of other countries of the world."[43] Administered by the Institute for International Education, the Fulbright Program has seen tremendous growth. In 1953, a few years after its inception, 974 Americans traveled abroad for study. Five decades later, approximately 279,500 students and scholars have participated in the program.[44]

At the same time this "soft" diplomacy got under way, the advent of the cold war provided a major impetus to the growth of university science and engineering. Amid much anxiety about America's competitive status vis-à-vis the Soviet Union, the National Science Foundation (NSF) was created in 1950, entrusted with advancing basic research. When the Soviet Union launched the *Sputnik* satellite seven years later, the NSF refocused its efforts on turning more academic institutions into centers of research and development. It broadened its criteria for scientific grants, for instance, awarding them to colleges and universities that badly needed to replaced outdated labs.[45]

These concerted national efforts, combined with huge funding increases, only increased the momentum of international student enrollment. In 1963, a record 74,814 foreign students studied in U.S. colleges and universities, a 16 percent increase over the previous academic year. Engineering was the leading field of study, followed by the humanities, and natural and physical sciences. In addition, 8,377 foreign scholars—faculty and researchers—along with 8,804 physicians were present in the United States, participating in internships and residencies, respectively.[46]

U.S. dominance in scientific research grew throughout the 1970s and 1980s, serving to accelerate America's status as an international scholarly destination. The percentage of doctoral degrees earned by noncitizens swelled from 15 percent in 1972 to 26 percent in 1990, with far higher proportions in scientific fields. In 1986, foreign grad-school applications outnumbered domestic ones at Ohio State University, home to one of the largest student populations in the country.[47] While home to more foreign students than any other nation, the United States arguably has plenty of room for further growth: international students make up 3.5 percent of all students on American campuses, a considerably smaller proportion than in other popular "receiving" countries.[48]

COMPETING FOR STUDENTS AND FACULTY

While American dominance of the international marketplace seems likely to continue in the near term, its long-term prospects are less certain as the global quest for talent becomes ever more competitive. Already, the U.S. share of all foreign students worldwide has dropped significantly since the 1980s.[49] And according to a recent report from the OECD, the U.S. market share of international students fell still further, by 4 percent, from 2000 to 2005. This decrease hasn't translated into fewer students in absolute terms, because the pie is getting bigger—the same report found a 5 percent increase in the total number of students studying outside their home countries during the same period.[50] What's happening is that the rate of growth of overseas student enrollment at U.S. universities is not keeping pace with some of the nation's competitors. During the 1999–2005 period, for example, overseas enrollments in the United States grew by 17 percent. Foreign enrollment in British universities grew by 29 percent during the same interval, in Australia by 42 percent, in Germany by 46 percent, and in France by 81 percent.[51]

Even countries that have seen growing foreign enrollment worry that this trend may not last. In an October 2008 report, for example, the British Council warned that the rapid expansion of higher education in countries such as India and China means that universities in the United Kingdom will have a harder time attracting students from abroad. (The Council suggested that British universities need to concentrate not only on student recruitment but on partnerships and research collaboration as well.)[52] In the past decade, for example, the number of Malaysian students at British universities has declined by more than 36 percent, as other nations such as Australia successfully woo these students.[53] Worried about this decline in enrollment from some nations, then prime minister Tony Blair initiated a program in 1999 that called for attracting an additional 271,000 foreign students to the United Kingdom—a quarter of all foreign students studying in primarily English-speaking countries.[54] The primary motivation for the initiative, which Blair later extended, was not bringing in tuition revenues but maintaining academic and economic competitiveness.

With universities around the globe vying for market share, recruiting students and fostering overseas partnerships have become de rigueur. In the United States, this involves not only individual universities—some of which hire recruiters to market their institutions to prospective students, and then to enroll them—but also higher education associations and the federal government. The U.S. Department of Education, for example, led a delegation of college presidents to China, Korean, Japan, and India in 2006, then took another group of university leaders to Chile and Brazil in the summer of 2007.[55] Similarly, in June 2008 the Institute for International Education led a delegation of college presidents to three relatively undiscovered but fast-growing markets for new students: Thailand, Vietnam, and Indonesia.

Beyond the United States, other Western nations are also energetic recruiters of foreign talent. Australia, for instance, which is particularly reliant on fees from international students, recruits heavily from China, Singapore, Malaysia, and the Middle East. As a result of those efforts, Australia—a country with a population only a bit larger than that of metropolitan New York—has attracted nearly one-third as many overseas students as the United States in the past couple of decades.[56] Overall, 20 percent of students in Australian universities are from overseas—making higher education the nation's third largest export after coal and iron ore.[57] In Scotland, too, universities are eager to enroll students from beyond their national borders. Nearly half of graduate students—and 20 percent of all students[58]—now come from overseas.[59]

Recruiting foreign students is increasingly a priority for non-English-speaking countries, too. Many that have long been mostly "sending" countries now want to attract foreigners themselves. Singapore is hoping to attract 150,000 foreign students by 2015; Malaysia is seeking 100,000 students (up from 45,000 in 2005); and Jordan wants to attract 100,000 international students by 2020. China, which already has 196,000 foreign students, mostly from Asian nations such as Korea and Japan,[60] is now seeking to enroll 300,000 overseas students by 2020. Japan is especially ambitious; it aims to boost its current overseas enrollment of 120,000 to 1 million by 2025.[61]

At times recruiting has become controversial, often due to the widespread practice—particularly among British and Australian universities—of offering per-student commissions to "agents" hired by universities to attract students. In some instances, recruiters have been given fees both by overseas students eager for Western credentials and by the universities seeking such students, creating concerns about financial conflicts of interest.[62]

Student recruiting can be so relentless that some entrepreneurial nations have adopted unconventional tactics. Not to be outdone by Australia's recruiting success, New Zealand recently launched (and then withdrew) steamy viral Internet ads aimed at young Asians. One video showed a young couple locking lips in a hot tub. The camera then pulled back to reveal their disapproving parents looking on. The words "Get further away from your parents" appeared at the bottom of the screen.[63]

While a plurality of students who cross national boundaries to earn degrees in other countries are undergraduates,[64] student recruiting is particularly fierce when it comes to top graduate students. This is usually not because of the tuition revenues they will bring—many are supported by fellowships—but because of their contribution to the research enterprise. "The battle for the knowledge of the future lies in recruiting postgraduate students," says Ellen Hazelkorn, the American-born director of research and enterprise, dean of the Graduate Research School, and head of the Higher Education Policy Research Unit at the Dublin Institute of Technology. "If you assume that we're in the middle of a knowledge economy, then you need to ask the question 'What will produce this knowledge? Where does it come from?' One of the biggest contributors to knowledge is universities. So then you ask, 'Who in higher education produces the knowledge and where does it come from?' Increasingly most of the work is done by researchers and their teams—and their teams are PhD students."[65]

Hazelkorn notes that EU governments have set out to double the number of PhD students throughout the EU by 2010 in an effort to create what she terms "the biggest knowledge center in the world." This ambitious goal, combined with the limited number of domestic undergraduates likely to continue their studies, has led to intense efforts to enroll more overseas students, including scholarships designed to lure top doctoral candidates faced with many options. "There's an effort to counter the brain drain to the United States," she says.

The advantage to Great Britain and Ireland of offering overseas students an English-speaking environment is diminishing, Hazelkorn notes, as a growing number of universities on the European continent offer graduate-level programs in English. Now, she adds, universities eager to compete with American universities for top graduate students are retooling their PhD programs into something closer to the American model. That means moving away from the model in which "you sit at the foot of the philosopher king and you learn, which was the old traditional European model of PhDs," she says. Instead, European universities are creating a system in which cohorts of doctoral students take coursework and gain research skills of the kind that they will need to contribute to the knowledge economies in which they will participate once they have earned their doctorates.

Inevitably, the new global academic marketplace includes not just students but professors and university administrators as well. Perhaps the emblematic example of this emerging worldwide university culture is a professor of mechanical engineering named Choon Fong Shih. The son of a Chinese father and a Malaysian mother who emigrated to Singapore, he grew up in that nation, earning his undergraduate degree there before following a fairly conventional East-to-West pattern of academic migration. After traveling to Canada to earn his master's degree at McGill University, he moved to the United States, obtaining his PhD from Harvard in 1973. He led a research group at the General Electric Corporate Research Lab, then went on to a highly successful career at Brown University, becoming one of the world's most frequently cited engineering researchers.

But in 1996, after several decades in the United States, Shih reversed course geographically and moved back to Singapore to found a materials science institute at the National University of Singapore. His star rose yet again in 2000 when he became president of the well-regarded university. Eight years later, like a professorial free agent in the rapidly changing global education economy, he was recruited away to become the founding president of Saudi Arabia's KAUST.[66]

While journeys as numerous and distant as Shih's may not be taken by very many professors and administrators, his experience nevertheless illustrates the new patterns of faculty and research mobility that are beginning to emerge. Several administrators at American universities have taken senior positions at venerable British institutions, for instance, including two native Britons. Yale provost (and chemistry professor) Andrew Hamilton was nominated to become vice chancellor—the equivalent of president— of Oxford University in 2008. He took over from John Hood, an Australian who had previously headed the University of Auckland.[67] Another Yale provost, anthropologist Alison Richard, was recruited to become vice chancellor of the University of Cambridge in 2003.[68]

This kind of globe-trotting is seen as increasingly desirable outside the English-speaking world as well. Institutions that have traditionally had fairly homogenous faculties now actively seek international diversity. South Korea, for instance, has only twenty-two full-time foreign professors in its twenty-three public universities. In an effort to raise those numbers, the government is supporting universities in their efforts to recruit more foreigners. The nation's leading research university, the Korea Advanced Institute of Science and Technology, which is pushing hard to become a more cosmopolitan and competitive institution, recently recruited Mary Kathryn Thompson, an MIT mechanical engineering professor, to its faculty.[69]

The same patterns can be seen in other nations as well. In China, for example, despite the considerable flow of students and faculty to the West, as the nation's own universities try to become more competitive, there are more instances of scholars relocating to those institutions from other countries. Canadian-born philosophy professor Daniel Bell has made just such a reverse commute after a worldwide academic journey. Born in Montreal with French as his mother tongue, he earned a BA at McGill, went to Oxford for his M.Phil and D.Phil in politics, and took his first teaching position as a lecturer at the National University of Singapore. Several visiting fellowships and jobs later (at New York University, the University of Hong Kong, and the Center for Advanced Study in the Behavioral Sciences at Stanford, among others), the fluent Chinese speaker is now a philosophy professor at Beijing's elite Tsinghua University.

In Italy, which has experienced a much-lamented brain drain, Bocconi University in Milan is doing its part to reverse the trend by recruiting some of the best foreign brains to its campus: it aims to hire at least half its new professors from abroad by 2010. This private university generally uses English as the language of instruction and tries to offer salaries competitive with those offered by American state universities. Still, many bureaucratic obstacles—such as visa difficulties—remain.[70]

Despite such impediments, these faculty and student examples suggest that the globalized academic community is creating swirling patterns of mobility that don't always abide by the traditional developing-to-developed world trajectory. In a recent paper, researchers Rajika Bhandari and Peggy Blumenthal of the IIE describe the phenomenon as follows:

> Although there are no hard data to support this assertion, anecdotal evidence suggests that international mobility or skilled migration no longer follows a strictly linear pattern where people move between just two countries, typically from South to North. In an increasingly connected and flattening world, a student from Asia, for example, might choose to obtain an undergraduate degree in her home country, a Master's degree in the U.S., and a doctoral degree in the U.K., returning home subsequently to work for a European multi-national firm.[71]

Blumenthal, the IIE's executive vice president and chief operating officer, and Bhandari, the organization's director of research and evaluation, believe the terms "brain circulation" or "brain exchange" provide a more nuanced description of today's patterns of academic mobility and migration of skilled workers than the oft-used phrases "brain drain" and "brain gain."[72] In the same vein, the University of Toronto's Jane Knight offers another new shorthand for multination study and work patterns: "brain train." Because of this phenomenon, she argues, the higher education sector is becoming a more important actor in public policy, and is increasingly likely to work hand in hand with science and industry, notably the technology sector, as well as immigration authorities, "to build an integrated strategy for attracting and retaining knowledge workers."[73]

As student and faculty mobility takes new directions, the shape of the academy is gradually being transformed by international mobility, particularly among elite scholars. A team of University of Warwick researchers recently completed a study finding that half the top physicists in the world no longer work in their native countries and that three-quarters of young economists in top U.S. universities earned their undergraduate degrees in another nation. The study also found that the United States and Switzerland are the largest importers of elite scientists on a per capita basis. "Talented researchers," the study's authors note, "are being systematically funneled into a small number of countries." [74]

Further evidence of the extent and impact of faculty globe-trotting is collected in a 2008 OECD report, "The Global Competition for Talent: Mobility of the Highly Skilled." The report observes, for example, that Australia has experienced fast growth in the movement of researchers into and out of the country. "The number of academics and scientists entering Australia on a long-term basis rose from 1283 in 1995–96 to 4823 a decade later," it notes. Departures of scientists and academics also rose during the same period, but at a slower rate.[75] In the United Kingdom, a report by Universities UK highlights the significant role in the academic workforce now played by professors recruited from abroad. During the periods 1995–96 to 2003–4, 806 academic staff came to the United Kingdom from Eastern and Central Europe; 3,018 from Western Europe and Scandinavia; 1,926 from Australia, the United States, Canada, and New Zealand; 526 from China, Japan, and East Asia; and 678 from the Middle East and Central Asia. And in Norway in 2001, some 16 percent of academic staff in the sciences were citizens of other nations.[76] A long time may pass before there is any authoritative answer to the question of whether and how the nature of academic work and knowledge production changes when increasing numbers of students, faculty, and even presidents are crossing borders to study, teach, and collaborate, when campuses themselves are becoming increasingly internationalized, and when online learning is spreading rapidly. But in the near term, evidence is emerging that, at the very least, globalization is having some practical intellectual consequences.

For one thing, the research community is on the road more than ever before. Research is "a globalized activity," says University of Warwick vice chancellor Thrift. "Many of my colleagues here spend as much time going overseas as they do at home." Little wonder, then, that cross-border collaboration is going up. A July 2007 study by Britain's Office of Science and Innovation, for instance, found that in 2001–5, the percentage of papers by American scientists written with coauthors from other nations rose to 25 percent, up from 19 percent during the 1996–2000 period. The degree of international collaboration rose even more in Britain, growing from 29 to 40 percent between the two periods.[77] Another study, which examined 2.4 million scientific papers written at 110 leading American research universities from 1981 to 1999, found increased collaboration in general—as scientific teams grew larger—as well as a greater degree of international collaboration. The authors write that "placement of former graduate students is a key determinant of institutional collaborations, especially collaborations with firms and foreign institutions."[78]

Does all this interaction across national boundaries actually affect the quality of academic work? It is hard to think of a research methodology that could provide a definitive answer to that question, particularly given that growing global collaboration is a relatively new phenomenon. Still, evidence suggests that international research experience is at least associated with higher quality. Well over half the highly cited researchers based in Switzerland, Australia, Canada, and Italy have spent time outside their home countries at some point during their academic careers, according to a 2005 study.[79]

Beyond physical mobility, another far-reaching change is taking place as well. Increasingly, academic mobility can be understood not just literally—as comprising the travels of students, professors, and administrators—but also metaphorically, as a state of mind. Universities now think of themselves as institutions that not only compete globally with other universities but are also increasingly internationalized in their own operations and ambitions.

Take Stanford University, which, like many of its peers, is making a concerted effort to take stock of where it is globally—and where it ought to go. The 124-year-old university already has a substantial international presence on its own campus simply by virtue of its faculty and student body. About one-third of faculty members are foreign-born (some have become U.S. citizens), while around 7 percent of undergraduates and 30 percent of graduate students are from overseas.[80] Most foreign faculty members tend to be of European origin, while most foreign graduate students come from countries such as China, Korea, Japan, and India. As at other prominent American universities, foreign grad students are especially heavily represented at the School of Engineering, the Graduate School of Business, and the School of Earth Sciences.

Notwithstanding this facts-on-the-ground international representation in Palo Alto, Stanford's board of trustees decided several years ago that the rise of globalization warranted considerably closer examination, both of what was happening at universities internationally and of Stanford's place in this fast-changing landscape. It brought in the consulting firm McKinsey and Company to prepare background research that formed the basis for a two-day board retreat, the upshot of which was a realization that the trustees lacked concrete information about Stanford's own global activities. Roberta Katz, then the university's associate vice president for strategic planning, was asked to prepare an inventory of what Stanford was up to. "It was hard to say we should be doing XYZ in the future if we didn't even know what we were [already] doing in terms of ABC," she says.[81] Her conclusion? Without any particular planning effort, Stanford's faculty and students were engaged in numerous activities, large and small, that placed the relatively young university squarely in the midst of the global academic revolution "The simplest way to put it is that we have a thousand flowers blooming," Katz says.

In addition to the many international faculty and students on campus, Katz found that Stanford professors of all nationalities are heavily involved in cross-border scholarly activities. Some 80 percent, she estimates, have "some global aspect" to their research and are in regular contact with colleagues from other countries—by traveling abroad as visiting lecturers or by supervising graduate students and postdocs from abroad. One example of a partnership with far-reaching implications: in several departments, including applied mathematics and computer science, faculty members have been intensely involved with establishing Saudi Arabia's KAUST. In addition to receiving personal compensation and a multimillion-dollar gift to Stanford in return for their participation, Stanford professors anticipate ongoing academic relationships and research collaborations with the new Middle Eastern institution.

As part of Katz's review, the university also examined ways in which undergraduates are engaged overseas. Perhaps its best-known program, more than four decades old, is the Bing Overseas Studies programs, which sends undergraduates to more than a dozen countries. Students work under the supervision of Stanford professors (sometimes in conjunction with professors from universities in the host countries) and receive Stanford credit for what is typically an academic quarter overseas. To be sure, the program is far from an immersion experience. "It's us taking Stanford students to another country and providing them with more or less a Stanford education," says Katz. Still, she believes it is valuable simply by virtue of exposing students to the varying perspectives and cultures of another country.

So what did the trustees recommend following Katz's review? Their conclusion was, in part, to do nothing. So much globalization is under way that for the time being, "the consensus view is 'Let's not put too much bureaucratic infrastructure in place over this because it's happening,'" she says. At the same time, the campus leadership is eager to expand undergraduate opportunities abroad. "Getting our students to have a global mind-set, from an educational perspective, is very important to us," Katz observes. In an effort to encourage all undergrads to have some kind of global experience, the university is hoping to create more foreign internships, as well as more alliances with peer institutions in other countries. It also hopes to use an existing campus international center, which has thus far facilitated visas and programming for overseas students, to create more opportunities for domestic students and foreign students to interact with one another.

On the faculty front, while existing activities are numerous, sometimes communication is lacking. "Someone from the law school who is going to some province in China may not be aware that someone from the biology department is working in the same vicinity," says Katz. The university will attempt to open up better channels of communication between its seven distinct schools, and also to provide improved nuts-and-bolts support about everything from telecommunications to health insurance for professors who want to set up research projects in other countries. Philosophically, Katz says, Stanford is determined to use the term "global" rather than "international." That's because the word "international" might imply that Stanford sees itself, and implicitly the United States, as "the hub of the wheel," she explains. By contrast, she adds, "If you have a global perspective, you understand that there are many nodes on a global network."

Like other elite universities, Stanford must also consider the matter of expansion overseas. A key question: whether making aggressive efforts to extend its presence globally could undermine the very quality that has placed it in the top ranks of higher education worldwide. "There's a distinction between building a brand and being a quality institution," Katz says. "Creating strong presences in other countries or having borders lifted is not necessarily a wise move when you already have a very strong brand." The stakes are particularly high for an institution like Stanford, which has much to lose if its reputation is eroded. Katz maintains that it can hold onto the value of its accomplishments in Palo Alto while still becoming a global university—but not necessarily acquiring foreign real estate. "You don't have to have a campus" in another country to be part of a global network, she says.

As Stanford was formulating its approach to globalization, its task force members consulted with Yale University president Richard Levin, an economist who is regarded as a leader in campus internationalization. So it is no surprise that Stanford is in many respects following Yale's lead. Yale is moving aggressively to embrace globalism in many forms, from physical mobility of students and professors through study abroad and joint ventures with foreign universities to a related attitudinal change that encourages students at the New Haven, Connecticut, university to see themselves as global citizens. "We want to do a good job of educating students for twenty-first century leadership, and you can't be cross-culturally illiterate and be a twenty-first century leader," Levin says.[82]

A key plank in Yale's platform is to send more of its students overseas. Already, the number of undergraduates doing study abroad has grown from 400 to 1,200 in the past five years, a figure that continues to grow. Because many students are reluctant to abandon Yale's rich course offerings and campus life during the school year, the university is placing a particular emphasis on sending undergrads overseas for study or internships during the summer. At the same time, Yale has made a concerted effort to recruit more international students: In the past twenty years, the proportion has jumped from one in fifty undergraduates to one in eleven. This has the effect of expanding Yale's search for top students, previously focused almost entirely on the United States, around the world. Admissions officials regularly travel to India, China, and beyond. "We want the best possible students that we can attract," Levin says. "There's just a bigger pool out there than the national boundaries define."

Moreover, in addition to boosting Yale's academic caliber, Levin sees the increased presence of foreign students as a means of exposing their U.S. counterparts to diversity, not only in culture but also in worldview. "It's the only way that American kids are going to, without going abroad, get real opportunities to learn about how people from different countries think differently than we do," he says. The growth in overseas students "already is having a big impact," he adds. "Everybody who graduates from Yale has an international friend."

The university cares about fostering leadership, too, both nationally and internationally. "We want to have an impact," Levin says, and Yale's long-standing traditional of preparing Americans for public service must now be extended worldwide. "We're in an interconnected world today," Levin says. "We're proud to say that we've not only educated four of the last six presidents of the U.S. but [also] a former president of Germany, two prime ministers of Korea, and a president of Mexico. We'd like to see that grow."

Other parts of Yale's internationalization agenda, outlined in a detailed strategic plan for internationalization that was released after a year of study in 2005, involve forging a wide range of institutional partnerships around the world. On the research front, the strategic plan makes the case that lower communication costs and lower barriers to trade and investment have created "huge potential gains in research productivity." The plan notes that other universities with which Yale competes have major partnerships in China—Johns Hopkins University completed a $21 million, 100,000-square-foot building at Nanjing University in 2006,[83] for example, and the

University of Michigan is expanding its joint undergraduate and master's programs with fast-growing Shanghai Jiao Tong University.

Thus, competitive forces are driving Yale's own efforts. The university has long-standing ties to China, and those now include extensive collaboration with Chinese research universities. Two key examples: Yale's Joint Center for Biomedical Research at Fudan University in Shanghai, and the university's Joint Center for Plant Molecular Genetics and Agrobiotechnology at Peking University. Both operate, the strategic plan observes, "at a scale that would be difficult in the United States." That's because both represent the academic version of global free trade, Levin says. "Facilities and laboratory technicians are cheaper in China than in the United States," he says. "We have one scarce factor of production [in China], which is the sophisticated knowledge worker who is the leader of the enterprise, whose research design is driving the system. And we're talking about experiments that are large scale and require a lot of lab technician support and a lot of space."

While Yale is enthusiastically pursuing partnerships around the world, it has been far more reticent than some other universities about creating branch campuses overseas. It came close to establishing an art institute in Abu Dhabi, but pulled out in 2008 after its Emirati partners insisted that Yale grant degrees, which the university was unwilling to do. But Yale has been far more eager to spread its teaching across borders through a virtual initiative that provides course content free of charge on the Internet. Each course includes not only a syllabus, as with the Massachusetts Institute of Technology's Open Courseware program, but also high-quality video and transcripts of lectures, which Levin is eager to point out are not typically provided for MIT's courses.[84] Twenty-five Yale courses are currently available, a number that is projected to grow. Levin is well aware that simply putting courses on the Internet is no guarantee that they will be used. Accordingly, Yale is working with seven universities around the world that will either offer the classes with support from teaching assistants or adapt some material from the Yale courses in their own classes. "I think we'll go heavier in that direction than we will in the establishment of these branch campuses," he says.

Mobility, evidently, takes many forms, both real and virtual. And the possibilities offered by technology, while yet to be fully realized, seem likely to play a decisive role in expanding higher education both within and across borders. Already, as former World Bank and Whitney International University official Ron Perkinson notes, online higher education is growing more quickly than any other segment of post–high school education.

But inevitably, many uncertainties and quandaries lie ahead. For one, are university leaders like Levin wise to expand their offerings overseas through distance learning? Some analysts contend that an expanded online presence is an attractive way for elite universities to burnish their reputations (in contrast to the widespread view that creating branch campuses is risky for top colleges because of the risk that their prestigious brands will be diluted as a result of problems with assuring quality control in foreign settings). Simon Marginson of the University of Melbourne, for example, argues that MIT's Open Courseware initiative will enhance rather than diminish the value of an MIT degree. Similarly, he says that Harvard strengthened its reputation when it made all articles by its arts and sciences faculty available on the Internet. "All else being equal," he believes, "Internet (or any) circulation of materials attached to a high-status brand augments the status of that brand."[85]

That said, Don Olcott, chief executive of the London-based Observatory on Borderless Higher Education (OBHE) maintains that global distance learning would be expanding even faster were it not for persistent concern over its legitimacy. Foreign students and universities who are paying to receive the benefits associated with Western universities, including academic programs, research, and technology transfer, value real-time, in-person contact over virtual learning. They are saying, in his words, "We will pay, but we want the real deal, not virtual expertise." This distinction may gradually become more and more blurry, however. Olcott notes that even on-the-ground overseas branch campuses of Western institutions are integrating "blended approaches" that include online learning as part of their course-delivery menu. "Campus faculty do this every day now, and it has become normative practice," he says.[86]

As universities everywhere contemplate globalization and take steps not to get left behind, old mechanisms of mobility are taking on new forms. Chief among them is language, the sine qua non of cross-border communication. When Western universities were first created, as noted by Philip Altbach, director of Boston College's Center for International Higher Education, the lingua franca that allowed students and professors from diverse nations to study together was Latin, the language of the Church and thus of scholarship. Today, of course, the universal language of scholarship is English. Notwithstanding the exhortations in English-speaking nations—particularly the United States—for young people to learn other languages, the reality is that English is the key to university access and scholarly collaboration everywhere. Researchers have already calculated that nonnative English speakers worldwide outnumber native ones by three to one.[87] As a result, not only must Chinese and Chilean students master English to study at Anglophone universities, but universities in non-English-speaking countries are offering degrees in English to cater to Anglophone and non-Anglophone students alike. "When the French start offering a master's taught in English, you know the world has changed," says Peggy Blumenthal of the Institute of International Education.[88]

In this evolving world, foreign students who once would have been unable to study at a German university without knowing German can now, for instance, enroll in an engineering master's program at the Technical University of Munich taught entirely in English. Similarly, English-language degrees are available in Scandinavian nations where it is hard to attract international students willing to learn Norwegian and Swedish. French and Spanish universities have begun offering English-language degrees, and the phenomenon is small but growing in Italy, Blumenthal says. The European Commission's Erasmus Mundus program, which gives scholarships to non-Europeans to do graduate work in EU universities, recently produced a booklet highlighting eighty-nine master's and PhD programs—in seventy-five of which the language of instruction is English. While the program is off to a fairly slow start, and must overcome the pull of brand-name elite universities outside the EU, collaborative efforts between universities, combined with an accessible language of instruction, will eventually lure students, predicts Blumenthal's colleague, IIE president Allan Goodman. "That is going to create, both within Europe and between Europe and the rest of the world, a whole new level of mobility."[89]

LOOKING AHEAD

Will the steady growth in academic mobility that has taken place over the centuries, with its vast acceleration in recent decades, continue in the future? And will the United States continue to be the most sought-after destination for students and professors alike? Some observers predict that today's waves of border-crossing students will seem small before long: one study estimates that by the year 2025, 8 million students will travel to another country for educational purposes—nearly three times more than today.[90] One underlying factor is the rise in the number of countries that have made K–12 education mandatory, creating huge numbers of graduates seeking higher education. "The massification of secondary education means that there are a whole lot of students seeking postsecondary education," says Peggy Blumenthal of the IIE. Indeed, 153 million students are now enrolled at universities around the world, a 53 percent jump in just nine years. With many nations unable to keep up with this growing demand, students have strong incentives to seek higher education wherever they can find it. An extra motivating factor is the perception that global aptitudes—linguistic, cultural, academic, or all three—are more and more necessary. "It's pretty clear that people realize their careers are going to be global," says Blumenthal. "They're not going to work for one company their whole lives. And whatever company they work for will probably be owned by a variety of multinational actors."

In countries such as India and China, which already account for some one-third of the world's tertiary students,[91] mobility is especially likely to continue, particularly as student populations grow. Altbach of Boston College estimates that the two countries could make up more than half the worldwide growth in student enrollment. Postsecondary capacity is growing in China and India, but to the extent both nations can't keep up with student demand—both in quantity and in quality—they will continue to be the largest sending countries. "In both countries, the upper middle class that can afford to send kids to Western countries, particularly to the U.S., is beginning to send them in significant numbers for undergraduate study, because there aren't enough quality places in either country, especially in India, for smart and reasonably well-heeled undergraduate students who want a good education," Altbach says.[92]

Student mobility won't just be one-way, however. Both nations are also increasingly looking to foreign universities to come in as providers (although given its unfortunate protectionist history, the effort is very much in its embryonic stages in India). And they are likely to attract more foreign students to their own institutions. They do so for the same reasons as many of their Western counterparts—foreign students impart an added international character to campuses while also serving as a source of tuition revenues. India doesn't serve nearly as many foreign students as China—about 20,000, compared to China's more than 200,000—but Altbach believes both countries are increasingly likely to attract international students as their economic ascent continues and they begin to be viewed as centers of academic excellence. China is likely to draw mostly students from East and Southeast Asia, he suggests, while India will be an attractive destination for students from South Asia.

The prospect that China and India may draw students largely from their own neighborhoods dovetails with a theory floated by Don Olcott of the OBHE. "There may be a new 'regional globalism' emerging where we will see more and more student mobility stay regional rather than involving large global distances," he says.[93] True, many international students will continue to head to today's most popular destinations: the United States, the United Kingdom, Australia, Germany, and France. But the emergence of regional agreements such as the EU's Bologna Process, has introduced a new model as well.

The Bologna Process, also known as the Bologna Accord, began in 1998 with a small group of countries and now includes forty-six participating nations. It standardizes degree requirements across the EU, making it much easier for students to move between member nations for study and work. The Bologna Accord creates, in effect, an academic and employment free-trade zone. That, Olcott, suggests, will not only facilitate inter-Europe student mobility but will also make Europe itself "a prime destination" for foreign students. Indeed, one goal of the accord was to improve the attractiveness of European universities to students from outside the EU. Over the longer term, the Bologna approach could spread to regions such as East Asia and the Persian Gulf, which might well wish to reap the benefits of easy internal scholarly exchange (which could keep more top students close to home), a strong regional knowledge base, and a greater ability to attract students from outside the region.

While more mobility seems inevitable over the long term, obstacles will surely be encountered along the way. To cite a well-known example, the United States experienced a slump in foreign enrollment after the 9/11 attacks, largely because of heightened security measures and resulting visa difficulties for many students.[94] Enrollment recovered within a few years,[95] but world events continue to have a huge effect on student movement. A worldwide pandemic or political instability could quickly alter the extent and direction of foreign study. And, of course, the global financial crisis that began in 2008 has already forced some students to change their plans. The *Chronicle of Higher Education* cites the case of Indian student K. Archana, who graduated first in her class from Osmania University in 2006 and was admitted to two American PhD programs in microbiology in 2008. The Hyderabad resident shelved her plans to study in the States, in part because the combination of a stronger dollar and a falling rupee would have raised her tuition costs. What's more, she would have needed to borrow some $42,000 to cover tuition and living expenses at a time when the dismal job outlook made taking on such a high debt load seem highly risky.

Archana is far from alone. India is the second-largest source of America's overseas students, sending more than 94,000 students to the United States in 2007. Worldwide, some 90 percent of Indian students rely on loans, the *Chronicle* notes. But the battered economy has meant that many are not only anxious about taking on debt but also having greater difficulty securing loans for foreign study. That could mean fewer Indian students at American universities.[96]

Similarly, tens of thousands of students in South Korea dropped or changed their overseas study plans in the wake of the worldwide financial meltdown. In a nation where studying abroad is increasingly regarded as necessary for professional success, the rapid decline of the won—it dropped by one-third in the last few months of 2008 alone—led many students to abandon their overseas ambitions. This was particularly true for the large numbers of students who sought to go abroad not for advanced degrees but to enroll in short-term programs, often to study English. "The global economy has not been good to me," Kang Youn-mo, a twenty-four-year-old French major who canceled plans to go to Paris, told the *New York Times*.[97]

Still, the economic crisis has by no means ended the appeal of foreign degrees. When job prospects at home are dimmer than before, the attraction of study abroad may be greater despite the cost. Just as U.S. students head to business schools when workforce opportunities are limited, a similar phenomenon occurs internationally. Blumenthal of the IIE explains, "When there are no jobs in India or China, people will say, and are saying, 'I might as well take that time to invest in getting a credential overseas that will help my career.'" At the education fairs held by the IIE to attract foreign students to U.S. universities, recent attendance has increased rather than dropped. "The major sending countries are in Asia," Blumenthal says, "and in Asia, culturally, parents consider investment in education the highest priority. Whatever resources they have left they'll put into educating their kids."

Indeed, in China, so-called overseas-study fever has continued unabated despite financial woes. Unemployment among recent college grads is 12 percent, household savings are high, the yuan has risen dramatically against the dollar, and families are intensely focused on their children's education.[98] Elsewhere, the economic crisis has simply led students to alter their foreign-study plans in favor of less expensive destinations. South Koreans, for instance, are shifting their sights away from Great Britain and the United States and toward such nations as Australia, South Africa, Malaysia, and the Philippines.[99]

Whatever difficulties are encountered along the way, over time the trend toward a near-borderless academic world seems inexorable. Whether motivated by the quest for intellectual enlightenment, career success, or both, students are more and more likely to have academic horizons that spread well beyond their home countries. As students continue to hopscotch across nations, behaving, in the words of the *Economist*, like "educational shoppers" in the "global supermarket,"[100] changes large and small are well under way. Ironically, for instance, German universities to which Americans once looked for guidance now send regular delegations of rectors to the United States to learn how to "brand" themselves and to recruit internationally with greater success. For their part, despite rising global competition for students, American universities may see their market share grow still bigger. U.S. institutions by and large have yet to follow the lead of their counterparts overseas and use "agents" to recruit international students. The practice has been controversial in the United States, but a new nonprofit recruiting group hopes to destigmatize the practice by creating a new code of ethics to which all its members must subscribe. If that happens, the *Economist* predicts, "the market in international students will be transformed."[101]

But the influence of Western universities will not ultimately rest on the number of students they attract, considerable though that number has become. The very concept of academic mobility is being redefined. On the one hand is the proliferation of efforts by universities to set up branch campuses where their potential students reside. But a still more far-reaching form of mobility is the way in which the idea of the university itself is being exported. More than ever before, the Western research university is being replicated around the world by societies that have realized that the road to economic success runs through college campuses.

Chapter Two

Branching Out

After the recruitment of students and professors from foreign countries, perhaps the most visible symbol of just how much universities are bending over backward to cater to a worldwide market is their establishment of branch campuses, or satellite campuses, abroad. These campuses are quite different from the study-abroad centers sponsored for years by universities such as Stanford and New York University, which are intended primarily for undergraduates who wish to spend a summer, semester, or year studying in a foreign country. Instead, despite occasional cross-pollination between home and overseas student populations, branch campuses are typically intended to cater to students from the immediate area or region, allowing them to enroll in a foreign university without uprooting themselves from their home countries. Such campuses, usually but not always established by Western institutions, can now be found from the Middle East and China to Southeast Asia.

Why are these campuses becoming so popular? In part because of some practical facts: growing demand for Western-style higher education, rising incomes in foreign countries that allow families to afford these more expensive Western universities, and lower logistical barriers to home-campus administrators and faculty spending time at satellite facilities. Even more important is how these factors combine to allow universities to behave like for-profit firms in seeking new markets. Today's cross-border outposts are "a classic stage in multinationalization," the University of Warwick's Nigel Thrift says.[1] In classic firm theory, he says, the first international activity is trade with overseas partners, which in the case of universities might involve exchanges of students and professors. Next, Thrift says, for-profit companies "start producing subsidiaries in other countries"—much as Britain's universities of Nottingham and Liverpool have established campuses in China. While some in higher education may deplore this rhetoric of consumerism, when customers want what universities have to offer, universities will find a way to reach those customers.

Any new or expanding firm must face the prospect of failure, of course. That possibility is certainly on the mind of John Sexton, the exuberant and ever-candid president of New York University (NYU). Sexton, who is widely credited with an entrepreneurial zeal that led him first to vault NYU's law school into the nation's top ten during his years as dean from 1988 to 2001, then to do the same with the entire university since assuming the presidency in 2002, is now in the midst of creating one of the most ambitious and audacious overseas campuses in Abu Dhabi. When classes begin in the fall of 2010, NYU Abu Dhabi proposes to offer not just a boutique program or major, akin to those many other satellite campuses provide to overseas students, but what it calls "a comprehensive liberal arts and science college" that incorporates "the research and creative power of a major research university." This full-service undergraduate institution will offer a wide range of majors in the arts and sciences. Still, Sexton is quick to acknowledge in one of several interviews that the bigger they come, the harder they fall. "We're first movers, which carries with it inherent risks." Fortunately, he adds, unlike Harvard, Princeton, and Yale, "the one great thing about NYU is its willingness to take risks."[2]

That's a good thing, because Sexton is by nature an evangelist and an optimist. In an interview in his spacious office atop NYU's Bobst Library, overlooking Washington Square, he emphasizes the transformational possibilities of the campus he is creating rather than dwelling on risks. For starters, he bristles at the common term for universities' overseas outposts being applied to his new creation. "We don't call them branch campuses. We certainly wouldn't call them satellites." Instead, Sexton—who before attending Harvard Law School earned a PhD in religious studies—holds up the model of religious ecumenicalism, his point being that each component of the new global university he wants to create ought to be equally prized and legitimate. Thus, he dislikes "the subordination principle" that he says is implied in the term "satellite campuses," with the "mother ship" campus viewed as superior to the overseas branches.

By contrast, Sexton is intent on creating what he calls a "global network university," in which students can study at a number of major NYU campuses around the world. Some would be considered full-service "portal" campuses, where students who wished to could spend all four years earning their undergraduate degrees. Others would be variants on NYU's current ten study-abroad campuses, where students spend a semester or a year studying and soaking up a foreign culture before returning to their home campuses. He says that NYU may have as many as four "portal" campuses by 2010, when its Abu Dhabi site is scheduled to open. Along with Washington Square and Abu Dhabi, additional sites might include one in Europe, perhaps in Berlin or Florence (Paris was considered seriously but was rejected, Sexton says, because of the difficulty of navigating French labor laws), as well as another in China, likely in Shanghai. Once the global network is fully established, students could crisscross the world, spending, say, five semesters in New York studying film, then continuing with a semester in Europe, another in Asia, and so forth. Sexton also envisions two dozen or so courses that would be common to all campuses, capitalizing on technology that would allow NYU students in multiple time zones to take classes together.

The end result, he believes, will be to make students of this new global university true citizens of the world—and to set a model for the transformation of other universities as well. "I feel very strongly that the top universities in the world will not be location-bound the way the Oxfords and the Cambridges and the Ivies have been," says Sexton in an interview in a coffee shop at the Abu Dhabi Sheraton. "Of course, those universities have tremendous magnet power, and they'll be able to draw conversations and talent to them by their tremendous magnetic power. But there's a tide . . . 97 percent of the high school graduates in the world graduate from schools outside the United States. Of the students that study outside their country for college, we're down to only 20 percent of them coming to the United States. What is it that makes Americans think that a preponderance of the smart professors in the world will want to move to the United States?"

Part of the global impact Sexton has in mind for his latest pet project, the Abu Dhabi campus, as well as other NYU portals, is that his university and others will help transform the cities where they are located into "idea capitals." Urbanologists, he says, often use the acronym FIRE when describing the forces behind the twentieth-century development of cities such New York and London. It stands for finance, insurance, and real estate. Today, he argues, FIRE is necessary but not sufficient. A great twenty-first-century city must supplement FIRE with ICE—the intellectual, cultural, and educational assets that help turn a metropolis into a center of ideas.

The world is likely to have only a limited number of idea capitals, Sexton maintains—"there's only so much of that talent at the top"—and cities that want to be contenders must not stint with cultural and intellectual resources. "The top places in the world are going to need it all. They're going to need Lincoln Center. They're going to need the Met. They're going to need a couple of great research universities because they've got to create the critical mass at the top that then feeds down the talent pyramid," providing an incentive to improve such vital institutions as K–12 schools and community colleges. In the case of Abu Dhabi, the critical mass will include not only a branch campus of the Sorbonne, which began classes in 2006, and a research institute affiliated with MIT, but also several cultural institutions on Saadiyat Island, the future home of NYU's campus. The island will include a 670-acre cultural district that will feature such projects as branches of the Louvre and Guggenheim museums, and a performing arts institute.[3] Several renowned architects will be designing these institutions: the master plan for NYU's campus will be developed by Rafael Viñoly.

An idea capital doesn't come cheap, of course. The leader of the oil-rich United Arab Emirates (UAE), Sheikh Zayed bin Sultan Al Nahyan, has made a massive financial commitment to luring the universities and cultural institutions that the ruling family sees as vital to helping the Emirates prosper intellectual and culturally. Even before NYU agreed to launch its Abu Dhabi campus, Sexton insisted on receiving a $50 million gift from the Emirates that he termed "earnest money" to demonstrate the UAE's seriousness about the project.[4] With an endowment significantly lower than the elite East Coast schools with which it aspires to compete, NYU is particularly conscious of the need to make sure its expansion to the Gulf does not drain resources from its other ambitious project closer to home. So it is no surprise that the Emirates are covering all the costs for the Abu Dhabi campus, from construction of a short-term and then a long-term campus, complete with athletic facilities, student dorms, and so forth, to building research labs and paying generous faculty salaries. Hefty subsidies will allow NYU Abu Dhabi to offer student financial aid that is often as attractive as the scholarship packages provided by the most highly endowed Ivy League colleges.

All these resources are intended to guarantee quality—one of the biggest concerns of top Western institutions that branch out around the world. The new NYU campus will grant degrees that are indistinguishable from those offered to Washington Square graduates. Sexton aspires to have Emiratis make up only a fraction of the student body; he aims to lure perhaps 40 percent of the student body from the United States, with the rest coming from the Middle East, India (Mumbai is a two and a half hour flight from Abu Dhabi), and other locations within striking distance of the region. To help accomplish these goals, an admissions director, Renee Dugan, was hired in the fall of 2008 from King's Academy in Madaba, Jordan, a recently established elite prep school often called "Deerfield in the desert."

Sexton says he wants students not only to meet but also to exceed the demanding admissions standards at Washington Square, where about 24 percent of applicants were accepted for the 2008 entering class. "As we've talked about the admissions process, what we've said is that the students at NYU Abu Dhabi will be students who fit comfortably into the top 1 percent of the talent pool of the world," he says. "We think there's a case to be made, which will be quite attractive to a group of students that I call the 'cosmopolitans,' who get the value proposition of the most ecumenical education available anywhere, with a student body that is the most cosmopolitan anywhere, drawn literally from the four corners of the world, set in the Fertile Crescent, the classic crossroads of humanity when viewed from anything but an American perspective."

Sexton's vision may prove too grandiose to be realized even in part. But if the leadership of the new campus is a mark of NYU's seriousness about quality, it is certainly off to a highly credible start. In the fall of 2008, the university announced that it had hired Alfred Bloom, who had been president of Swarthmore College since 1991. It would be hard to find a better pedigree for the head of a liberal arts institution that aspires to be globally distinguished.

Still, even more important to a university than a high-powered president or talented students is the faculty. Thus, attracting high-quality professors is seen by NYU as a make-or-break proposition. "The quality of this institution will stand or fall by its faculty. If you can't get the faculty, you can't have a high-quality institution," says Mariët Westermann, a distinguished art historian and NYU–Abu Dhabi's provost, who moved with her family to Abu Dhabi for the 2008–9 academic year and became the university's senior representative on the ground as plans for the campus proceeded at a furious pace.[5] Bringing the university's best professors to the Gulf—and attracting other top candidates from the region or beyond—is vital to making sure that NYU's new campus is not seen as second-best, as has happened to some other branch campuses around the world. "You want to create a club that people from around the world want to join," says Sexton. Preserving the brand, in other words, is paramount.

While persuading professors to teach in Abu Dhabi might seem to be a hard sell, Sexton maintains his recruiting efforts are going well so far. "The faculty response is overwhelming," he says. Some professors are attracted to the idea of being part of a new and exciting entrepreneurial endeavor. Others are drawn to the region because of their research interests in, say, Islamic art or literature. The professors who make up NYU's advance team may have spouses who are simply adventuresome, or whose careers (banking, for instance) make a relocation to the Gulf relatively easy to manage. Moreover, many arrangements are possible that stop short of requiring professors to relocate completely to the Gulf—from taking part in short-term lecture series to one- or two-semester stints teaching regular courses. Beyond all this, of course, are the significant financial incentives available to faculty in Abu Dhabi, including the standard expatriate benefits of salary supplements (NYU declines to specify their exact amount), subsidized housing, free private school tuition for children, and an annual business-class trip back home.[6] Sexton and other NYU officials insist, though, that many professors will be attracted to Abu Dhabi not by money and other benefits but by professional opportunities, from extensive lab facilities not available in Washington Square to the chance for interdisciplinary and global collaboration not found as easily in New York.

Sexton himself is leading by example, augmenting his presidential duties in Washington Square by teaching what amounts to a prequel class to NYU's nascent program, a seminar on the First Amendment offered to a handpicked group of Emirati students. On a balmy evening in November 2008, Sexton arrived in Dubai with his chief of staff, Diane Yu, after a twelve-hour and forty-five-minute flight from New York in the first class section of Emirates, the airline of the UAE. Following the two-hour drive to Abu Dhabi, he sat down for a late-night dinner with a few colleagues and Democratic political analyst Bob Shrum and his wife, Mary-Louise Oates. Shrum, a lifelong friend of Sexton's, was in town to participate in a panel discussion dissecting the results of the recent U.S. presidential elections, to be held the following evening under the auspices of the NYU Abu Dhabi Institute. The institute began establishing an NYU presence in Abu Dhabi through a series of public lectures and cultural events, long before the first one hundred or so students (out of a target student body of 2000) are projected to begin classes in the fall of 2010. The institute also worked with local officials and universities to develop the Sheikh Mohamed bin Zayed University Scholars Program, whose sixteen students are all enrolled in Sexton's seminar, "The Relationship of Government and Religion." His course focuses on the Supreme Court's treatment of the separation of church and state. In most respects, it is identical to a class Sexton has taught to NYU undergraduates for many years (he is unusual among college presidents in routinely teaching a full load of three classes every year).

Just how different the seminar is becomes clear when Sexton teaches the two-hour course the next afternoon. Following coffee with a visitor in the lobby of the Sheraton Abu Dhabi, where several NYU colleagues join the conversation as they come and go, Sexton is driven to the Intercontinental Hotel, where his students are meeting with two teaching assistants who have flown in from New York for the class. After a group lunch in the hotel restaurant, the students assemble in a plush conference room that serves as their classroom. As the 1:30 p.m. beginning of the seminar approaches, young women in head-to-toe black abayas gather around the table (none wear veils, and several wear jeans beneath their robes), along with a smaller group of young men—one in Western clothes and several in the traditional long white robe known as a *dishdasha*, worn with a head-dress called a *tailasan*. The juxtapositions seen everywhere in this region are apparent in the classroom, too, as one woman in a black abaya with bright blue sleeves begins playing with her iPhone, while others send text messages on their cell phones.

As the class gets under way, Sexton begins a steady stream of affectionate banter with his students (who, at his request, call him by his first name). For starters, he tells them to turn off their cell phones and urges one woman, who is drinking a Red Bull energy drink after staying up all night studying for an exam, to be sure to get some rest before she attempts her long drive home after class. Then it is on to business. "What's our basic text?" he asks. "I want you in the mode where you're thinking the sixteen words and nothing more than the sixteen words." He is referring to the so-called establishment clause of the First Amendment to the Constitution: "Congress shall make no law respecting an establishment of religion, or prohibiting the free exercise thereof." The two landmark cases under discussion today are *Engel v. Vitale*, the 1962 ruling that said state officials could not require public school students to recite an official school prayer, and *Abington Township School District v. Schempp*, a ruling issued the following year in which the Court said that school-sponsored Bible readings in public schools were unconstitutional.

It soon becomes clear that Sexton is a masterful teacher, prodding students with repeated questions about different scenarios that might or might not trigger a violation of the First Amendment's establishment clause, and entertaining them with vignettes about the politics of Supreme Court nominations. He urges students to interrupt him with questions or if they disagree with something he has said. At times the class resembles U.S. Civics 101 as Sexton coaches students on some basics: "Remember, what's the most important number in the Supreme Court?" "Nine?" offers one student. "No, five!" replies Sexton, referring to the number required for a majority decision. Throughout the seminar, the Brooklyn native gestures expansively and speaks in a dense, layered style, full of lengthy meanderings. He makes no secret of his liberal politics, mocking what he characterizes as the intolerance and homogeneity of 1950s *Ozzie and Harriet* America as he establishes the sociological framework for pre-1960s First Amendment jurisprudence. (He does not appear attuned to the irony of delivering this judgment around a seminar table of Emiratis in traditional dress. Some of the young women in his class would never be permitted by their families to travel out of the country without a male escort. And, needless to say, separation of church and state is truly a foreign concept for these students.)

Sexton demonstrates particular concern about showing students how the ecumenicism he favors in U.S. civic life ought to apply to the world stage: "How do we create a world where we don't look at things through a single window, but embrace all the ways of looking? That's going to be the challenge of your century. Will it be a clash of civilizations? Or interconnected elements of a watch where we have a whole that's greater than the sum of its parts?" He returns to discussions of court rulings and dissents, then concludes the class by saying "For Thanksgiving, I want to thank the Lord for the gift of you people."

The appreciation is reciprocated by the undergraduates, who seem to value this taste of a U.S.-style Socratic seminar for a combination of reasons: pedagogical, political, and social. Afterward, twenty-two-year-old Ayesha Alateeqi says that the class is much more challenging than what she is used to at HCT in Al-Ain, one of sixteen institutions that make up the Higher Colleges of Technology at assorted locations around the UAE. In Sexton's seminar "we get to think outside the box," she says. "We're more active in this class. In our other classes [at the students' universities] we're more passive—we're spoon-fed."[7] Another undergraduate, Alia Rashid Al-Shamsi, a fourth-year student at Zayed University in Dubai, says she has had some experience with interactive classes in her public relations and advertising major. Still, she says Sexton's approach is distinctive. "He captures your attention, definitely. He has charisma. He is an amazing storyteller." His only flaw, she adds, is a tendency to launch into interesting digressions that aren't easy to connect—at least right away—to his central subject.[8]

One of the perks of the Sheikh Mohamed Scholars Program is a full scholarship for graduate study at NYU's Washington Square campus for those who excel.[9] That is definitely an attraction for students like Alia, though it comes with one important catch. When asked whether her family would permit her to study in New York, she says the answer is yes, "but it would probably mean that one of my family members has to come with me." True, not all parents would insist on an escort, but many young women in this traditional society must balance a sometimes uneasy tension between their lives outside the family fold and the restrictions placed on them at home. "The families here are very overprotective, especially of females," Al-Shamsi says. "I mean, we're very modern and up to date, but when we go back to our families . . . we have certain things in our culture that have not changed. . . . It's very similar to, like, the Victorian era." For this reason, she thinks NYU's Abu Dhabi campus will fill an important niche for female students whose families would never let them study overseas. "Basically, instead of us going somewhere, it's coming to us," she says. "So this is perfect."

On the political front, too, the freewheeling approach taken by Sexton—and presumably by professors of future NYU courses—has great appeal to some Emirati students. Khulood "Eternity" Al-Atiyat, a twenty-one-year-old public relations major at Zayed University, says the "healthy disrespect for authority" preached by Sexton reminded her of the university classes she took in the United States under a State Department–sponsored summer program. By contrast, she says, her professors (many of whom come from outside the UAE) tend to self-censor and avoid potentially touchy subjects. "The professors at our university . . . there's this notion or idea that they cannot say whatever they want because 'Oh, we might get deported from the country, or maybe the government will hear about it and then we can't delve into this topic of so and so,'" or "'No, we can't talk about this topic, about politics—no, we can't.' So there are certain guidelines that are not written on paper, but it's just in the air." Al-Atiyat believes that the support Abu Dhabi's ruler, Sheikh bin Zayed, has given to NYU's new campus is a healthy sign that the ruling family wants to encourage greater political liberalization.[10]

Still, NYU's critics, both within and outside the university, are deeply skeptical about whether the 51,000-student university can or should establish a presence in places like the UAE. At NYU, critics of Sexton's mission have decried everything from the Emirates' treatment of women and gays to its lack of a free-speech tradition appropriate to the open inquiry that students and faculty ought to expect from a Western university. The political part of this debate falls along familiar lines, writes Andrew Ross, a professor of American studies at NYU: "Is it better to try to influence the political climate in illiberal societies by fostering collegial zones of free speech, or is it the instinct to engage student elites in such societies a naïve or, at worst, colonial instinct?"[11] Then there is the criticism that Sexton, an impressive figure who can also be needy and voluble, is on a mission to build an empire. A harshly critical *New York* magazine story about the project was titled "The Emir of NYU."[12]

Sexton and others who are part of the NYU Abu Dhabi project reply emphatically that their new campus is part of the solution, not part of the problem. For one thing, Sexton says, many of the questions critics have raised about the lack of political and social liberalization in Abu Dhabi apply equally to places like Singapore, China, and Ghana. "It's an argument that doesn't apply in a unique fashion here," he says. But after conversations with NYU faculty and with Emirati officials, he concluded that Abu Dhabi was in fact a place where an "iterative process" of liberalization was most likely to take hold with NYU's involvement. Moreover, he says, bedrock academic values will not suffer in the Gulf kingdom. "There can be no compromising of free speech in NYU Abu Dhabi."

On the gender front, many Americans have misconceptions about just how constricted the role of women is in the Emirates, says Mariët Westermann. "Everybody has asked, 'Do you wear an abaya?' " she says. Women in particular were curious about how Westermann—who is tall, striking, and blonde—would fare in an Arab culture. "It was amazing to me, frankly, how parochial some of the reactions were," she says. "It made me realize how poorly understood this region is." Westermann wears normal business dress to appointments, she says. "I would be laughed out of court if I were wearing the abaya." And as the senior NYU official on the ground, she says she is treated with great deference because of the norms of Arab culture. "The thinking is so hierarchical, for better or worse, but for women there can be an advantage," she says. "When I show up in a meeting—it typically is a bunch of guys—and they will turn to me first, because I'm the boss." That isn't always true in the United States, she notes, where she has occasionally attended meetings at which her interlocutors assumed that her lower-ranking male colleagues were the ultimate decision makers.

As for unfettered free inquiry, it was a nonnegotiable matter for NYU, Westermann says. "The key walk-away issue for us was academic freedom. That's, after all, what's essential to operate an academic institution. And if we are going to be some kind of positive change agent, which the Emirates understand us to be, they understand that we come with that risk. They know what NYU is." At the same time, however, she acknowledges that NYU walks a fine line in just how broadly its freedom is defined. "We have to be able to exercise academic freedom, but that comes with responsibilities, too, as it does in the United States. And just as we can't give a blank check to anyone in Washington Square to do whatever they wish without regard for the laws of the land, we can't have that immunity in any of our abroad sites—including Abu Dhabi."

Her statement could be seen as an evasion—or just a statement of reality. But Westermann also insists that NYU is committed to recruiting students and faculty according to no other principles than "standards of

academic quality and promise to succeed in the institution." Immigration
restrictions may be a problem, she concedes, just as it would be hard to
bring an Iranian physicist to teach in the United States. What about Israeli
passport holders? In the short term, she says, the best way to make that
happen is by using backchannels rather than direct confrontation with
Emirati authorities. "We will advocate and make a point that we need
a person, and then offline I will say that I am very hopeful that we will
be very successful in bringing Israelis here." In fact, she says, NYU has
already done so, bringing Ron Rubin, associate dean of NYU's Steinhardt
School of Culture, Education, and Human Development—and an Israeli
citizen—into Abu Dhabi. "It isn't a cake walk," she says. "He had to be
whisked through. You end up not even showing your passport because
it isn't recognized. . . . Nobody wants to come in that way, but he came,
and he was fine with it." Indeed, NYU officials note that its Abu Dhabi
campus has received support from the likes of Abraham Foxman of the
Anti-Defamation League[13] and Itamar Rabinovich, Israel's former ambas-
sador to Washington (and an NYU "global professor"[14]).

For now, the initial model of Sexton's seminar certainly suggests that
Emirati students—at least an elite segment of those students—are experi-
encing an intellectual atmosphere that is, by the standards of the region,
remarkably open. Still, these questions are likely to linger until the NYU
campus is up and running and boosters and critics alike have an opportunity to see how their hopes and fears play out in practice.

EDUCATION CITY

The sort of active learning and liberalization that NYU says it has in mind
is already on display in Doha, Qatar, another oil-rich kingdom that lies
187 miles northwest across the Gulf from Abu Dhabi. On the 2,500-acre
grounds of Education City, a similarly lavish experiment in bringing elite
Western higher education to the Gulf is well under way. Six American
universities—Texas A&M University, the Georgetown School of Foreign Service, Weill Cornell Medical Center, Northwestern University's
School of Communications and Medill School of Journalism, Carnegie
Mellon University, and Virginia Commonwealth University's School for

the Arts—have been invited by the royal family of Qatar to establish outposts designed to provide the best of American education for students
from Doha and around the region.

On the edge of the construction-filled, traffic-congested boomtown of
Qatar, Education City is itself filled with dust and cranes as it adds buildings to house its growing number of university tenants. In addition to the
six campuses already in the complex (which includes many other buildings,
including the opulent headquarters of the Qatar Foundation for Education, Science and Community Development, two schools, a RAND office
focusing on education research, and the offices of Al Jazeera Children's
Channel), the foundation is in advanced talks with a major American law
school and one other university.

Just as in John Sexton's Abu Dhabi seminar, the juxtaposition of cultures here is hard to miss. At the entrance to the Texas A&M building,
three young women in black abayas leave through an impossibly tall
doorway that looks as if it were modeled after the entrance to an ancient
Mesopotamian temple. Yet the street they approach outside the building
is adorned, Texas-style, with banners that say "Welcome Home, Aggies."
Once inside the lavish structure, made of more than 44,000 square meters
of rosa travertine marble mined in the mountains of Turkey (clearly, no
expense has been spared for any Education City building), more Aggie
banners are soon in evidence. So is a prayer room, with separate entrances
for men and women, that helps students meet their obligation to pray five
times daily. Yet perhaps in deference to the ubiquity of American fast food
in the Middle East and beyond, student dining options are distinctly non-
multicultural. The Carnegie Mellon building next to Texas A&M houses
a Subway sandwich shop, while the Liberal Arts and Sciences building
features a Starbucks where guys in traditional robes and young women in
abayas chat happily while sipping their lattes.

Beyond these surface impressions, the Qatari government's motivations
for establishing this academic outpost are serious indeed. The royal family,
which funds Education City under the auspices of the Qatar Foundation
(which is headed by Sheikha Mozah bint Nasser al Missned, wife of the
Emir of Qatar, Sheikh Hamad bin Khalifa Al-Thani), is well aware that
the tiny nation's vast wealth from gas reserves will not last forever. Thus,
through a range of reforms that encompass K–12 education, its own university system, and the importation of handpicked U.S. university "fran-

chises," the government of Qatar is attempting to move "from petrodollars to human capital," in the words of Robert Baxter,[15] a former journalist who now serves as a communications adviser to the Qatar Foundation. This human capital strategy involves both improving the educational pipeline for all students and ensuring that enough elite educational opportunities exist to keep the nation's most talented students in the country.

To make this happen, ensuring quality is vital. Baxter points to huge differences between the Qatar Foundation's approach and the freewheeling "shopping mall" environment of the higher education complex in Dubai known as the Knowledge Village, where any rent-paying university is welcome. By contrast, Qatar Foundation officials in Doha researched U.S. university partners exhaustively and cherry-picked programs that they viewed as among the best in the world. Thus, rather than offer a full-service smorgasbord of majors, each university in Education City offers the typical variety of general-education classes (English, U.S. government, and so forth), after which each student majors in one of the subjects for which the campus is renowned: engineering at Texas A&M, journalism and communications at Northwestern, foreign service at Georgetown, and so forth. Undergraduates (there are so far no graduate students in Education City, although Texas A&M plans to open a master's-level program) may cross-register for about twenty courses at other institutions. But academic schedules often don't dovetail, so not many do so; over time, Education City officials hope to standardize schedules and build more synergies between campuses, creating something like a super-university.

Beyond the choice of U.S. partners, perhaps the most important step to ensuring quality is the Qatar Foundation's insistence that every degree issued by a university in Education City be identical to those issued at the home campus. "Your diploma doesn't say Georgetown-Qatar, or Georgetown-lite," says James Reardon-Anderson, dean of Georgetown's Qatar campus.[16] With no indication on a diploma that it was issued in Doha rather than in Evanston or Pittsburgh, the reasoning goes, American institutions will have a strong incentive to self-police to ensure that their brand is not diluted. "That condition was put there for a reason—in order to guarantee that these universities have something at stake here," says Sheikha Al-Misnad, the president of Qatar University and an influential figure in the establishment of Education City as a board member of the Qatar Foundation.[17] In principle, admissions standards are just as rigorous as those at the universities' home campuses. In practice, however, professors and administrators acknowledge that the curve of abilities is a bit lower than at home, partly because of the uneven preparation of students who have come from schools in the region.

Another factor influencing quality is pressure to enroll Qataris: American administrators and Qataris alike insist that there are no rigid quotas, but those paying the bills would like to see at least 50 percent Qatari enrollment. A few professors say that it can be hard to insist on academic rigor for some wealthy students, mostly young Qatari men, who have grown up with a strong sense of entitlement. For now, most students are non-Qatari; they tend to come from a range of other countries in the region. When Cornell University's Weill Medical College graduated its first class in May 2008, for instance, the class comprised nine women and six men from Bosnia, India, Jordan, Nigeria, the Palestinian territories, Qatar, Syria, and the United States.[18]

Further complicating matters is the question of language. Education City classes, with the exception of foreign language instruction, are all taught in English. But while many students have attended English-speaking private secondary schools, in many cases their written English lags behind their speaking abilities. "They struggle at learning to write in English to our standards. The Medill School of Journalism standard is pretty high, we think, and we're holding them to that standard," says Richard Roth, associate dean of journalism at Medill's Qatar campus.[19] "We've put in many more hours as a faculty than we would in Evanston." Still, he is quick to note of his undergraduates, "they're otherwise intellectually inquisitive, intellectually capable students," and are in some ways far more worldly than their counterparts in Evanston.

As at NYU, bringing home-campus faculty to universities' Gulf locations has been a priority in Education City, part of the push to keep standards high and equivalent to those in the United States. Generous compensation packages, which include salary boosts (one Texas A&M professor reports nearly doubling his compensation; a 30 percent increase is more typical), free housing, round-trip travel home, and more, are designed to make a posting of one, two, or more years in Doha attractive. In part as a result of such benefits, more than 50 percent of Georgetown's Qatar faculty comes from its Washington, DC campus. "It would be disingenuous to say that anybody in Education City, whatever role they're playing, is not here in part because of the material rewards," says Reardon-Anderson, whose own $600,000 salary in 2007 (a figure that includes housing and other benefits) was approximately the same as the president of Georgetown's, according to nonprofit disclosure forms.[20] Faculty recruiting has been less of a problem than he expected, Reardon-Anderson says, with some top Georgetown professors willing to transplant themselves to Doha.

Still, Reardon-Anderson acknowledges that money isn't enough to lure most of his colleagues to the Middle East. "It's striking to me how few of my colleagues at Georgetown consider this a sufficient reason to come. Because most people don't want to come here," notwithstanding the incentives. In addition, he is concerned that it has been easier to recruit home-campus professors in fields such as English and philosophy than in the program's core areas of international politics and economics. At Texas A&M, some say faculty recruiting has fallen short of expectations. According to John Bryant, an engineering professor who moved to Qatar from College Station, administrators never succeeded in realizing their plan of attracting a critical mass of professors from Texas to Qatar.[21] The result has been a heavier reliance on faculty from the region who are hired on short-term contracts—the equivalent of the adjuncts often used to supplement core faculty on U.S. college campuses. That in turn raises questions about whether the experience offered at A&M's Qatar campus is truly equivalent to what Aggies find in College Station. For his part, Mark H. Weichold, dean and CEO of Texas A&M–Qatar, says he is pleased to have some 25 percent of his faculty members from College Station.[22] The remainder of the faculty is hired directly into the Qatar campus. Most, he notes, have U.S. or British PhDs.[23]

Along with aiming for high standards for students and faculty, Qatar Foundation officials make no bones about their hope that their educational experiment can shake up the Gulf nation's sometimes conservative establishment. Accordingly, political liberalization is very much a part of their agenda. "The vision of the leadership was that education is the best leverage to make change possible," says Dr. Fathy Saoud, president of the Qatar Foundation, speaking in his office in the foundation's lavish building on the Education City grounds.[24] The high quality that Education City sought from the beginning (it had talks with Oxford, Harvard, and Yale, among others) would never be possible "except if you have the right environment, where people can talk freely, can debate, can express their opinion, you see?" says Saoud. "We believed, actually, that this was part of preparing the country for the democratic process." From the U.S. universities' point of view, guarantees of academic freedom were a must. In a country where potentially sensitive or controversial Web sites are still blocked by the government, for example, no such restrictions exist on computers at branch campuses. Deans and professors say they haven't been subject to any kind of political interference.

Indeed, the Qatar Foundation is intent on fostering the kind of debate for which this part of the world is not famous. Posters at various buildings around Education City advertise a series of monthly debates in the format used by the Oxford Union, featuring prominent speakers and televised by the British Broadcasting Corporation. The debate proposition for November 2008 was hardly low-key: "This house believes Gulf Arabs value profits over people." Perhaps even more surprising, it passed by a margin of 75 to 25.[25]

In a similar, if less visibly provocative, vein, the presence of Northwestern's journalism school in Education City is intended to bring freewheeling American-style journalism—and thus gradual social transformation—to a country that has little tradition of a robust free press. Already, since Medill's journalism program began in September 2008, Roth has visited many local newspapers and, in his words, "agitated for a more free press." He notes that until just twenty-five or so years ago, a censor literally sat next to the editor in the newsroom. But although the Emir outlawed censorship when he took power in 1995, self-censorship remains widespread: "There's still stuff that's not being published," says Roth, himself a seasoned journalist at various U.S. newspapers. He has quietly lobbied the newspapers—many staffed by Indian journalists—to stop such practices as running a picture of the Emir on the front page every day. Some have even run controversial stories.

Roth believes the Qatar Foundation is serious about improving the Qatari media. A senior foundation official, he says, told Northwestern administrators that "if we wanted to have a controlled press, we wouldn't have [invited] a school of journalism." Indeed, the Qatar Foundation's Saoud, who is sometimes called the father of Education City, says emphatically that opening up a traditional society was a key goal of inviting Medill school to Qatar. "You know what media power is in making change," he says. But, he is asked, is the foundation really ready for robust investigative reports that criticize government officials, when public questioning of authority has not previously marked the region's political culture? He does not hesitate. "That's what we want to do here. We want to change that culture."

A further sign of liberalization is the fact that all courses offered at Education City campuses—except physical education and Islamic studies—are taught in coeducational classrooms. "Women are the big beneficiaries," says Sheikha Al-Misnad. Undergraduate classes on her own campus, she notes, are completely segregated by sex. Like NYU's campus, Education City also offers young women from traditional, protective families the opportunity to study at elite U.S. universities, which many of them could not otherwise do because of cultural barriers against traveling solo overseas.

While the different cultures on the Qatar campuses of Texas A&M, Georgetown, and other universities generally blend harmoniously, there are nevertheless occasional clashes. During a campus interview, John Bryant of Texas A&M lamented that students don't always show the same willingness to learn to function in a transplanted Western environment that professors from the West are expected to show in the Middle East. "To me it's largely a one-way street," he said. Bryant spoke ruefully of an incident in which, by the engineering professor's account, his hand accidentally brushed a female student's hand while he was reaching for a computer mouse to demonstrate something to his class. After the young woman complained, Texas A&M reprimanded Bryant for sexual harassment. "I've gotten myself in major hot water a couple of times culturally here," he said. Despite his disappointment with the way the incident was handled—he said he received "zero advocacy" from administrators—he later added that it was "isolated" and shouldn't be overblown. "In the cultural context, I'm sure that the Qatari female student thought she had been 'violated' by an unrelated male and was upset and/or embarrassed," he wrote in an e-mail message. "The only recourse through the Texas A&M system is through the sexual harassment route."[26] Bryant says he is glad he retained the protection of tenure at the main campus, but he emphasizes that he has enjoyed his time in Qatar and has no immediate plans to return to College Station. After four years in Qatar, he recently extended his contract for another three years.

As Education City shows much early success, but also weathers some unavoidable growing pains, one of the biggest questions for its long-term success is whether its model is financially sustainable. For one, its lavish facilities don't come cheap. Nor does its policy of giving Qatari students free tuition and offering interest-free loans to expatriates through the Qatar Foundation. The costs of salaries and lavish benefits for faculty, staff, and administrators are enormous, too. By design, there is no cost to home campuses for any of their Qatar satellite costs—and in fact, departments at U.S. universities may save money if a professor spends one or two years at Education City where his or her salary costs are covered. "The price per student for running this operation is beyond any rational analysis," says Reardon-Anderson. "If I had to give a gut number, I'd guess it's a half million dollars a year per student."

Given the investment required to keep Education City going, the key factors behind the survival of this experiment in transplanted Western education are both economic and political. "One never knows—the price of oil and gas could change dramatically and priorities could change as a result," says Mark Weichold of Texas A&M–Qatar. A related question, of course, is just how committed the government is to retaining and sustaining the campuses it has recruited. "Right now, today, I would bet that in thirty years we'd still be here." Reardon-Anderson shares that optimism, based on Georgetown's experiences so far. When his university was negotiating with the Qatar Foundation, "there were five areas of risk," he says. "That we wouldn't get faculty, that we wouldn't get students, that we would suffer financial risk, that there would be a security problem, and that the reputation of the university would be harmed." So far, he reports, "none of that has come about."

EXPANDING OUTPOSTS

While U.S. universities are major players in the satellite-campus world, institutions from many other nations are extending their presence in regions well beyond the Middle East. These branch campuses are numerous—and take many shapes and forms. To complicate matters, there are multiple definitions of what constitutes a branch campus. According to two Australian academics, Grant McBurnie and Christopher Ziguras, authors of *Offshoring Higher Education*, a "full-service" branch campus can be defined as a "bricks and mortar presence, wholly or jointly owned and operated by the awarding institution, providing degrees face-to-face, supported by traditional physical infrastructure including library, laboratories, classrooms, and faculty and staff offices. Ideally research and community engagement should be part of the profile, as well as teaching." Some fall far short of this standard, they note, ranging from storefront operations that function primarily as marketing offices for enrollment at the main campus to online course offerings that have no in-country physical presence beyond a local P.O. box.[27]

Using a fairly rigorous definition, the London-based Observatory on Borderless Higher Education reported around 100 branch campuses worldwide as of June 2005.[28] A more recent study by the same group found there are now 162 such campuses; an increase of about 60 percent in just a few years.[29] Established mostly since the mid-1990s, the largest concentrations are in the Middle East and Southeast Asia, with particularly strong growth taking place in India, China, and Central Asia.[30] American and Australian universities sponsor the largest number of satellite campuses, McBurnie and Ziguras report, with a smaller number of branch campuses operated by British, Malaysian, and Singaporean institutions.

To take just a few examples of non-American universities now active in the branch-campus boom, the Sorbonne has joined NYU in establishing an outpost on Abu Dhabi, while Scotland's Heriot-Watt University has a campus in Dubai, and another Scottish institution, Queen Margaret University, has a branch in Singapore.[31] For its part, Australia's Monash University has a campus in South Africa in a suburb of Johannesburg[32] (in addition to its branches in Malaysia and Italy).[33] Another Australian institution, RMIT International University, which is associated with the Australia Royal Melbourne Institute of Technology, has about 3,800 students in its campuses in Hanoi and Ho Chi Minh City.[34]

In China, where huge numbers of students have shown an interest in acquiring Western diplomas, U.S. and non-U.S. universities alike have flocked to fill the demand. Britain's University of Nottingham established a branch campus in the port city of Ningbo in 2005, billed by the *Economist* as "the first foreign-run university campus in China since the Communist takeover in 1949."[35] Noteworthy for a campus that aims to replicate the British architecture and atmosphere of its home campus, the University of Nottingham, Ningbo, offers courses entirely in English and represents an effort by the parent campus (which also operates a branch in Malaysia) to expand its global profile. Among American universities, probably the best-known presence in China is a joint Johns Hopkins–Nanjing University program that has been in place for twenty years. The State University of New York–Stony Brook has initiated a dual-degree partnership with Nanjing University in which students divide their time between SUNY–Stony Brook and Nanjing.[36] And in the for-profit sector, Kaplan, Inc., said in December 2007 that it would be significantly expanding its educational programs in China.[37] Between the pure satellite programs—still relatively rare—and the much more numerous partnership efforts, the Western university presence in China has become very large. One report found that as of August 2006, more than 1,300 joint programs were in operation, with another 378 in the works.[38]

Another massive market for university education can be found in India, whose extraordinary economic growth has created a significant middle class and a hunger for higher learning. With the exception of a relative handful of elite institutions such as the Indian Institutes of Technology and the Indian Institute of Management, Indian universities are generally of middling to poor quality. They also have a woeful lack of capacity to enroll the soaring number of young people seeking degrees. Little surprise, then, that India is the world's second-largest sender of students to overseas universities after China[39] and the single largest source of international students in the United States.[40] Like the Middle East and China, India has attracted enormous interest from foreign universities hoping to set up shop on India soil as well. But regulatory obstacles are particularly significant in India. For starters, foreign universities can't operate independently. Georgia Tech, for instance, hopes to establish an offshore campus in the southern state of Andhra Pradesh, offering several undergrad degrees. But it can't do so until Parliament passes new legislation permitting a freestanding satellite campus. Meantime, many institutions—130 by one count—have entered the Indian market through partnerships or "twinning arrangements," whereby students study in India with local private institutions for part of their program (usually using the U.S. college's curriculum) and in the United States for the rest. Participants in such programs range from North Dakota State and Western Michigan University to Carnegie Mellon and Clemson.[41]

Another model lets Indian students earn an American degree without ever leaving the country. The highly regarded S. P. Jain Institute of Management and Research, for example, has partnered with Virginia Tech to offer a dual master's degree program. Students accepted into the program spend two years earning an S. P. Jain diploma in systems management while also studying for a master's in information technology from Virginia Tech's Pamplin College of Business. Students don't need to spend any time at Tech's Blacksburg, Virginia, campus; instead, they attend all of their classes in S. P. Jain's modern building in the northern suburbs of Mumbai. U.S. professors work with "co-instructors" from the S. P. Jain faculty, make use of audio software to offer some lectures with slides, and fly in once per semester for an intense week of in-person classes and meetings. All final grades are determined by Virginia Tech faculty. While class sizes tend to be large by U.S. standards—sixty-plus in some cases—the program has proven extremely popular so far. S. P. Jain officials say applications rose from around 100 for the first cohort of students to some 2,000 for the fourth cohort. And they note that the placement rate for graduates of the program has been very high.

On a late January morning in 2008, Virginia Tech professor Steven Sheetz—jet-lagged after flying in for a week of classes—says Virginia Tech's motivation for the partnership is less about grand notions of globalization than dollars and cents. "I can speak to why we do it: it's generating revenue," he says. With state appropriations dwindling since 2001, Tech is scrambling to find new ways of funding its operations. Catering to student demand in India helps fill the budget hole. For its part, S. P. Jain touts numerous virtues of the arrangement, including allowing students to receive a U.S. degree while avoiding the visa restrictions that periodically make travel to the United States difficult. "Sitting in India, we get the top professors from Virginia Tech to teach us about the latest technology and trends," says student Anamitra Ghatak.[42] (Despite these benefits, the partnership was terminated after the 2007–8 academic year. According to Sheetz, the Indian government refused to let the arrangement continue because it objected to a foreign university taking profits from such a venture outside the country. With a new higher education minister more friendly to foreign universities now in office, Virginia Tech officials remain hopeful that the alliance may be revived.)

Even as they proliferate, and notwithstanding tuitions that are often lower than the amount charged on the universities' home turf, branch campuses have faced plenty of obstacles. These range from financing and luring home-campus faculty to remote outposts to gauging student demand

and ensuring that the valuable brand identity of well-regarded universities is not diluted in the process of creating new branches. Branding, while a term that university officials don't always care for, is often a major consideration, especially for top-tier institutions.

Yale's negotiations with Abu Dhabi officials broke down over whether a proposed Yale art institute in that tiny Emirate could grant degrees identical to those earned at the university's home campus. "We told them right from the outset, 'We're not going to give Master of Fine Arts degrees, normal Yale degrees there, because we can't provide a faculty of comparable quality to what we have in New Haven,'" said Yale president Richard Levin in an interview in his office at the heart of Yale's campus.[43] More broadly, he counts himself a skeptic of the satellite model as currently conceived. "The fundamental problem is universities are communities of scholars that build up over decades. And to really get a critical mass of high-quality faculty to go to some new location, it's going to take a long time to build up a teaching faculty of the quality you have at the top schools. And so I'm somewhat skeptical that we can actually do that effectively."

College presidents who are less skeptical than Levin may nonetheless find their branch-campus dreams dashed. One potential stumbling block: home-campus worries over human rights and free speech. Such objections don't apply only to illiberal regimes in the Middle East. The University of Warwick, which prides itself on an entrepreneurial, globally oriented culture, spent months in prolonged discussions with officials in Singapore over what it hoped would be the university's first satellite campus. Ultimately, however, it abandoned the plan in 2005 after the faculty senate voted to reject the proposed 10,000-student campus, amid concern by students and faculty alike about maintaining academic freedom in a nation that limits freedom of speech, assembly, and the press.

Concerns about political freedom were intertwined with disagreements over finances in preventing Warwick officials and their Singaporean interlocutors from coming to terms. "We got about 65 to 70 percent of the way," says Edward Harcourt, head of Institutional Relations at Warwick.[44] But a long-term, secure source of funding from Singapore was particularly important to Warwick. Unlike some heavily fee-driven Western universities in China and Malaysia, it wanted its first outpost to be above all research oriented. "The proposition they put to us wasn't particularly attractive, because we would only develop a campus overseas if we could be as research intensive and as excellent and as high-end an academic proposition over there as we were here," Harcourt says. "They wouldn't commit to a funding methodology that would give us the confidence to go forward. And the fact that they wouldn't do that raised the academic freedom concern that we would become closely aligned with Singaporean public policy, because they would only fund stuff that they liked." With a Singapore campus off the table, Warwick has no other plans to establish satellite locations.

Other obstacles can include not only financial risks but also regulatory, cultural, and logistical problems. In China, such barriers are legion. The Chinese Ministry of Education is notoriously slow to grant approvals, and identifying the Chinese institutions required as partners can be difficult. The University of Montana, for instance, had so many problems getting approved that the campus for 2,000 Chinese undergrads it planned to open in fall 2006 still hasn't started classes. Neither has Kean University, which announced in May 2006 that in September 2007 it would be the first American university to open a brand-new campus in China.[45]

The difficulty of gauging student demand is a further barrier. One of the most spectacular flameouts to date occurred when Australia's University of New South Wales, which opened a brand-new campus in Singapore in 2006 with hopes of enrolling 15,000 students, shut its doors a year later having enrolled only 150 students. Some attributed the failure to the significant competition the Sydney-based university faced from the numerous other Western institutions that have established partnerships in the city-state in the past decade. (As Singapore has sought to become a center for global higher education, it has forged collaborations through its own universities with many Western institutions, including U.S. universities such as Carnegie Mellon, Cornell, the University of Chicago, Duke, the University of California at Berkeley, Stanford, and the California Institute of Technology.)[46] Perhaps the most notable failure of branch campuses came when American universities flocked to Japan in the 1980s and 1990s, when that nation seemed to be the next model for world economic prosperity. Yet the popularity of U.S. branch campuses was short-lived; today only one satellite campus, that of Temple University, remains.[47]

For other institutions, moving overseas simply isn't part of their core mission. Philip Altbach points to his own university, Boston College, which has frequently been approached about establishing a satellite campus but decided against such a move. "It's too complicated and we do well enough in our own markets," Altbach says.[48] Instead, Boston College pursued a different internationalization strategy, sending more students abroad and recruiting more foreign students.

A clear possibility is that the global economic downturn will lead to the expansion of branch campuses as some students decide to stay closer to home for financial reasons but are still eager to earn degrees from Western institutions. However, that expansion might not be a good thing if it severely compromises quality, as Olcott of the Observatory on Borderless Higher Education believes it might. "I suspect some institutions that are desperate for alternative revenue streams will consider playing in the global sandbox," he says. "Many of these institutions have no business in the business of global higher education." These universities are underresourced and won't be able to sustain programs over the long term, he suggests, and many lack any expertise in delivering their courses off-campus.[49]

Indeed, some analysts argue that location itself is a crucial part of what gives a university its identity. Kris Olds, a professor of geography at the University of Wisconsin–Madison, says even his university's long tradition of overseas programs and research initiatives, not to mention the sixty-eight languages taught on campus, doesn't mean it has strayed from its origins as a public land-grant university. "I'm remarkably struck by how rooted in place it is," says Olds,[50] who runs a well-regarded blog, *Global-HigherEd*, together with a colleague at the University of Bristol.

What's more, proponents of any significant branch-campus initiative at Wisconsin would have to jump through many hoops to get approval: the faculty senate, the Board of Regents, the state legislature—not to mention negotiating the university's famously contentious campus politics. "I just don't think we have the resources and institutional culture and capacity to do it," Olds says. Costs alone could sink even more modest joint degree projects, let alone full-blown satellite campuses, he says.

"I think American public institutions aren't really going to get significantly involved overseas unless somebody is going to bankroll it from outside the institution—for example, state economic development initiatives or the State Department," says Olds. "In Europe, millions are going into the Erasmus Mundus initiative to facilitate the establishment of joint degrees with European institutions. In Asia, lots of funding comes through ministries of education. My sense is that unless some other actors with larger-scale resources start getting involved in the United States, I imagine all we're going to see are niche, well-resourced initiatives by interesting universities like NYU."

Still, amid this uncertainty it is worth noting that even in the face of branch-campus failures, determined universities often find ways to continue forging cross-cultural partnerships. A good case study involves George Mason University, a fast-growing institution in Fairfax, Virginia, about thirty minutes from Washington, DC, that has made a conscious effort to spread its offerings both close to home and overseas. In addition to the university's main campus, which offers a range of general subjects, it has a nearby campus in Arlington, Virginia, devoted largely to law and public policy. Another branch in the exurbs of Prince William County, Virginia, focuses on the biological sciences. And in 2005, after much debate among its trustees, it decided to expand its presence still further by opening a small satellite campus in Ras al Khaimah,[51] one of the United Arab Emirates.

George Mason's president, Alan Merten, says he and his colleagues felt it was important to treat the new campus as just one more component of its network. "We created the concept of the 'distributed university,'" he boasts.[52] "We're almost fanatic," he adds, echoing NYU's John Sexton. "We don't like the word 'satellite.' When someone refers to one of our campuses as a satellite, no matter if it's Arlington or if it's United Arab Emirates, we correct them because we believe that how you name something, particularly in higher education, sometimes has more of an impact than we're willing to admit." In a March 2008 interview, Merten said this integration across national boundaries can occur in ways large and small. The night before, he explained by way of example, the George Mason men's basketball team was taking part in the NCAA Selection Show. Along with the crowds of supporters on the Fairfax campus, a group of students in Ras al Khaimah joined the festivities via satellite link. "They were cheering," say Merten, "and our players were cheering when they cheered, and everybody cheered here."

This vision of cross-cultural understanding (at least on the basketball court) came to an abrupt end a year later, however. In February 2009, the university announced that it was closing its small but closely watched Gulf branch, largely because of disputes between George Mason and its Gulf partner, the for-profit firm Edrak, over who would provide academic oversight and how soon the campus could reasonably be expected to become profitable.

Merten was undeterred, however. In a conversation five months after the closure, he spoke energetically about the success of a U.S.-China program collaboration known as the one-two-one program, in which George Mason and other U.S. universities participate. It works as follows: Chinese students attend any of 1,200 or so participating universities in China for their first year of study, then travel to George Mason for their second and third year before returning to their home campus for their final year. "It seems to be working," Merten says. "It gives us exposure all over China without having to have a lot of overhead—we don't have to set up a campus in China."

George Mason isn't shying away from new satellite campuses either. Merten also waxes enthusiastic about Mason's role as one of seven or eight Western institutions (including the University of Delaware and North Carolina State) that will create branch campuses in South Korea's Incheon Free Economic Zone. The new complex being created around a massive new international airport about one hour from Seoul is in an ideal location, says Merten. While the collection of campuses—analogous to Qatar's Education City—initially aims to cater primarily to South Koreans, it hopes to eventually lure students and research from all over Asia to attend U.S. university campuses. "You've got to have the right partner when you do it internationally," Merten says. "We think that this South Korean enterprise has much more of a government commitment and much more money behind it than maybe what we saw in the United Arab Emirates."

Whether the obstacles and complications facing branch campuses are sufficient to thwart their growth will not become clear for some time. Decades of experimentation will likely take place along the way. For example, while collegiate entrepreneurs in the West explore ways to spread their offerings closer to potential students, more traffic is also beginning to develop in the opposite direction. Non-Western countries are improving their own postsecondary capacities, both in the traditional research university sector and in more targeted markets. Thus, new "reverse branch campuses" may emerge in the future. Already, a Malaysian for-profit university, Limkokwing University of Creative Technology, has opened branches in seven countries, including Cambodia, China, Indonesia, and Malaysia, with twenty more in the works over the next five years. Its recently established London branch is the first non-American foreign university to open a campus in the United Kingdom.[53]

Meanwhile, as evidenced by the plans of George Mason and others, the rise of the new global campus is likely to create a range of other permutations and combinations, some more radical than anything being contemplated today. Continuing his analogy between universities and the business world, Nigel Thrift of the University of Warwick argues that the next step for universities "ought to be to think about some form of consolidation with other universities around the world to get an organization that really works." This would be a giant step beyond campus-to-campus partnerships, which he calls "an intermediary stage." If universities behave as firm theory would predict, he concludes, "the logical end point of what's going on in higher education at the moment is that institutions will actually start merging across borders."

Whatever new forms the global presence of the world's most successful universities may take—up to and including international mergers—some bumps in the road are certain. But in an ever-flattening world, the sweeping popularity of Western institutions, along with the ideals and excellence they represent, seems only likely to grow.

Chapter Three

Wanted: World-Class Universities

Globalization doesn't necessarily mean operating campuses across national boundaries. Nor must it involve recruiting students and professors from other countries. While those phenomena are obviously widespread, still another form of globalization involves a nation's concerted effort to compete internationally by creating world-class universities. Such institutions are not clearly defined; as Boston College's Philip Altbach memorably observes, "Everyone wants one, no one knows what it is, and no one knows how to get one."[1] Still, the widely shared understanding is that world-class institutions will be closely modeled on the Western research university—and in particular on the hugely successful American research university.

Why are so many countries interested in seeking world-class status for at least some of their universities? Because, says Jamil Salmi, coordinator of Tertiary Education at the World Bank, of "the general recognition that economic growth and global competitiveness are increasingly driven by knowledge, and that universities can play a key role in that knowledge.[2] Amid ever-more-ferocious academic competition around the world, the quest for world-class status can take many forms, from expanding existing institutions, and improving their quality, to building brand-new universities. From China, India, and Singapore to Germany, France, and Australia, national governments are convinced that competing on the world stage by building great universities will keep more students at home, perhaps attract more from abroad, and above all create innovative and prosperous economies. For Americans, increasingly fretting over whether their hard-earned place at the top of the intellectual pecking order is now vulnerable, this movement could instead be read much more positively: imitation, after all, is the sincerest form of flattery.

One of the most ambitious and widely followed efforts to create a new group of elite universities is taking place in China, a country whose higher education system had, as one observer put it, "ground to a halt"[3] during the horrors of the Cultural Revolution. China has long been the largest exporter of students in the world and, after India, the second-largest sender of students to the United States. With demand for Western degrees high among Chinese students, it has also become home to many satellite campuses and partnerships with foreign universities. Now it exemplifies all three main forms of campus globalization: in addition to the first two forms, the world's most populous nation is embarking on a plan to create homegrown excellence, boosting enrollment throughout its higher education system and singling out a group of universities to receive significant extra funding and attention, all in the hope of creating a group of world-class institutions.

This plan could be said to have its roots in the reform agenda put into place by Chinese leader Deng Xiaoping following the death of Mao Zedong in 1976. Deng wanted to see China catch up and compete with the rest of the world in a number of sectors, including science and technology and industry. Universities were key to his vision: they would produce the research and human capital needed to jump-start China's economy. Accordingly, the campus curriculum moved from political indoctrination to more scholarly training.[4]

But it was not until the 1990s that the Chinese initiated a much more far-reaching effort to boost both the quantity of its university enrollment and the quality of those institutions. In 1993, then president Jiang Zemin announced the creation of Project 211, which was implemented two years later and provided an infusion of $20 billion in government funds to one hundred Chinese universities. The initiative did everything from upgrade buildings and laboratories to develop capacity in key academic disciplines such as basic science, health and medicine, and technology. The Project 211 universities, according to the government-published *People's Daily*, now train four out of five doctoral students and 30 percent of undergraduates in the nation.[5]

In an intensified effort to create a small group of elite research universities in China, Jiang announced a second initiative in 1998 during Peking University's centennial celebration.[6] Dubbed Project 985, the new program was initially targeted at ten elite universities, among them Beijing, Tsinghua, Fudan, Zhejian, and Nanjing. To allow these universities to build new research centers, hold major international conferences, and attract top faculty and visitors from overseas, they were given significant additional funding: Beijing and Tsinghua each received $225 million over five years. Shanghai Jiao Tong University and Nanjing University each received $150 million. In 2004, twenty-six more universities were added to the program, bringing the total number to thirty-six.[7] Five years later, in 2009, nine elite universities banded together to create an academic conference known as C9. Focused on graduate education and easier transfer of credits between member institutions, it quickly became known as China's Ivy League.[8]

Not only is China physically expanding its universities, it is also aggressively recruiting overseas Chinese to return to their homeland, in an effort to spur what some have dubbed a "reverse brain drain." In the past, luring expats back to China was often a tough sell, for academics and nonacademics alike. Between 1978 and 2005, 770,000 Chinese students went overseas; less than 1 in 4 returned. However, when the country's massive economic growth began to create significant new job opportunities, many more expatriates began to return. The majority of the 770,000 returnees came back after 2000.[9] To give added incentives to professors, the government has worked in partnership with private donors to provide hefty salary increases for new recruits. In 1998, for instance, China's Ministry of Education, together with Hong Kong billionaire Li Ka Shing, inaugurated the Cheung Kong Scholars Program, which gives annual bonuses of up to 100,000 yuan, or $15,000, to professors recruited from public universities overseas. More than eight hundred foreign-educated professors have returned to Chinese universities through this program since 1998.[10]

These academics are known as "sea turtles"—the Mandarin word for sea turtle, *haigui*, as the *Chronicle of Higher Education* notes, is a homonym for "returnee." Among the prominent recruits from elite American universities now at Peking University are Chen Shiyi, a former Johns Hopkins University professor who heads Peking's Engineering Institute; Yi Rao, once a Northwestern University professor and now dean of the School of Life Sciences at Peking; and C. S. Kiang, formerly a Georgia Tech professor and now dean of the College of Environmental Science. Similarly, the already rarified ranks of Tsinghua University have been further enriched by former University of California, Berkeley, economist Quan Yingyi, now dean of the School of Economics and Management; and Shi Yigong, a onetime Princeton University professor who is now vice president of Tsinghua's Institute of Biomedicine.[11] There is also strong interest in business and finance professors. At Shanghai Jiao Tong University, Chen Fangrou, a tenured professor at Columbia who has a PhD from the University of Pennsylvania's Wharton School, is on a three-year detail as dean of the business school, where he is busy recruiting forty faculty members from overseas.[12]

China's efforts to lure back overseas faculty—and to vault its universities into the ranks of the top institutions in the world—have been accompanied by a push to have professors spend more time on scholarly research. Some universities go so far as to require professors to publish in at least three international journals in order to keep their jobs. Others have stopped awarding tenure to all but the most senior professors in an effort to foster a more competitive environment.[13] In many respects, these reforms seem to have borne fruit. China is now one of the world's largest producers of scientific research as measured by its share of the total number of peer-reviewed scientific articles.[14] In 2004 it ranked fourth in the world, with 6 percent of the world's scientific output, at a time when both U.S. and European Union shares of global scientific research have been declining. Indeed, it has been much noted that China's emphasis on science and technology education means that by 2010 it will overtake the United States as the world's largest producer of PhD scientists and engineers.[15]

Those PhDs are accompanied by a range of degree holders of all kinds, as China has tried to bring broader access to its rapidly growing postsecondary system. Between 1999 and 2005, the total number of undergraduate and graduate students earning degrees from Chinese colleges and universities quadrupled, jumping from 830,000 to 3.1 million. And the number of new entering students reached close to 5 million in 2005, according to a recent analysis by the National Bureau of Economic Research.[16]

Boosting mass access while aiming for academic excellence has paid dividends beyond research citations. China has become a major destination for overseas students, both in the region and around the world. In fact, contrary to its image as primarily a source of students for other nations, China now takes in more students from overseas than it sends abroad. Over just a decade, from 1997 to 2007, the number of international students at Chinese universities rose from 39,000 to 195,000—a figure the government would like to raise still further. Already in 2007, China ranked sixth in the world—after the United States, Britain, France, Germany, and Australia[17]—in its enrollment of foreign students. Part of the nation's success in attracting students—about two-thirds of whom come for nondegree programs—is its creation of English-language programs in fields such as business and medicine.[18]

Notwithstanding China's success in upgrading and expanding its postsecondary system, many obstacles remain before its universities are truly globally competitive. Some observers fear that rapid expansion has reduced quality. A case in point: despite significant spending on Project 211 and Project 985 institutions, overall funding has not kept up with rapidly increasing enrollment. According to former education minister Chen Zhil, the central government's budget allocation for universities declined from an average of $847 per student in 1998 to $672 per student in 2005. Diminishing government funding has, in turn, forced universities to borrow some $25 billion from banks since 1998.[19]

In an effort to reduce this debt, universities began to raise tuition. But after the government ordered a five-year tuition freeze at public universities in 2006, they turned to yet another revenue source. Many universities set up affiliated colleges that charged higher fees to students who did not pass the famously competitive exams for public universities.[20] But the three hundred or so of these colleges that now exist in China are viewed as subpar, and their growth threatens the quality and reputation of the mainstream universities with which they are affiliated.

A more fundamental challenge for Chinese universities on the road to international competitiveness is whether they can embrace a core tenet of the Western research university: academic freedom. While some criticism of the government's economic policies has been permitted, the government has a track record of interfering with the activities of visiting scholars and closely monitoring the discourse of students and professors. As the *New York Times* has reported, the government also routinely censors online discussion groups. All this means that it may take time to make the shift to the freedom of inquiry that is required for true excellence. "Right now, I don't think any university in China has an atmosphere comparable to the older Western universities—Harvard or Oxford—in terms of freedom of expression," Lin Jianhua, the executive vice president of Peking University told the *Times*. "We are trying to give the students a better environment, but in order to do these things we need time. Not 10 years, but maybe one or two generations."[21] In the meantime, Chinese universities are not waiting that long to follow the American research university model in another, quite different, way: institutions like Fudan University are now seeking alumni donations for the first time.[22]

India, another emerging titan of the twenty-first-century global economy, would also like to join the ranks of the world's best higher education systems. Yet despite an immense population hungry for educational opportunities—and a rigorous tradition of free speech—India is far behind China and other nations. It has yet to create a university infrastructure that caters to its huge pool of talented human capital while also competing at the highest levels with the rest of the world. With the exception of a handful of prestigious and sought-after universities, notably the Indian Institutes of Technology (IITs), the Indian Institutes of Management (IIMs), and the All India Institute of Medical Sciences, the rest of the country's postsecondary system is both mediocre in quality and inadequate in capacity, given the vast demand. As Boston College's Altbach points out in an article coauthored by N. Jayaram, dean of the School of Social Sciences at the Tata Institute of Social Sciences in Mumbai, none of India's 348 universities ranks among the top 100 in the world. What's more, India educates just half as many university-aged students as China. It also falls behind most Latin American and other middle-income nations in college access.[23]

The need for reform is apparent in many academic sectors, including engineering. "We need to focus both on quality and on quantity," says Narayana Murthy, the cofounder of Infosys and a legendary figure in India's high-tech renaissance.[24] In his own field, he says in an interview on Infosys's massive Bangalore campus, heavy demand for engineers has led to highly attractive salaries. But quality is extremely uneven, leading to the paradox of high unemployment among technology grads even as jobs go begging to be filled. Without an adequate supply of well-trained new engineering graduates, Murthy says, "you're hardly left with anybody to build bridges, to build power plants, to run nuclear plants, for the chemical industry, etc." That poses a threat to India's storied economic growth, he suggests. "Given that the country is growing at 9.2, 9.3 percent a year," he adds, "we need engineers in every sector of the economy."

Even at the IITs, a small group of elite campuses around the nation that are often regarded as the pinnacle of higher education in an engineering-obsessed land, challenges to world-class excellence abound. For one thing, high-level research has been given short shrift in recent years. In the early days of the institutes, which were created by India's first postindependence prime minister, Jawaharlal Nehru, each of the IITs was established in partnership with top-notch Western institutions. Thus, IIT–Kánpur worked with a consortium of American universities, including MIT; the California Institute of Technology; the University of California, Berkeley; and Purdue University. Other IITs received similar support from the governments of Germany, Russia, and Great Britain. But although the IITs were intended to supply not only well-trained graduates but also top researchers, that promise has not been fulfilled. "Today some of the IITs have lost out on research," says Murthy. "Somehow that focus has been lost. Now they're trying to bring it back, which is good. But I wouldn't say we are out of the woods yet."

There are many reasons for this dearth of influential scholarship, beginning with the difficulty the IITs have attracting top graduate students. Their own undergraduates, who undergo a grueling selection process (the pass rate on the national entrance exam is about 2.5 percent), have appealing opportunities to go to graduate school overseas, often in the United States. At the same time, lucrative professional prospects abound for those with bachelor's degrees. Multinational consulting firms like McKinsey & Company routinely recruit from the top of the class on IIT campuses. The appeal of such opportunities significantly lessens the likelihood that the best students will stay on for IIT graduate degrees.

Similar constraints apply to building a strong faculty at the IITs. Without many top-notch graduate students, developing a distinguished faculty roster is a tough challenge. And, as with luring undergrads to PhD programs, low salaries are a huge barrier: professors can often earn many times their current salaries by taking jobs in industry. Because of rapid economic development, says IIT–Madras director M. S. Ananth, "the salaries in industry have gone far beyond the salaries in the academy. There is a difference always, even in the West, but the issue is much higher here. As a result, fewer people are coming for PhDs—fewer people want to."[25] Faculty shortages are rampant at the IITs and beyond, as is the problem of subpar qualifications. One in four faculty slots nationwide is vacant, according to a recent government report, and more than half of all professors have neither a master's degree nor a PhD. Laboratory facilities, too, have fallen into disrepair, even at institutions considered elite by Indian standards.[26] The faculty shortage, in turn, makes the profession still less desirable because of heavy course loads and large class sizes.

Adding to the difficulties faced by Indian universities as they strive to improve their academic standing is a rigid affirmative action system for members of "backward castes" who have historically faced massive discrimination. A substantial portion of slots—around 22 percent—are reserved for both students and professors who are members of these so-called scheduled castes. While university applicants must meet minimal academic requirements, the bar is set very low, which means many students coming from disadvantaged castes are poorly prepared. The system, which has a counterpart in other public sector fields such as the massive Indian civil service, is widely accepted. But it gives rise to frequent grumbling, akin to objections voiced in the United States over race-based admissions and hiring preferences at universities. This is especially true when populist political parties attempt to substantially increase the percentage of reserved slots, even when few qualified applicants are available to fill them. After the percentage of reserved faculty slots at the IITs was raised to 50 percent in 2008, ferocious protests led to the policy being reversed.[27]

Against this gloomy academic backdrop, and after years of study by groups such as the National Knowledge Commission, headed by telecommunications czar Sam Pitroda, India's prime minister Manmohan Singh recently launched what has been called "the boldest educational reform program since Jawaharlal Nehru."[28] Anxious to overhaul what Singh has called India's "dysfunctional" university system, the government plans a broad range of initiatives. Most boldly, it wants to create thirty world-class universities (starting twelve new institutions along with the eighteen currently existing central universities), and build eight new IITs and seven new IIMs in the next five years. It plans a big infusion of resources, at least by Indian standards, to accomplish this goal. The central government has pledged $2.22 billion[29] toward its higher education effort, to be earmarked for everything from building twelve new central universities to raising faculty salaries by as much as 70 percent.[30]

There has long been agreement at the highest levels of India's government that major improvements in the nation's universities are needed.

But in an interview in his Delhi office conducted before the prime minister's new initiative was announced, Montek Singh Ahluwalia, deputy chairman of India's Planning Commission, the nation's influential economic-policymaking body, cautioned that the process will not be easy. "You don't create a good university in ten years," he said. The sprint to establish new campuses "is just a matter of paying out money," he noted. By contrast, establishing world-class institutions is a vastly greater challenge. "We have three or four really good universities that we want to take to ten." Moreover, at a time when economic growth has skyrocketed from 5 or 6 percent annually to 9 percent, he explained, the demand for skills has also shot up and will require excellent academic preparation on a large scale. "We need to upgrade thirty or forty of the existing universities to something much better. Now the easiest is the expansion. The most difficult is getting to the top."[31]

Already, however, in its hurry to clone its handful of elite institutions, the government has made numerous missteps. In 2008, when the government launched its plan to more than double the existing network of seven IITs, the first six of eight new planned IITs were opened with students but no faculty, no permanent campuses, and no construction under way on new campuses.[32] (Students had to double up at existing campuses, or start at temporary facilities to which professors were temporarily detailed.) Moreover, limited research opportunities will continue to make faculty recruiting an even greater problem, with a projected fifteen IITs needing to recruit five hundred professors with engineering PhDs over the new decade. Add to that India's ever-present political patronage system, which has led to plans to locate IITs in remote states, and prospects for successful expansion seem bleak. Indeed, while the vast number of students who apply for the IITs (320,000 applied in 2008 for some 8,000 places) lead some to argue that room should be made for the many promising students who don't currently make the cut, others believe exclusivity is the hallmark of a top university. They argue that the very value of IIT degrees will be diminished if they become more common. "Have you heard of anyone wanting to multiply Harvard or Oxford even though they face a heavy demand for admissions?" asks P. V. Indiresan, a former director of IIT–Madras. "Value is proportional to scarcity: Make anything easily available, and its value collapses."[33]

As India pushes to expand its pockets of quality into a system of widespread excellence, critics warn that willy-nilly expansion is doomed to fail without first engaging in careful self-examination followed by systemic reform. "If India invests large amounts of money and human capital into academic improvement and expansion without undertaking strategies to ensure that the investment will yield results," write Altbach and Jayaram, "resources will be wasted and failure will be assured. . . . Just pumping money and resources into a fundamentally broken university system is a mistake."[34] The problems that must be overcome before India can create a world-class system are numerous, they maintain. First, there is what they term the "sclerotic bureaucracy" for which India is infamous—with few incentives for the kind of innovation that is a crucial prerequisite for top-flight academic research. Then there is the problem of the professoriate, which is not limited to low salaries. Indian academics have no financial incentives for productivity, and by the same token it has been very difficult to pay top researchers the highly competitive salaries that would be required to keep them on campus.

Not surprisingly, then, universities in India are also marred by what Altbach and Jayaram term "a culture of mediocrity." Conversely, they say, the meritocracy that is the fundamental hallmark of world-class universities is rare in Indian academia—as exemplified by the pervasiveness of the reservations system, troubling favoritism in faculty appointments, cheating on exams, and so forth. Then, too, there is the paucity of truly research-intensive universities. To create them, Altbach and Jayaram contend, will require not only a massive infusion of resources but also an abandonment of the illusion that creating a system based on the American model means treating all universities equally.[35]

India is fortunate to have a vigorous free-speech tradition and a population that is eager for academic opportunities. The nation's enthusiastic campaign to create world-class universities—including its efforts, like China's, to recruit more faculty from overseas—are a sign of just how deeply governments have embraced the belief that academic excellence and innovative economic growth go hand in hand. At the same time, the many barriers Indian universities face suggest that the road to excellence may be a bumpy one indeed.

If India's higher education push is driven in part by concerns that too many top students are leaving the country, notwithstanding its more attractive economic climate in recent years, the same is doubly true for South Korea. Well-known as one of the fastest-growing Asian tigers,[36] the thriving economic power has by no means given short shrift to its universities, at least in economic terms. In recent years, it has spent 2.6 percent of its gross domestic product on higher education, a figure that is twice the average of most Western nations and second only to the United States. Nevertheless, South Korea lost nearly 220,000 students to overseas study in 2007, nearly twice the number that went overseas ten years earlier. Most of those students went to the United States, where they now make up the third-largest group of foreign students. In economic terms, education can be viewed as a service export, with nations either gaining or losing depending on their balance of trade in students. Through this lens, South Korea has an estimated educational trade deficit of $3 to $4 billion annually, according to Pilnam Yi of the education ministry's University Policy Division. "We are extremely worried," he told the *Chronicle of Higher Education*.[37]

To keep more students at home while also fostering economic growth, South Korea has embarked on an ambitious plan to create an international hub of research excellence that can compete with the best institutions in the region and in the United States. It is creating what amounts to an academic free-trade zone in what is known as the Incheon Free Economic Zone, a 52,000-acre complex near the Incheon International Airport. There, South Korean officials have begun luring what they hope will eventually be several dozen high-level research institutes, as well as seven or more foreign campuses, beginning with the State University of New York at Stony Brook and North Carolina State University. Government hopes for establishing a regional and even global academic power are rooted in part on South Korea's existing Western-educated elite and its favorable geographic location, with Beijing and Tokyo each just a two-hour flight away. Its reforms involve a hearty embrace of English, too. In an effort to prepare students for a globalized society in which English has become the lingua franca of both the scholarly and business worlds, the top private university in South Korea, Yonsei, has created a new all-English liberal arts college. Underwood International College hopes to attract both foreign students and Koreans who might otherwise go abroad.

English will also be mandatory for all undergraduates at the Korea Advanced Institute of Science and Technology (KAIST), South Korea's leading research university, which is undergoing sweeping changes as its new president pushes it toward becoming one of the world's best scientific institutions. Nam Pyo Suh, the relatively new president of KAIST, is taking no prisoners as he tries to shake up the campus culture. Rather than treat professorships as sinecures, as had been traditional in Korea, he denied tenure to one-third of all applicants in 2007. He revamped admissions, too, mindful of the need to turn out graduates who not only are smart but also have the creativity needed to prosper in a fiercely competitive economy. Top exam scores no longer suffice; he has introduced essays and personal interviews to the process. Once on campus, students now need to earn at least a B average if they want to avoid significant extra fees. Suh, who was educated in the United States and still divides his time between KAIST and Boston, also wants to recruit top professors from overseas (he has already lured MIT mechanical engineering professor Mary Kathryn Thompson). Suh, himself a former MIT mechanical engineering professor, plans to add new medical and law schools as well. His ultimate goal: to make KAIST, which came in 132nd in the 2007 *Times Higher Education* ranking, one of the top 10 science universities in the world.[38]

Part of South Korea's plan, like those of many other nations who want to jump-start their research campuses and help them reach the top tier of global universities, is to rely heavily on partnerships with top foreign academics—particularly U.S. researchers. In January 2008, South Korea launched its World Class Universities program, an $800 million, five-year effort to import foreign professors, usually on a part-time basis, to teach and conduct research. The Korea Science and Engineering Foundation, which administers the program, said 1,000 foreign academics had applied for the program in its first ten months. More than 40 percent came from the United States, including eleven Nobel laureates and eighteen members of the U.S. National Academy of Engineering. Economic growth is a core goal of the program, foundation spokesman Woo Hyun Cho told the *Chronicle of Higher Education*. "Our focus is on supporting new growth-generating technologies that will spearhead national development," he said. While some skeptics doubt that the faculty partnership program will foster true collaboration rather than short-term stays, South Korea hopes that some of its new recruits will establish specialized research programs or new university departments in fields such as nanotechnology, nano-science, and ocean-systems engineering.[39]

It is no doubt true that South Korea's hopes may turn out to be overblown, given the academic competition it faces just in its own region, let alone worldwide. Still, that so many government and campus officials view world-class status as a necessity for their universities and their nation's economy is a signal of just how powerful the global yearning for university excellence has become.

That intense desire is certainly on display nearly 3,000 miles away in Singapore, where a concerted effort has been under way to turn the island city-state into a global intellectual powerhouse. In 2002, a government-sponsored economic panel concluded, like so many similar analyses elsewhere, that an overhauled and high-powered postsecondary system would be needed to keep up with the growth in international education around the world and to keep the country at the forefront of the global economy. The panel cited the reputation of Singapore's universities and its English language strengths as reason for confidence in its ability to bring in foreign institutions and students. It set a goal of attracting 150,000 foreign students by 2015. The dividends, it said, would be considerable: creating 22,000 jobs and boosting the contribution of the nation's education sector from 1.9 percent of GDP (18 billion U.S. dollars) to 5 percent.[40]

Already, five years earlier, the government had announced an initiative to bring ten world-class universities to Singapore within a decade. Its efforts were remarkably successful: as of 2005 it had surpassed its target by six universities. International partners that have established either joint degree programs or satellite campuses in Singapore include the University of Chicago Graduate School of Business, Johns Hopkins University, Carnegie Mellon University, and INSEAD, the international business school,[41] which began in Fontainebleau, France, but now considers its decade-old Singapore campus to be coequal with its original facility. The partnerships have been eased by the tax-free status offered to foreign universities, favorable real-estate terms, and the Singaporean government's reputation for quality control.[42] A particular coup for Singapore's effort to become a world-renowned educational hub came in 2007 when MIT established a research center at the National Research Foundation's Campus for Research Excellence and Technological Enterprise, or CREATE.[43] Singapore views the project as emblematic of its commitment to international research and collaboration.[44]

In addition to creating synergies of academic excellence by working with elite foreign universities, Singapore has also nurtured its own institutions. Recognizing the value of talented graduate students for incubating research excellence, for instance, Singapore has followed the example of other nations and established lucrative graduate fellowships. In 2007 it introduced an award known as the Singapore International Graduate Award (SINGA), which is open to international students who want to pursue postdoctoral studies at the National University of Singapore or Nanyang Technological University.[45] Following a tough application process, some 240 SINGA scholarships are awarded each year.

All these efforts seem to have paid off so far. Some 90,000 foreign students representing more than 120 nationalities now study in Singapore. And the burgeoning number of partnerships with world-class foreign universities, and branches established by them, is expected to act as a magnet that will raise those numbers still further.[46]

As its drive to be an international hub gains steam, Singapore, like China, has also begun adapting another Western innovation: raising money from alumni. Its colleges and universities, which have traditionally relied on government funding, are now moving away from this model. Nanyang Technical University (NTU), for example, hired the former development director at Northern Kentucky University in 2005 to run its new fund-raising office. Her efforts soon bore fruit. When she was hired, only 143 of 90,000 alumni had donated to their university. Two years later, more than 4,000 NTU graduates had contributed, helping bring the university's fund-raising total to $27 million. Most of this amount was earmarked for NTU's endowment, on the theory—widely shared by other universities in the region—that U.S. universities' dominance of global research is closely linked to their massive endowments.[47]

For all its progress toward global academic excellence, Singapore has certainly had its share of setbacks. Some partnerships simply never came to fruition; the University of Warwick's plan to build a campus in Singapore fizzled when long negotiations broke down over financial terms and human rights concerns. Others have fallen apart more dramatically. In 2006, the Singaporean government and Johns Hopkins University ended a joint research and education program amid considerable acrimony. The partnership, which had received $50 million in funding over eight years, collapsed because it failed to meet recruiting goals, fell short on transferring technology to local industry, and became mired in disputes over subsidies.[48] The following year brought another high-profile disappointment. Just four months after matriculating its first class of 148 freshmen, the Singapore branch of Australia's University of New South Wales closed its

doors, victim to what administrators said was a combination of low enrollment and high operating costs.[49]

Singapore also faces the same difficulty other would-be global hubs
must confront—the challenge of attracting a finite number of top faculty in a hugely competitive global marketplace. To lure the most sought-
after intellectual talent, universities and research institutes must often pay
huge salaries that constrain their spending in other key areas.[50] Then, too,
there are constraints on academic freedom in what remains an authoritarian state[51]—a barrier to true excellence comparable to the limits on free
expression that exist in other aspiring world-class academic centers such
as China and Saudi Arabia. "Singapore does have a bit of a brand image
problem in the global schoolhouse," says Edward Harcourt, head of Institutional Relations at the University of Warwick. "They hang people, they
ban homosexuality, they whip students if they misbehave—that kind of
thing."[52] Still, despite these considerable obstacles, Singapore's savvy use
of financial resources and its strategic partnerships with premier foreign
institutions seem to bode well for it to continue on its path to becoming a
global academic crossroads.

While China, India, South Korea, and Singapore have garnered plenty
of attention in their efforts to become heavy hitters in the global academic
game, perhaps the most audacious attempt to create a world-class university from scratch is taking place in Saudi Arabia. In September 2009, the
King Abdullah University of Science and Technology, or KAUST, opened
its doors. It aspires to become a top-flight graduate institution, with an
elite faculty of scientific researchers and close connections to the top universities whose ranks it hopes to join. Its establishment also hearkens back
to the Islamic Golden Age. At KAUST's opening ceremonies, its architect and benefactor, Saudi Arabia's King Abdullah, compared the fledg-
ling university to the House of Wisdom, the celebrated center of research
and education that flourished in Baghdad from the ninth to thirteenth
centuries.[53] Today, the oil-endowed desert kingdom, which has become
immensely wealthy since World War II, is looking beyond its massive pe-
troleum revenues to a future in which ideas will be the most important
currency. It is no surprise then, that higher education in general—and
KAUST in particular—has become a top priority for the Saudis.

For evidence of the nation's commitment to KAUST, one need look
no further than King Abdullah's personal $10 billion donation to his pet

project. That start-up funding amounts to the sixth-largest university endowment in the world,[54] and over time the endowment is expecting to grow still further to $25 billion, which would make it second only to Harvard's.[55] At the same time, King Abdullah has ensured that the new university is not run by the education ministry, with its reputation for bureaucratic inefficiency. Instead, it is being created by Saudi Arabia's national oil company, Aramco, which is highly regarded for its businesslike habits. A further symbol of the university's global ambitions: its decision to recruit its first president, Harvard-educated engineer Choon Fong Shih, from the National University of Singapore, which made great strides toward becoming a worldwide intellectual hub during his presidency.

But the key ingredient in the KAUST formula is its extensive partnerships with some of the best Western institutions in the world. It has negotiated carefully tailored agreements with individual departments in areas where KAUST hopes to immediately establish high-level expertise. Initial partners include the mechanical engineering department at the University of California–Berkeley; the Institute for Computational Earth Sciences and Engineering at the University of Texas at Austin; Stanford University's computer science and applied mathematics departments; the biosciences and bioengineering departments at the University of Cambridge; and the departments of chemical engineering, materials science, and engineering at Imperial College, London. KAUST will also have oversight from a blue chip international advisory board that includes such elder statesmen of science as Frank Rhodes, president emeritus of Cornell University, Frank Press, president emeritus of the National Academy of Sciences, and Richard Sykes, the rector of Imperial College.[56] In keeping with its aspiration to an intellectually open Western atmosphere, KAUST will be coeducational—a big step in a country where female students have often been taught by men via closed-circuit television.[57] It will also offer lucrative fellowships—covering tuition in full, along with a living stipend—to top undergraduates from around the world who enroll in KAUST's graduate programs.

As with all world-class university ventures, attracting top-flight researchers—whether as partners or as full-time faculty members—is crucial. New York University officials, for instance, are well aware that their Abu Dhabi venture is dependent on luring these professors, and the same holds true for KAUST. Even as the new university began building what amounts to a city some fifty miles from Jeddah, it was also deeply immersed in building the core of professors that is the backbone of any great university. With no existing faculty to engage in their traditional role of recruiting and hiring new professors, KAUST essentially subcontracted the task to its Western partners, who were also charged with the responsibility of designing the curriculum in their respective fields of expertise. To recruit faculty, the partner institutions have conducted interviews around the world and given KAUST advice about important inducements to lure top candidates, including modest teaching loads and an opportunity to work with faculty from world-class partner institutions. Final hiring decisions are made by KAUST, which negotiates financial packages and must persuade candidates to relocate for at least part of each year to Saudi Arabia.

The challenge would seem to be steep: working with an institution halfway around the world, in a desert country known for authoritarian rule and an austere, rigid form of Islam might not at first blush seem attractive to academics in the United States, Great Britain, and beyond. Social constraints outside the university grounds are likely to be a significant barrier to faculty recruitment. Alcohol is prohibited in the kingdom. There are no movie theaters (religious authorities have only recently begun to moderate the decades-old ban with occasional public showings of preapproved films).[58] Women are forbidden to drive and must cover themselves almost completely in public. "Women are not going to be rushing there in a hurry," says Walter Murray, a computational mathematics expert at Stanford University who is part of the team working with KAUST. "There will be a lot of reluctance—simply because of the horror stories you hear about Saudi Arabia."[59]

Nevertheless, the start-up of KAUST quickly attracted faculty interest. Jean-Claude Latombe, another Stanford professor who is working with KAUST, says he organized an 8 a.m. faculty meeting that attracted fifteen professors. "Getting fifteen professors from computer science is [always] very difficult," says the native of France, who has joint appointments in the School of Engineering and computer science departments, "but at 8 a.m. it is almost impossible. This showed there is interest."[60] Indeed, across the San Francisco Bay at the University of California, Berkeley, the mechanical engineering department voted 34 to 2 in favor of an agreement with KAUST.[61]

Some of that interest might be attributed to the hefty research funding that KAUST offered to faculty at other institutions who are helping with its start-up. The university partners themselves are also receiving considerable funding from KAUST: upwards of $25 million over five years, split between $10 million for home-campus research, $5 million for research at KAUST, and $10 million in outright gifts, along with administrative costs.[62] Still, Stanford's Latombe insists that money is not the principal factor driving faculty interest in the new project. "Of course we're getting quite a bit of money from this agreement," he says. "But the main interest of my colleagues who are working on this project is the impact this can have on the region."

For starters, creating a university from scratch is a daunting but, for some, an appealing project—all the more so in Saudi Arabia. "To create an open university with no barriers based on race, ethnicity, national origin, religion, is a very big challenge," says Latombe. And notwithstanding the difficulties, Latombe, like other advocates of bringing Western-style universities to the Middle East, is convinced that if KAUST becomes a top-ranked university, it will change Saudi life: he and others cite the cosmopolitan effect of having Saudi students mix with others from around the world; the eye-opening experience of coeducation; the pride of seeing Saudi Arabia as a producer and not just a consumer of cutting-edge knowledge. Latombe even thinks Saudi Arabia's notorious hostility to Israel may be softened because of the inevitability of academic collaboration between the two nations. "What are the closest major academic centers to KAUST? They're all in Israel, so they'll have to establish contact—maybe at first with American or European universities as intermediaries."

Despite such optimistic visions, U.S. universities' partnerships with KAUST and similar ventures have caused controversy at home. At the University of California, Berkeley, for instance, a number of faculty members expressed worries about whether academic freedom could really be possible in Saudi Arabia and also voiced concerns about the treatment of women, gays, and Israelis in a kingdom not famous for religious or social tolerance. William Drummond, the chairman of Berkeley's academic senate, wrote to the *Contra Costa Times*, a local newspaper that had reported on the issue, to insist that, while the concerns had merit, an internal committee had quizzed the mechanical engineering department carefully on these matters and had been satisfied. "The purpose was to find out if the rights and privileges of Berkeley faculty (women, men, Jews, and gentiles) would be protected," Drummond wrote.[63]

He did not seem to give the project a resounding vote of confidence, however. "The collaboration is not being undertaken because of a secret fondness for a notoriously authoritarian regime," Drummond said, but because of the need for the campus to seek outside funding in the face of reduced state subsidies. He concluded by noting that the deal must be watched "vigilantly" as it unfolds, observing bluntly: "We are walking down a dark street at night in an altogether strange neighborhood."[64] Similar concerns were raised at another public university, California Polytechnic State University at San Louis Obispo, when it entered a $5.9 million, five-year partnership with another Saudi university, Jubail University College. Only men can teach or take engineering classes at the campus, which has separate classes in other fields for women. "No matter how you cut it, we're supporting the oppression of women," one professor told the *Los Angeles Times*.[65] As at Berkeley and elsewhere, however, senior administrators point to pledges by the Saudis that U.S. faculty will be able to teach at Saudi institutions regardless of gender, religion, or sexual orientation. More broadly, they make the case that islands of Western academic excellence such as KAUST, in what has previously been an uninspiring intellectual environment, will inevitably spread liberalization of both scholarly and social varieties. One early sign of the Saudi regime's commitment to greater openness: after a Saudi cleric criticized KAUST's coeducation policy as "evil" when the new university opened its doors, King Abdullah quickly removed him from the council that sets religious policy for the kingdom.[66] However ambitious the promise of KAUST in academic terms, it seems that its potential political and social repercussions are greater still.

WORLD-CLASS IN WESTERN EUROPE

While a rush to create top-tier institutions continues in the Middle East and Asia, which have not traditionally been centers of scholarly excellence and are striving to catch up with the West, a different kind of race is taking place in Western Europe. There, in an ironic reversal, campuses that were crucial to the development of modern universities, that were once held up as models for today's global leader, the United States, have in some respects descended into academic mediocrity. No longer on the cutting edge of global research, no longer the most appealing destinations for international students, these universities are in the midst of a far-reaching and sometimes contentious effort, spurred by their national governments, to restore their lost luster. The two best examples: Germany and France, each of which is in the midst of a government-led overhaul of its higher education system.

In Germany, where the Humboldtian university of the nineteenth century pioneered such hugely influential concepts as academic freedom and the combination of teaching and research in one institution, a very different picture had emerged by the 1970s. As recounted by Daniel Fallon, author of *The German University* and an emeritus professor at the University of Maryland at College Park, the social unrest of the 1960s, combined with the transformation of German universities from elite to mass institutions, resulted in highly regulated, dysfunctional universities. The universities had too many students, too few professors, and little differentiation by mission. Doctoral-granting comprehensive universities became the norm around the country, regardless of the nation's economic needs, and by the late 1980s foreign enrollment had declined significantly both qualitatively and quantitatively. In sum, few or no incentives to excellence were in place.

"Although many factors contributed to the sluggishness of the Germany university," Fallon writes, "the most obvious was the tenacity of adherence to the idea that a German university must be the same wherever it was located, offering essentially the same full range of study, by faculty who were treated essentially the same everywhere."[67] As of 2008, Germany had eighty-eight "research-intensive" public universities with authority to award doctoral degrees, a number that Fallon says is "untenably large" and "implausibly supportable at a high level of quality." German universities are notably absent at the top levels of global college rankings.[68]

Against this backdrop, in 2004 Germany's federal minister for higher education gave a speech decrying the state of the nation's universities and calling for a targeted effort by which the government would identify, and lavishly fund, six campuses believed to have the potential to become world-class. Less than two years later, the Excellence Initiative was launched with funding of 19 billion euros, divided 75:25 between the federal government and the states. After significant opposition, the program was broadened considerably, focusing on improved research and better doctoral education at a wider range of institutions. Nonetheless, it was a revolutionary break from the egalitarian norms of Germany's postwar universities. "You couldn't even use the word 'elite' until a couple years ago," said a California-based consultant who advised some of the universities competing for the new awards. "It was *verboten*."[69]

The program was divided into three contests: one for graduate schools, one for "clusters of excellence" in which institutions combine high-quality academic programs to promote interdisciplinary research, and one "futures concept" category intended to promote radical reorganization of the university in order to compete at the highest levels internationally. To be eligible for the final category, universities had to win at least one award in each of the first two contests. While the government carefully avoided using the terms "elite" or "best" in discussing the competitions,[70] their true meaning was lost on no one. "The German world of universities will change in the future," said Horst Hippler, rector of the University of Karlsruhe, when his campus won one of the first three $26 million excellence awards in 2006. "The wish has always been that all universities are equal. This has never been true and now has been accepted politically."[71]

The process for awarding performance-based funds to German universities is both highly competitive and explicitly intended to subject the federal republic's campuses to global standards. Fallon, who served on the twelve-member committee that evaluated "futures concept" proposals, notes that he was accompanied on one three-day site visit to a finalist campus by a high-powered committee of scholars from around the world: "an Arabist from Yale, an American historian from Princeton, a mathematician from Oxford, a dean from Indiana University, a prize-winning young scientist from Göttingen, a former university chancellor from Switzerland, and two directors of independent research laboratories in Germany."[72]

But even as Germany taps international expertise on its path to improvement, it still faces the formidable task of recruiting more foreign students and scholars, a goal that is part and parcel of its effort to make the country's universities more globally competitive. On the one hand, the number of international students in Germany has risen every year for a decade or so. A recent report by Germany's Federal Ministry of Education and Research noted that Germany is one of the top higher education destinations in the world, lagging only behind the United States and Great Britain.[73] However, its share of students from China—its prime source of overseas students—dropped slightly in the most recent survey. As Chinese enrollment abroad has soared, Germany's share of those students grew in absolute terms from 17,000 in 2002 to about 27,000 in 2005. At the same time, more Chinese students chose to study elsewhere, leading to a decline in percentage terms from 7.7 to 6.7 percent.

Overall, the report found, "only 43 percent of the foreign students surveyed indicated that Germany was their first choice."[74] Moreover, Bulgaria, Poland, and Russia—countries that, after China, send the largest numbers of students to Germany—all project population declines. Then, too, Germany has a major shortage of engineers and researchers.[75] All in all, the urgency of sustaining the nation's competition-driven overhaul is increasingly clear.

France's effort to restructure its own public university system came several years after Germany's. It has been just as sweeping and controversial, overturning many of the same assumptions of equal funding that had characterized Germany's universities. The first step in France's new regime came in 2007 when the National Assembly passed a broad range of reforms championed by newly elected president Nicolas Sarkozy. The bill gave the nation's eighty-five universities significantly greater autonomy, including control over their finances and more leeway in personnel decisions. As in Germany, opponents raised the specter of the eventual privatization of universities, while supporters of the new regime maintained that adherence to the principle of equality for all had in fact translated into mediocrity for all.

Within a year, Sarkozy's government had announced the first six campuses to receive considerable extra funding under "Operation Campus," his five-billion-euro initiative to bring French universities to a world-class standard. Like its German counterpart, the program uses a competitive process, asking universities to develop ten centers of excellence likely to bring international renown.[76] The first six winning centers, in Bordeaux, Grenoble, Lyon, Montpellier, Strasbourg, and Toulouse, each consist of a combination of research and higher education institutions. "The competitive character of this selection is very modern, and in line with the spirit of autonomy for the universities as they are the ones who developed their projects, and not the ministry," Valérie Pécresse, Higher Education and Research Minister, told *Le Monde*.[77]

Despite the rapid implementation of Sarkozy's election promise to reform French universities, the changes did not appear to move far enough and fast enough to satisfy him—even as his critics continued to raise alarms over both his rhetoric and his actions. In January 2009, the French president blasted what he termed an "infantilizing system" of "weak universities." France has fallen behind other nations in research and innovation, he argued, because it has shrunk from the task of reforming its higher education and research infrastructure. Far from being revolutionary, he declared, his moves toward greater individual campus control of budgets, hiring, and more are par for the course in the countries with which France competes. "Autonomy is the rule" in all nations with world-class universities, he said. "There is not a single example in the world of great universities that are not autonomous."[78] For its part, the protest group Sauvons la Recherche ("Let's Save Research") called Sarkozy's remarks "lies and insults." Still, for now at least, it seems likely that his approach to university reform will prevail.

While France's large public postsecondary sector undergoes a significant globalization-driven shake-up, colleges in France's much smaller system of elite *grandes écoles* are also eyeing their place on the world stage. While these highly selective institutions already enjoy huge prestige within France and, in some cases, worldwide renown as well, many are anxious to follow the internationalization model of other elite universities around the world. This aim is driven by a combination of factors, including the desire to prepare students for a global marketplace, and the sense that a cross-border presence, whether through student exchanges, partnerships, or both, is now de rigueur for an institution that wants to join the company of world-class universities.

A case in point is the Institut d'Études Politiques, known as Sciences Po, a highly regarded Paris-based university that focuses on social science research. Sciences Po has long been a beacon of excellence within France but has been less well known in Europe and around the world. Since 1996, however, it has become globalized with a vengeance. About 40 percent of its 6,700 students are international.[79] It has exchange partnerships with some three hundred universities globally, most notably with the London School of Economics (LSE) and Columbia University's School of International and Public Affairs. Fifteen foreign languages are taught at Sciences Po, which since 2000 has required all undergraduates to spend a year abroad and also requires all master's graduates to learn at least three languages.[80] Like so many elite universities in other countries, it draws heavily on international faculty, hosting ninety-two visiting professors from foreign countries each year. Unsurprisingly, then, the university is not monolingual: one-third of its lectures and seminars are taught in languages other than French—in English, of course, but also in German, Spanish, Portuguese, and other European languages. Its two-year Master of Public Affairs with LSE and Columbia is taught in English, for example, while other degrees, such as an MBA program, are taught bilingually.

Much of this global flavor can be traced to the efforts of Richard Descoings, who became president of Sciences Po in 1996. Before long, he made his mark with a multipronged campaign to reform a university that he saw as out of step with the era of globalization. Along with a range of new measures that led critics to charge that he was Americanizing a cherished French institution—private fund-raising, affirmative action in admissions based on social disadvantage, and linking tuition to family income—he launched a new focus on internationalization. His premise is that luring students with worldwide horizons will require serious effort. "The age of globalization means comparisons," he says. "We have mobility of students, of professors, of research, so we are compared." This is a generational change, he suggests. "In my generation, I didn't know it was possible to be educated at Oxford, or Harvard, or in Asia. I was French, so I went to a French university."[81]

Descoings is also on the record in favor of greater use of English in a nation famously attached to its *langue maternelle*. "English is not a foreign language—it is *the* international language," he says in an interview in his office on Science Po's central Paris campus. "When I go to Germany and I meet my colleagues, the presidents of the German universities, we speak English. We have to stop saying that English is *one* of the languages. It is *the* language of international exchange: commercial, military, and also intellectual and scientific. How can an economist not speak English? That's it. It is no longer an object of debate." He suggests that the resistance of some French academics to the dominance of English in scholarship sometimes stems from defensiveness and thwarts French universities' international competitiveness. "It can camouflage a certain mediocrity,"

Descoings argues. "When a professor says that one thinks in the language that one speaks, does he say that really out of conviction? Or is it a way of escaping being read, and thus criticized and evaluated?"

Another key player in Sciences Po's efforts to internationalize was Pascal Delisle. Previously head of the university's American Center, where he helped establish partnerships with U.S. universities, Delisle is now cultural attaché at the French Embassy in Washington DC, where he is in charge of strengthening U.S.-French academic cooperation. Had Sciences Po not made significant changes, its progress as an institution would have been limited, he says. "If we had stayed in the situation we were in ten to fifteen years ago, we would still be a very good school in France. But we would have missed the train of globalization. And it would have been very hard to catch up."[82] The imperative driving the change is the same one heard over and over at universities around the globe: "Our students will do work everywhere in the world," Delisle says. "It was important to prepare our students for a globalized economy."

Building the university's own reputation is a significant factor as well. The proliferation of student exchanges is mutually beneficial for students and the university, says Francis Vérillaud, a vice president of Sciences Po in charge of international affairs and exchanges and a national expert on academic globalization. "It's fruitful for the students studying a year at Yale or in China or wherever in good universities,"[83] he says. At the same time, Sciences Po's own reputation is enhanced when its high-quality students serve as ambassadors to other universities. By the same token, exchange students help Sciences Po's reputation when they report back to their home universities on the strengths of its programs. "This network is a sort of network of excellence," says Vérillaud.

Similarly, brand-building is also a key part of Sciences Po's strategy. While the university is constantly approached by other institutions about creating dual-degree programs, it selects partners carefully, forging alliances only with the best universities in the world. This choosiness helps extend the institution's reach when it tries to enter new markets where it is less well known than in France and Europe. The university's joint-degree programs with leading universities such as LSE and Columbia University make Vérillaud's job easier in places like India, he says. "We have ten dual degrees with these [prominent] institutions. I don't need to explain very long in India who I am, what I'm doing, what Sciences Po is."

More broadly, he explains, the dual-degree programs lead each institution to take a more innovative approach to its mission. Each can begin to conceive of the partnership not simply as serving one another's students but as attracting a worldwide student population with a degree that is truly cross-institutional. "We go to LSE and jointly say, 'We are going to do a dual degree, not for the LSE students, not for the Sciences Po students; we are going to do a dual degree to target students wherever in the world.'" Already, the five joint degree programs between LSE and Sciences Po mean they share three hundred students who are not linked to one institution any more than to the other. In other words, partnerships initially built on the mutual advantage to each institution of "co-branding" can lead to the creation of universities, or divisions of universities, that are no longer closely linked to their respective home campuses but are instead truly transnational—perhaps an increasingly good fit with an increasingly transnational world.

The Uncertain Path to Success

From France and Germany to India and China, evidently numerous paths lead to the global recognition so many universities now seek. What so many higher education systems around the world have in common is that they are under unprecedented pressure, often from their government funders, to demonstrate that they are providing value for money—particularly in the form of the scientific and technological accomplishments that are so closely associated with innovation and economic prosperity. "To a certain extent, we are victims of our success," said Jan Sadlak, director of the UNESCO–European Centre for Higher Education, at an October 2008 conference on world-class universities hosted in Shanghai by Shanghai Jiao Tong University. "Higher education became too important to be left just to academics—and also has a very important role in the innovation chain." The result, said Sadlak, a leading figure among those seeking to document and analyze the drive for world-class universities: "Companies, universities, research centers, and whole countries are in pursuit of and trying to attract the best brains."[84]

Despite tremendous global efforts to create top-tier research universities, some analysts caution that the enterprise may turn out to be remarkably difficult. "It's a lot harder to create world-class universities than other people think," says George Mason University economist Tyler Cowen. A look at lists of top U.S. universities in 1900, 1920, and 1940, he contends, when compared to today's top schools, shows "basically no change" outside the growth of some elite institutions in California. "The lack of turnover is remarkable. If you compare what's in the Dow [Jones Industrial Average], it's totally different."[85]

Cowen quickly ticks off a list of reasons he believes the lack of turnover within the United States will be seen globally. Top-notch universities require "broad institutional" commitments that are present only in the United States, Great Britain, Canada, and a few other countries, he contends. Universities can't become great without complete free speech, autonomous faculty governance, and high levels of trust in that governance, "so the university is not treated just like a branch of the civil service, and if you make a deal with an institution you can be sure it will be honored."

Countries that have those norms, such as Canada and England, he says, are able to compete with U.S. universities—although not with notable success. But those marked by excessive bureaucracy and intermittent corruption, among other woes, are unlikely to fare well at all ("Look at Italian academia," Cowen exclaims, "it's a nightmare!"). While he calls the explosion of high-quality Chinese research "the best thing that's happening in the world," he is doubtful that recent gains among Chinese universities can be counted on to last, citing the country's turbulent history (and, he might have added, its uncertain commitment to academic freedom).

Moreover, simple geography may play a significant role in the concentrations of universities that have proven to be most successful, according to Cowen. "There are a number of endeavors that are naturally concentrated," he says. Banking is likely to found above all in New York and London for some time to come, while moviemaking will thrive in Hollywood, Bollywood, and perhaps Paris. By this logic, then, sheer synergies of location are likely to clinch U.S. dominance of higher education, notwithstanding growth in mobility of students, professors, campuses, and ideas. The one exception Cowen will make is in individual fields, where a French or German university might create a standout department in, say, mathematics. "But a whole school that's across the board better than [for instance] Boston University—the closest you get is in England, and they don't compare all that well."

Others offer a considerably rosier view of the prospect that globalization and the recognition of universities' importance to economic growth could shake up the existing pecking order. "Nothing is forever," says Jamie Merisotis, a longtime higher education analyst in Washington, DC, who is now president of the Indianapolis-based Lumina Foundation for Education, which promotes college access and also underwrites research on university globalization, including world rankings. Unlike Cowen, Merisotis believes that a new setup of top-notch institutions may emerge within the next decade. "We've had a fairly defined set of world class universities for a while, but I think that the case of China, the case of King Abdullah University in Saudi Arabia, what we're seeing in terms of the retooling of some of the European universities, all that is likely to result in the emergence of some set of new world-class universities that aren't really on the radar screen right now."[86]

Venturing into the territory of sacrilege, Merisotis contends that some much-vaunted universities already have lost some of the prestige they once held: "It has been quite a while since Oxford and Cambridge were believed to be the best universities in Europe." And he suggests that the example of Stanford University, which Cowen portrays as the exception to the rule of a remarkably stable list of academic front-runners over time, in fact shows that public policies can make a big difference in determining which universities thrive. "Before the federal government made massive investments in infrastructure, Stanford wasn't considered one of the best universities."

Is there a third way between these divergent assessments of the intense drive worldwide to create great research institutions? Altbach of Boston College offers a highly plausible scenario that acknowledges today's changing academic world without giving too much credence to the grandest aspirations of some up-and-coming universities. Fifty years from now, he says, a greater number of serious research universities will surely be established in many more countries. But, he adds, "I don't think KAUST, to take that example, or Seoul National University in Korea, or Nehru University in India, are ever going to be Harvard or Oxford. Because it's just too difficult to do that, especially in smaller countries that aren't English-speaking, that aren't so much linked in with the global higher education system." A much more likely outcome is that many universities will be good but not great—a form of differentiation that is well established in U.S. higher education and should not be viewed as failure by postsecondary institutions around the world. "They should look at Indiana University as a model," Altbach says, "which is a wonderful place, and not be disappointed if they can't get above that."[87]

By way of illustration, Altbach describes a recent meeting with a group from Kazakhstan that is eager to build a top university there. He says their prospects are dim. "They can probably have a research university in Astana—probably not as good as Indiana—in twenty years, but they're not going to have Harvard. Ever. No matter how much money they spend," Altbach says. "It's not just money. It's location. It's the size of the intellectual community in your country," along with many other factors. Some countries, such as Cambodia, just won't be able to develop research universities, he maintains. But there's nothing wrong with establishing divergent academic goals in which not everybody aspires to be part of the elite. "The institutions lower on the totem pole need to have a mission that makes sense for them and makes sense for society," he says. Indeed, in his thoughtful how-to manual, *The Challenge of Establishing World-Class Universities*, World Bank higher education expert Jamil Salmi writes that governments and institutions eager to move into the upper echelons of global scholarship should begin by asking themselves why their country needs a world-class university in the first place: "What is the economic rationale and the expected added value compared with the contribution of existing institutions?"

For those governments that are determined to move ahead, Salmi outlines three basic strategies: "Picking winners," that is, improving a small group of existing universities that hold the promise of excellence (as France and Germany are now doing through an unprecedented process of singling out a handful of promising campuses for extra funding); a "hybrid formula," which involves encouraging "a small number of existing institutions to merge and transform themselves into a new university," one that would benefit from the same sort of synergies typically associated with top research institutions; and a "clean-slate approach," in which governments attempt to create from scratch brand-new world-class universities, as with KAUST.[88]

None of these approaches guarantees success. But as Altbach told the same Shanghai audience addressed by Sadlak, "All of us must play in the knowledge league of the twenty-first century. All of us can't play at the top of that league, and must be realistic, but all of us must participate." There are, after all, only a finite number of top researchers at present—all with a disproportionate influence in the academic world and beyond. But perhaps the best eventual measure of the global scramble to create world-class universities will be whether and how the precious resource of knowledge has been expanded.

Chapter Four

College Rankings Go Global

It would be hard to overstate just how contentious rankings of U.S. colleges and universities have become in recent years. As editor of the *U.S. News & World Report* college guides in the mid-2000s, I became accustomed to a steady stream of college presidents and admissions officials visiting the magazine's Washington, DC offices to complain about the publication's influential college rankings. Some thought outsiders—especially journalists—shouldn't be ranking colleges at all. Some took exception to one or more aspects of the methodology used to calculate each college's standing. Others insisted that if only their own data had been properly tabulated by the magazine, their ranking would be higher. Outside the magazine's offices, of course, those that fared well in the rankings often trumpeted the results on their Web sites.

Several years later, the rankings debate had spread far beyond United States. In the fall of 2007, I listened intently—from the sidelines, mercifully—as the elegantly dressed director of the École Normale Supérieure, Monique Canto-Sperber, addressed an international conference hosted by Shanghai Jiao Tong University. An expert in Greek philosophy, she delivered a meticulous demolition of the university's closely watched global college rankings, explaining why they couldn't possibly do justice to the strengths of her celebrated institution. The only difference from the debate in the United States was that U.S. universities at the very top of the pecking order tend to publicly ignore the rankings, whereas in Shanghai the president of an elite institution made clear that, for her university, the global rankings are a serious business indeed.

The colloquy that took place in Shanghai is by no means an isolated one. In recent years, college rankings have experienced explosive growth around the globe, as the same calls for accountability and objective evaluation seen in American higher education have become ubiquitous. Rankings now exist in more than forty nations,[1] whether established by journalists, government agencies, nonprofit organizations, or universities themselves. There are global rankings too, of course. All are closely watched and are also a source of great controversy, in part because of the serious consequences that sometimes result for universities that are deemed not to measure up. All this should come as no surprise. Students everywhere increasingly behave like consumers. At the same time, governments closely follow the extent to which the universities they fund are contributing to innovation and national economic growth. As students become more mobile, universities move across borders, and competition for world-class status becomes ever more intense, little wonder, then, that college rankings have gone global. They are an unmistakable reflection of global academic competition. Many would say they fan that competition as well. Rankings seem destined to be a fixture on the global education scene for years to come. Detractors notwithstanding, as they are refined and improved they can and should play an important role in helping universities get better.

BIRTH OF THE RANKINGS

In the United States, whose college rankings have been uniquely influential, a number of efforts at evaluating colleges long predate those inaugurated by *U.S. News* in 1983. Some, intended earnestly, look rather whimsical in retrospect. In the 1895 *Illustrated History of the University of California*, a detailed chart[2] offers a "before" and "after" snapshot of the fitness level of the men of the then-young university, comparing the physical prowess of its undergraduates to those at three of the university's well-established East Coast rivals: Yale, Amherst, and Cornell. Upon entering the university, the illustrated chart demonstrates, the average UC man had biceps, chest, thigh, calf, and arm measurements, plus strength in various body parts, well below the average of a sample of 15,000 of his blue-blood competitors. But following two years of calisthenics in the healthy California air,

the chart shows, brawny Berkeley students had surpassed their effete East
Coast counterparts. Perhaps this early cross-college comparison is more
analogous to today's intercollegiate sports ratings than to any academic
ranking. Still, its focus on how much students improve while in college is
striking for the way it foreshadows the value-added analysis that is much
sought after in today's higher education world.

That outcomes-oriented approach was only hinted at in the earliest
truly academic college rankings in the United States, which date back to
the turn of the twentieth century.[3] They focused simply on which universities produced the most distinguished graduates, following the example of
an Englishman named Alick Maclean. In 1900 Maclean published a study
called *Where We Get Our Best Men*, which looked at the characteristics of
the eminent men of the day, including nationality, family, birthplace, and
university attended. In the back of the book, he published a list of universities ranked by the number of their prominent alumni. The first U.S.
ranking in 1910 took a similar "reverse-engineering" approach, examining
successful individuals and crediting their alma maters for their eventual
success. A number of different rankings were attempted over subsequent
decades, most looking at graduate-level education and almost all continuing the emphasis on either some version of the "great man" theory of
educational quality, or, in one case, of how well a college's graduates performed in graduate school.

By the early 1960s, however, survey-based reputational methodology
began to supplant the rankings' earlier focus on outcomes. Soon, almost
every published ranking was based on an institution's reputation among
its peers rather than the accomplishments of its graduates. Interest in examining undergraduate education reemerged during that time, too. And
with the emergence of commercially successful rankings such as Allan
Cartter's discipline-by-discipline *Assessment of Quality in Graduate Education*, which sold 26,000 copies and received great critical acclaim, reputation-based college rankings began to come into their own.

Nevertheless, rankings were still scrutinized mostly within the guild of
academe rather than in the wider world of college-bound students and
their families. That would soon change. By the late twentieth century, attending college had become a mass phenomenon. By 1972, nearly half of
all high school graduates continued directly to either a two- or a four-year
institution.[4] And while most U.S. undergraduates have always attended

public institutions near their homes, the growth of meritocratic admissions at the nation's elite universities led to growing competition for admissions slots. Where selective colleges were once fed largely by a small number of Eastern prep schools, the opening of those colleges to a broader swath of society—beginning in the 1960s and continuing at a faster pace during the 1970s—led to wider interest in how to make a sound college choice, and, in an increasingly competitive admissions climate, how to get in.

Against this backdrop, a number of different efforts emerged to inform students and parents about their college choices. One, *The Gourman Report*, was published from 1967 to 1997, ranking colleges to within two decimal places despite having a methodology that was shrouded in mystery.[5] A far more credible effort was launched in 1981 by Edward T. Fiske, then education editor of the *New York Times*, under the title *The New York Times Selective Guide to Colleges* (a name that was later changed, when the guidebook became too controversial for the *Times*, to *The Selective Guide to Colleges* and then *The Fiske Guide to Colleges*). Like its main competitor, the *Yale Daily News's Insider's Guide to the Colleges*, Fiske's guide was compiled with the help of a network of student reporters at campuses around the nation. It profiled several hundred colleges, using a narrative feature-article style to paint a picture of academics and student life at each university. The guide, which remains popular today, uses a version of the Michelin star system to rate the social life, academic rigor, and "quality of life" at each campus, with a maximum of three points available in each category. Perhaps because it is a rating rather than a ranking—there is no ordinal numbering of top, middle, and bottom colleges, and many colleges can earn a two- or three-star rating in a given category—it has never been as controversial as other efforts to see how colleges stack up against one another. "I originally got a lot of flack, since colleges were used to doing the judging of students, not being judged," Fiske says. "But *U.S. News*, bless its heart, took the pressure off me. People love rankings, which is not really what I do, and the way people use the rankings really irks colleges and, for that matter, college counselors."[6]

Indeed, the *U.S. News* rankings were contentious from the very start. Launched in 1983, the rankings began simply enough as an outgrowth of another journalistic project for which the newsmagazine had received significant attention: a survey asking U.S. leaders to identify the most influential Americans. In a detailed account written by the late Alvin Sanoff, the longtime managing editor of the rankings project,[7] he says the magazine's editors at the time were hoping to gain similar notice—and, to be sure, sell some magazines—with an effort to identify the best colleges in the United States. Although today's *U.S. News* rankings are often criticized for focusing too heavily on reputation rather than actual accomplishments, the magazine's first rankings were exclusively based on reputation. *U.S. News* surveyed college presidents around the country, asking them to identify the nation's best universities. It published the results in a regular issue of the magazine, first in 1983 and again in 1985. It was only in 1987 that the magazine published a separate guidebook entitled *America's Best Colleges*, extending its reach to include not only undergraduate education but also law, business, medical, and engineering schools.

The debut of the rankings was well timed, coming at the height of the U.S. consumer movement. "A generation of parents who were college-educated brought both pragmatism and status-seeking to the college search process," writes Sanoff. "While many members of earlier generations were simply pleased that their children were going to college, members of the Baby Boom generation cast a more critical eye toward higher education. They wanted value for their money." The first generation of *U.S. News* rankings catered to that appetite in a fairly simple way. The presidents surveyed were asked to pick the ten colleges that provided the best undergraduate education in the academic category to which their university belonged. These nine categories, based loosely on the so-called Carnegie Classifications established by the Carnegie Foundation for the Advancement of Teaching, included National Universities, National Liberal Arts Colleges, Southern Comprehensive Institutions, Eastern Liberal Arts Colleges, and so forth. In the first two, most closely watched categories, the magazine published a ranking of the top twenty-five institutions. In the remaining categories, it ranked the top ten. This straightforward early effort—a fairly standard journalistic approach to a consumer-advice story—had within a few years become more complex, more popular, and more contentious. "No one imagined that the rankings would become what some consider the 800-pound gorilla of American higher education," writes Sanoff, "important enough to be the subject of doctoral dissertations, academic papers and conferences, and endless debate."

When the first full-fledged *U.S. News* guidebook was published in 1987, a delegation of college presidents and senior administrators met with the magazine's editors and asked that the rankings enterprise be stopped. Purely numerical indicators are an inappropriate way to measure the varied institutions and missions of U.S. higher education, they argued (as would umpteen critics in years to come). Moreover, the reputational survey of college presidents amounted to nothing more than a beauty contest. The *U.S. News* editors listened, but rather than do away with their already flourishing enterprise, they made significant changes to the rankings instead. As Sanoff recounts, they consulted with outside experts and decided to divide the rankings into two components. The reputational survey was revamped to include not only college presidents but also provosts and deans of admission who would bring a broader base of expertise to the task. At the same time, a range of quantitative measures was introduced, each requiring data collection followed by the application of a weighting determined by the magazine's editors. The objective data included several components: (1) student selectivity measures, such as a college's acceptance rate and the average SAT or ACT scores of the entering class; (2) student retention data, notably the graduation rate and the percentage of first-year students who returned for their second year; (3) institutional resources, mostly consisting of research spending; and (4) faculty quality, including average faculty salaries and the percentage of faculty with PhDs.

In one form or another, the basic structure of the rankings has remained roughly similar ever since, notwithstanding the addition of a few supplementary factors, changes in data sources (the quality of the magazine's data is widely regarded to have improved), and tweaks to the weighting of each category. *U.S. News* has also made a concerted effort to be more transparent with its methodology and to take suggestions from critics. The magazine invites a group of admissions deans to its offices every year to serve as an informal advisory board. And despite bouts of defensiveness, it does make changes that it believes improve the rankings. One example came in 1997. Detractors had argued for years that the rankings focused excessively on "inputs" rather than "outputs" by giving colleges credit for admitting well-qualified students rather than for how well they actually educated those students. In response, the magazine expanded a so-called value-added measure (now referred to as "graduation rate performance"), accounting for 5 percent of the total ranking in the "National University" and "National Liberal Arts College" categories, which assesses graduation rates on a curve, taking into account students' incoming qualifications and socioeconomic back-grounds. This measure of persistence controlling for social and academic backgrounds doesn't really capture how much students learn—an elusive question that is in many ways the Holy Grail of college rankings—but it does reflect an effort to fine-tune the rankings where possible.

Still, criticisms of the rankings have continued unabated. Colleges eager to present their numbers in the most flattering possible light have fre-quently been accused—sometimes with good reason—of gamesmanship or outright fraud. In one recent instance, the former director of Clemson University's Office of Institutional Research declared at a June 2009 con-ference that senior administrators at the school had deliberately given low "reputational" scores to rival universities in their zeal to help Clemson rise in the rankings. (The officials denied the charge.) Fierce battles have also been waged over methodology. Detractors note, among other things, that because of the inclusion of research spending and average class size (which is expensive for colleges to achieve), the rankings invariably reward well-endowed private institutions and punish public universities—many of which, ironically, were ranked far higher when *U.S. News* considered only reputation rather than including quantitative variables. More gener-ally, the argument goes, the factors used in the rankings provide colleges with perverse incentives to focus on the factors that are measured rather than taking on the more elusive task of providing the best possible educa-tion for their students. "The *U.S. News* methods are really indefensible," says Fiske. "They ask the wrong question. The issue is what is the best college for any particular student, not what is the best college in some abstract sense. . . . You cannot quantify the really important questions like matters of fit."

In a sense, the *U.S. News* editors who designed the rankings became paradoxical victims of their own earnest efforts to make the rankings more rigorous. What began as a fairly conventional journalistic parlor game—a simple survey seeking the views of college presidents—had morphed into an exercise that took on many of the trappings of social science, with na-tionwide data collection, a detailed methodology, regression analysis, and so forth. But at heart, the rankings remained a journalistic rather than an academic exercise. Thus, it was not much of a surprise when the Chicago-based National Opinion Research Center, an outside consulting firm hired by *U.S. News* in 1997 to evaluate the ranking methodology, reached a conclusion that gave further fuel to critics. "The principal weakness of the current approach is that the weight used to combine the various measures into an overall rating lacks any defensible empirical or theoretical basis," it said. To be sure, the report also noted that the weights might not be off-base. But it said they could not be defended "on any grounds other than the *U.S. News* staff's best judgment on how to combine the measures."[8]

U.S. News editors have continued to defend the rankings vigorously, challenging the magazine's role as stock villain in the competitive world of college admissions. They argue that the characteristics measured—from research spending to class size to graduation rates to alumni satisfaction to qualifications of incoming students—are all factors that prospective college students and their families might reasonably want to know about. And they point out that the rankings always come with a cautionary note and accompanying articles that stress the importance of finding the right "fit" in a campus, and tell students they should use the rankings only as a starting point. Whatever ranking decisions the magazine makes, it is left in a no-win situation: When it changes the methodology, it is accused of seeking to sell more magazines by shaking up the previous year's pecking order. When the formula goes unchanged from the previous year, the magazine remains vulnerable to the charge that it has done nothing to correct the rankings' many imperfections.

Moreover, while the rankings certainly have many flaws, some popular critiques have proved to be urban legends. For years college officials alleged that *U.S. News*, by including "yield" as a factor in its selectivity measure, was stoking the surge in binding "early decision" admissions programs. Early decision requires students to attend a college to which they have applied and been admitted early. Yield refers to the percentage of students offered admissions who decide to attend. Early decision is controversial because it has often been blamed for adding stress to an already frenzied admissions process and for disadvantaging low-income students, who lose the ability to compare financial-aid packages from multiple schools in the spring when they are required to say yes to an early admissions offer in December. Because binding early decision by definition results in 100 percent yield, the use of yield by *U.S. News* was said to give colleges an incentive to boost their yield stats by relying more heavily than ever on early decision. This argument had one flaw, however: first, yield counted for only 1.5 percent in the ranking methodology. More important, when the magazine decided to remove itself from the controversy by removing yield from the ranking equation, early decision continued unabated. Rarely did critics acknowledge that universities have many self-interested reasons for maintaining a practice that, in an age when "enrollment management" is extremely important, permits them to predict more accurately the size and composition of incoming freshman classes.

As the debate continues, one thing is certain: more than twenty-five years after they were inaugurated, the rankings are routinely cited as having transformed the world of U.S. college admissions. In 2009, for instance, the University of Chicago announced the retirement of Theodore "Ted" O'Neill, the university's longtime dean of admissions, who is best known for introducing Chicago's quirky "uncommon application," which asks applicants to write essays on offbeat topics. (A sample question: "Chicago professor W.J.T. Mitchell entitled his 2005 book *What Do Pictures Want?* Describe a picture and explore what it wants.") O'Neill presided over a huge increase in applications as Chicago, notorious for its demanding academics, worked hard to expand its recruiting net to a broader range of students. But he bemoaned the increased pressure on universities—citing *U.S. News* in the process. "At some point, we were put on this nationally observed competition for numbers," O'Neill said. "*U.S. News* did that, or we did it to ourselves. There's this grander competition that is about numbers and ratings. Some of us resist that, some go along with it, but it affects us all."[9]

The *U.S. News* college rankings were preceded by, or in some cases joined by, a vast array of other college guides and rankings, including the silly (the *Princeton Review*'s annual "top party schools"); the cut-and-dried (the phonebook-sized *Barron's*, *Peterson's*, and *Lovejoy's* guides); the niche-oriented (guides identifying the best colleges for African Americans, Christians, and conservatives, for instance); and the serious-minded (assorted efforts to measure the student experience and academic strengths of campuses around the United States without sorting the results into ranked order, as with the National Survey of Student Engagement [NSSE] and Web-based report cards developed by groups such as the Association of Public and Land-grant Universities and the National Association of Independent Colleges and Universities).

With the exception of NSSE, which is aimed primarily at universities that wish to improve their own efforts to educate students, all these efforts cater, in one way or another, to the huge hunger of educational consumers for more and better information about educational quality and value for money. But whatever their strengths and credibility within academic circles, it is probably fair to say that none has had the sheer influence and popularity of the *U.S. News* rankings, their faults notwithstanding.

RANKING THE WORLD

That influence goes well beyond U.S. shores, which should perhaps be no surprise given that some of the same factors that made rankings ubiquitous in the United States have led to their rapid spread elsewhere. Often called "league tables," the same term used in Europe for sports rankings, university rankings at the national level became common in the 1990s.[10] The forty-plus national rankings that now exist around the world[11] can be found from Eastern Europe and the Middle East to Latin America and sub-Saharan Africa. By 2007, according to the region-by-region tally of Jamil Salmi, the World Bank's Tertiary Education coordinator,[12] countries with rankings included Argentina, Australia, Brazil, Canada, Chile, China, Germany, Hong Kong, India, Italy, Japan, Kazakhstan, Korea, Malaysia, Mexico, the Netherlands, New Zealand, Nigeria, Pakistan, Peru, Poland, Portugal, Romania, Russia, Slovakia, Spain, Sweden, Switzerland, Thailand, Tunisia, Ukraine, the United Kingdom, and the United States.

The groups that prepare the rankings are as varied as the nations where they have emerged. Rankers include newspapers or magazines, accreditation organizations, universities themselves, and, increasingly, government agencies such as higher education ministries. Thus, country-level rankings in Britain, Germany, Canada, Italy, and Mexico are published by the *Financial Times* and the *Sunday Times*, *Der Spiegel*, *Macleans*, *La Repubblica*, and *Reforma*, respectively. Government and higher education organizations that rank institutions include Germany's CHE (Center for Higher Education Development), India's NAAC (National Assessment and Accreditation Council) and NBA (National Board of Accreditation), Turkey's Council of Higher Education (YOK) and TÜBİTAK (The Scientific and Technological Research Council of Turkey), and the Philippines' PAASCU (Philippine Accrediting Association of Schools, Colleges and Universities). There are also many commercial guides, including Australia's

Good Universities Guide, Germany's Bertelsmann Stiftung, and Canada's Re$earch Infosource Inc.[13]

The factors included in these rankings vary, of course, as do the weightings, but they typically include indicators that should be familiar to any student of the *U.S. News* rankings. Institutions are usually ranked from highest to lowest based on a combination of quantitative and qualitative measures, including core statistics from universities about their research and teaching outcomes, along with surveys of students, peers, or outside analysts. Ellen Hazelkorn, director of the Higher Education Policy Research Unit at the Dublin Institute of Technology, notes that these national rankings, like those pioneered by *U.S. News*, began as a consumer information tool to provide students and parents with information, comparable across institutions, that was often not easily obtainable from universities themselves.

Over time, however, more evidence has accumulated suggesting that rankings are being used by a much wider variety of users, including government policymakers and industry officials. "Undoubtedly, part of the increasing credibility of league tables and rankings," Hazelkorn writes, "derives from their simplicity and the fact that they are perceived as independent of the higher education sector or individual universities."[14] Despite profound worries over methodological shortcomings and misuse of rankings, just as in the United States, analysts such as Boston College's Philip Altbach acknowledge that the assorted forms of rankings and league tables found around the world "serve a useful role" because of the spotlight they shine on "key aspects of academic achievement."[15]

At the same Shanghai meeting of ranking experts where Canto-Sperber voiced her dismay at the way the École Normale Supérieure fared in global rankings, a number of other education officials detailed their own nations' efforts to develop indicators of excellence, some quite different from one another. In Taiwan, for instance, Tamkang University published the country's first national college ranking in 1993 with a twofold aim: understanding the overall academic performance of Taiwan's 139 varied institutions and creating a useful self-improvement tool for Tamkang University itself. The creator of those rankings, Angela Yung-chi Hou, formerly a professor at the university's Graduate Institute of Higher Education, notes that they were explicitly modeled after those created by *U.S. News*, with multiple criteria established—both quantitative and survey-based—and then weighted in order to rank each institution in one of eight categories. College rankings remain controversial in Taiwan, she concedes. But, she maintains, "it is expected that the quality of Taiwanese higher education could be improved through rankings."[16]

In Romania, too, where no fewer than three rankings have been inaugurated, a group of researchers who have studied the classifications concludes that "ranking makes universities aware of their very weak and strong points and prepares them to measure up to competition under the circumstances of liberalizing the education and labor markets, once Romania accedes to the European Union."[17] Similarly, in the Republic of Kazakhstan, the Ministry of Education and Science directed its National Accreditation Center to conduct rankings of the nation's universities beginning in 2006. The goals of the initiative, as in other nations, are to help provide decision-making tools to students and parents, government workers, employers, and international organizations; to promote competition between universities; and to encourage quality assurance within universities.[18]

Even in places where rankings have not yet penetrated, it seems, there is a hunger for them—at least among some. In Greece, two other researchers explained, rankings are strongly discouraged. Indeed, researchers are typically restricted from classifying and evaluating public universities, thanks in part to opposition from student groups and unions representing academic staff. Nevertheless, they suggested a number of possible approaches to ranking Greek universities, arguing that such measures could be useful to a number of groups: students seeking reliable information about campuses, universities seeking a diagnostic tool and measure of quality, the government, and society more generally.

While national-level university rankings have continued their seemingly relentless march around the world, probably the most influential comparisons between postsecondary research institutions are the global rankings that have emerged and become popular in the past fifteen years. The first international ranking was conducted in 1997 by *Asiaweek* magazine, but it was limited to universities in Asian nations.[19] Five years later, in 2002, the Swiss Centre for Science and Technology Studies released its "champions league," which ranked universities and other research institutions on the basis of their research journal publications.[20] However, the first closely watched worldwide ranking to appear on the global scene came the following year with publication of the *Academic Ranking of World Universities*, produced by Shanghai Jiao Tong University's Institute of Higher Education, which some view as the most influential international ranking. First released in June 2003, the Shanghai rankings had their origins several years earlier in 1999. Shanghai Jiao Tong administrators, worried about the university's decline from its once-exalted position in prerevolutionary days, began a series of planning meetings aimed at assessing where the university stood compared to others, particularly in the key area of research productivity.[21] One particularly active participant, a professor of chemistry and chemical engineering named Nian Cai Liu, was drafted as the university's first-ever director of strategic planning. His first task? Compiling a report comparing his university's performance to that of others in China and elsewhere.

Liu's timing was good. The rankings prototype, initially circulated privately to administrators and campus officials, came as China was embarking on a broad, ambitious, and expensive initiative to create a much-larger group of high-level research universities. Even well-known institutions had set ambitious targets to reach the much-coveted "world-class" status quickly: Peking University set its sights on 2016, for instance, while its crosstown rival Tsinghua University aimed for 2020. But without benchmarking against universities at home and abroad, determining just what was meant by "world-class" would have been difficult. That was where Liu's work came in, and it was quickly expanded to include a much larger number of institutions around the world. That broader scope permitted the entire nation, not just Shanghai Jiao Tong, to figure out where it stood vis-à-vis universities around the world—and just how far it would have to go to close the gap.

Although the early rankings were aimed at a small audience, after Liu posted them online the demand—and controversy—soon became enormous. By his count, 4 million people have visited the Shanghai rankings Web site since 2003—an average of 2,000 per day.[22] Liu and his research team pride themselves on having developed a transparent methodology, clearly explained on their Web site, that requires no complicated (or costly) survey research and instead relies on a range of publicly accessible indicators. His rationale for the Shanghai approach rests on several premises. First, while universities' impact on economic development has become well established, "it is impossible to obtain internationally comparable indicators and data" of that contribution. Furthermore, while education is certainly "the basic function of any university," differences across national systems make qualitative comparisons unworkable. The best approach, Liu concludes, is to look objectively at the research performance of universities, which he argues can be standardized and compared globally, providing a good indication of the relative standing of different institutions.

The Shanghai rankings begin by examining any university in the world whose faculty includes Nobel laureates; winners of the Fields Medal, granted every four years to a handful of elite mathematicians age forty and younger; and researchers who have published papers in *Nature* or *Science*, or whose work is frequently cited by others. It also looks at the overall number of academic papers at universities around the world indexed in the Science Citation Index Expanded (SCIE), the Social Science Citation Index (SSCI), and the Arts and Humanities Indices (ACHI). The World University Rankings researchers examine more than 2,000 universities and rank more than 1,000, posting the top 500 on their Web site.

The methodology itself bears some surface resemblance to the *U.S. News* ranking system in that it assigns varying weights to each of the factors measured. That said, unlike *U.S. News*, its research-intensive approach pays no attention to undergraduate-oriented measures such as student qualifications, class size, student retention, and graduation rate, nor to peer reputation. It assigns a weight of 10 percent for the number of an institution's alumni who have won Nobel Prizes and Fields Medals since 1901; 20 percent for university staff winning those honors (with higher weights assigned to more recent winners); 20 percent for the number of highly cited researchers in a range of fields, including life sciences, physical sciences, medicine, engineering, and social sciences; 20 percent for articles published in *Nature* and *Science* within the past five years; 20 percent for the total number of articles by university faculty indexed in the SCIE, the SSCI, and the ACHI within the past year; and 10 percent for a size-adjustment measure that attempts to gauge per capita research performance by dividing each subtotal indicator by the number of full-time faculty and academic staff at each university.

Liu exhibits a refreshing lack of defensiveness when discussing his rankings, making the case for their strengths while cheerfully acknowledging their weaknesses. In some cases, he and his team have attempted to improve their methodology in response to critics. A case in point: Many detractors have complained about the Shanghai rankings' bias toward science. After confirming that academics in the humanities typically have lower rates of publication than scientists, Liu doubled the weighting of articles that appear in the SSCI. The rankings are still viewed as heavily tilted toward science ("the easiest way to boost rankings is to kill the humanities," one university rector told Hazelkorn). Still, Liu says he is glad to receive more suggestions for improvement. "We love those ideas," he told the *Chronicle of Higher Education*. "We may not be able to implement all of them, but they're great."[23]

The institutions at the very top of the Shanghai rankings come as no great surprise; the global pecking order closely resembles the one that exists within the United States. Thus, the top ten universities in 2008 were Harvard, Stanford, Berkeley, Cambridge, MIT, Caltech, Columbia, Princeton, Chicago, and Oxford. That all but two of the top ten institutions are U.S. universities reflects the massive dominance of the American research model on the world stage—all the more so, of course, when the scientific and technological accomplishments most closely associated with that model are so richly rewarded by a ranking methodology like Shanghai's. At the same time, the rankings can provide bragging rights for those well beyond the inner circle—the University of Maastricht, for instance, is categorized in the band of universities between three hundred and four hundred (there are no numbered rankings beyond the top one hundred), along with institutions such as the University of Oregon and the University of Stuttgart.

One year after the debut of the Shanghai rankings, a second global effort to compare university systems was launched by a British publication, the *Times Higher Education Supplement* (THES). The World University Rankings quickly began vying with their Chinese rivals for influence on the world education scene. Views are mixed as to which ranking has garnered more attention from students, universities, and government policymakers, but it is broadly accepted that the THES assessment has far surpassed the Shanghai rankings in generating controversy.

The THES rankings were launched by John O'Leary, the onetime education editor of the London *Times*, who had previously overseen the national league tables produced by the *Times*, as well as a spinoff publication called *The Times Good University Guide*. In 2008, just before the magazine released its fifth annual rankings, O'Leary published an article that declared the ever-increasing importance of such global measures. "Particularly where research is concerned, Oxford and Cambridge are as likely to compare themselves with Harvard and Princeton as with other UK [institutions]," he wrote. "And governments all around the world have expressed an ambition to have at least one university among the international elite." The league table exercise was conducted during its formative years in conjunction with the research firm Quacquarelli and Symonds (QS) and thus formally called the *THE-QS World University Rankings* (after a change of ownership the THES was renamed Times Higher Education [THE]). Its goal: to give a "rounded assessment" of top universities "at a time of unprecedented international mobility both by students and by academics."[24]

O'Leary's reference to a "rounded assessment" is an unmistakable allusion to one of the key features differentiating the THE rankings from their Chinese counterpart. In contrast to the almost exclusive focus on research in the Shanghai rankings, the *Times Higher Education* methodology counts a much wider range of factors. Academic peer review is at the heart of the THE approach. It is based on about 9,400 responses over three years to an online survey distributed to academics worldwide, with the results weighted at 40 percent of the total[25]—by far the largest factor (and considerably larger than the 25 percent that *U.S. News* devotes to its peer survey, a weighting that itself is often criticized for its disproportionate influence on the magazine's college rankings).

The magazine's rationale for such heavy use of a subjective reputational measure is that it avoids penalizing universities with nonscience strengths. Unlike the citations-per-professor score, the World University Rankings Web site explains, "the peer review component offers an even-handed perspective on the various broad subject areas—with institutional strengths in Arts & Humanities and Social Sciences able to contribute significantly to the overall view of an institution." Somewhat undermining this defense, however, is the magazine's acknowledgment in the very next sentence of its "frequently asked questions" that if it could identify "additional reliable measures of institutional quality," it would likely reduce the weighting of peer review.[26] Still, it does make good on its promise of scrutinizing universities' strengths in a variety of disciplines: in addition to its master rankings of universities worldwide, it also publishes tables each year, based on the peer review survey, that list the best institutions for arts and humanities, social sciences, life sciences and biomedicine, natural sciences, and engineering and information technology.

The second component of the THE methodology is "employer review," weighted at 10 percent, which was introduced in 2005 and is based on a survey distributed to public and private sector employers around the world. In 2009 this score was based on about 3,300 responses over three years. An additional 20 percent is devoted to student-faculty ratio, based on the assumption that this measure serves as the best available proxy for an institution's commitment to teaching. Next, THE uses citations per faculty member, weighted at 20 percent, to assess each university's research prowess. Relying on Scopus, the largest database of abstracts and citations in the world, it draws on the most recent five years of citation data. The use of a per-professor measure is intended to control for institutional size. The measure doesn't carry greater weight, the magazine explains, because it tends to be weighted toward research in scientific and technical fields. Finally, the magazine measures the percentage of international students and faculty at a university, on the grounds that this serves as a market test of an institution's ability to attract brainpower in an ever-more globalized world. International students and faculty are each weighted at 5 percent for a total international measure of 10 percent.[27]

Like the designers of the Shanghai rankings, the journalists and researchers behind the THE rankings say that they try hard to make the factors behind their evaluations easily accessible to the public. "It's important that we get it right and that it is utterly transparent," says Ann Mroz, the current editor of the THE, over lunch at a London restaurant.[28] She is also, like Shanghai Jiao Tong University's Liu, quite happy to discuss misgivings about her publication's rankings and entertain criticisms or suggestions for improvement. "I'm very keen for there to be a debate about it," she says. "Any criticisms I'm quite happy to print. I would prefer that people came to us and there was some sort of debate about it and see whether maybe we have got a few things wrong. Until we discuss it, we're never going to know." Mroz herself says that she is "uncomfortable" with the faculty-student ratio, for instance. "It's so crude. Does it tell you how good the teaching is?" She would like to use a better measure, she says—if one can be found.

Even as she acknowledges shortcomings in the rankings, however, Mroz firmly defends their usefulness. "If you're talking about the students, what else do they have to go by?" she says. "There's very little information, especially for foreign students. How are you going to try to compare a university of one country against another if you want to go abroad and study? I don't think you should probably base your entire decision on the rankings, because that would be daft. You have to do a lot more research, but this is a good place to start." Universities, too, rely on the rankings, she notes, whether as grist for marketing efforts when their standing rises or as a gauge of whether a prospective international partner has comparable worldwide standing.

While the THE is proud of its aspiration to create a more "holistic" assessment of universities than the Shanghai ranking, critics like Simon Marginson of the Centre for the Study of Higher Education at the University of Melbourne view its methodology as more problematic on a variety of grounds. They often fault the THE's index for its high volatility, particularly vis-à-vis its relatively stable Shanghai counterpart. This was particularly true in 2007, when changes in data and methodology contributed to Stanford University's drop from number 6 to number 19, the National University of Mexico's plunge from 74 to 192, and the National University of Singapore's decline from 19 to 33. "Think 'yo-yo' and you've about got it," Marginson writes.[29]

In some sense, of course, the charge of volatility punishes rankers for attempting to remedy their past sins. Large changes in an institution's ranking typically come when the ranking organization—whether *U.S. News* or *Times Higher Education*—makes methodological changes in response to previous criticisms. In 2007, for example, THE prevented reviewers from assessing their own universities, changed its citation database to reduce what it called a "pronounced bias" toward U.S. institutions, and began using statistical normalization to control for outlier scores.[30] Still, to Marginson the frequent changes in the *Times Higher* rankings are highly suspect, as is the survey's dismayingly low response rate (as little as 1 percent, he states).

Marginson also objects to what he terms a regional bias in which the survey's "pool of responses was heavily weighted in favor of academic 'peers' from nations where the *Times* is well known, such as the UK, Australia,

New England, and Malaysia." Because of the survey's "composition bias," he argues, British institutions are vastly overrepresented. In 2007, "an amazing nineteen" U.K. universities placed in the top one hundred, compared to thirty-eight U.S. universities, a relatively modest showing given that fifty-four American universities placed in the top one hundred of the Shanghai rankings in the same year.[31]

In 2008, the very top of the THE and Shanghai lists overlapped significantly—seven of the ten universities were the same. But four British institutions placed in the THE top ten, while just two made it to the top of the Shanghai rankings. The *Times Higher*'s top ten in 2008 were Harvard; Yale; Cambridge; Oxford; Caltech; Imperial College, London; University College, London; Chicago; MIT; and Columbia. British institutions inched up still further in 2009, when they occupied four of the *Times Higher*'s top six slots. Meantime, U.S. superiority dwindled considerably: The number of North American universities in the *Times Higher* top one hundred dropped to thirty-six from forty-two the previous year.[32] But the pecking order could well be shaken up even further in the future: several weeks after releasing its 2009 rankings, THE announced that it would end its partnership with QS. It said it would develop a brand-new ranking methodology in consultation with Thomson Reuters, a prominent data research firm, together with its academic advisory board and readers. "We acknowledge the criticism and now want to work with the sector to produce a legitimate and robust research tool for academics and university administrators," Mroz said.[33] For its part, QS said it would continue to publish and circulate its own rankings, an indication that rankings proliferation shows no signs of letting up.[34]

Even as the comparative strengths of each major global ranking continue to be debated—or as each is emphatically rejected by some university officials and students of higher education—their influence seems to be ever greater. In addition to consumer uses of the world rankings, they are increasingly an object of anxiety for universities—and a significant factor in their decision making. In a study commissioned by the OECD, the Dublin Institute of Technology's Ellen Hazelkorn surveyed university leaders from 202 higher education institutions in forty-one countries, both new and old, teaching- and research-intensive. Rankings, she found, had become a hugely important factor in self-perception and decision making. "Despite the existence of 17,000 higher education institutions worldwide, there is now a near-obsession with the status and trajectory of the top 100," she wrote in a summary of her findings.[35] Across a wide range of institutions, she told *University World News*, "there is enormous attention given to every league table that is published as well as its quality ranking. And they are taken seriously by students, government and especially by the media. Because of this, they have a huge influence on university reputations and thus they promote competition and influence policy-making."[36] One manifestation of this intense interest in rankings: controversial efforts to "incentivize" administrators with cold hard cash to boost their institutions' standing. For example, in Australia a number of vice chancellors have received salary bonuses predicated on their success in nudging their campuses up in the rankings.[37]

Hazelkorn's multination study found that 58 percent of respondents were unhappy with their current ranking, that 70 percent wanted to be in the top 10 percent of their national league table, that 71 percent wanted to be in the top 25 percent internationally, that 57 percent had a formal mechanism to review where they stood in the rankings, and that 57 percent thought that the willingness of other universities to form partnerships with them was influenced by their position in league tables and rankings. These perceptions aren't just idle musings. Hazelkorn found that universities have often backed them up with concrete actions. Some go out of their way to hire more Nobel laureates, for example, given that this is a metric in the Shanghai rankings. More broadly, entire nations have paid special attention to revamping their university systems in the hope of achieving higher stature in the rankings. "Excellence initiatives in Germany, Russia, China and France are policy responses to rankings," Hazelkorn writes. "The pace of higher education reform is likely to quicken in the belief that more elite, competitive and better institutions are equivalent to being higher ranked."

Beyond survey data, it isn't hard to find ways in which the siren call of rankings is heard far and wide. In India, both the THE and Shanghai rankings are scrutinized at the highest levels of government, according to Montek Singh Ahluwalia, who heads the nation's Planning Commission. "We know about these lists. We look at them," says Ahluwalia in an interview in his New Delhi office.[38] The Oxford graduate, whose formal title is deputy chairman of the commission, says the rankings serve in part to confirm India's sense that some of its elite institutions—the Indian Institutes of Technology, the Indian Institute of Science, the Indian Institutes of Management, Jawaharlal Nehru University, and Delhi University—have earned a legitimate place among the world's best. "If tomorrow they were to drop all of them, we would say it's all biased and useless," he quips.

At the same time, the rankings provide a gauge whereby a nation that urgently wants to increase both the quantity and quality of its institutions can measure its progress. "Assuming we have about four or something like that [among the several hundred top institutions in the global rankings], everybody in India thinks that in ten years we should have at least ten and hopefully twenty," he says. "That's not easy to do, because you don't create a good university in ten years. But maybe you can upgrade some of the existing ones and so on." Improvement at the elite levels is even more daunting than improving mass access to higher education, he says. "Taking the number from four to ten will require some of the brightest brains in government to do some very innovative thinking on reforms for universities."

In addition to serving as a broad measure of quality for nations intent on improving their international standing, rankings can also act as a great leveler. In the best-case scenario, they allow individual institutions or programs to prove their worth against better-established competitors. This can be seen particularly clearly in the case of business schools, which were early adapters to globalization.

As goods, services, and people started to move ever more freely across borders, a far-reaching market for globally literate MBAs soon emerged. Business schools began to market themselves aggressively to foreign students, to start branch campuses, and to forge alliances with their counterparts in other nations. The results of all this internationalization were striking. To take a few examples: Between 2004 and 2008, the number of U.S. MBA applicants sending scores on the Graduate Management Admissions Test to non-U.S. programs increased by 35 percent. At INSEAD in Fontainebleau, no more than one in ten faculty members comes from any single country. Madrid's IE Business School has recruitment offices in Berlin, Dubai, Lisbon, and Singapore. And Alpina, a dairy and beverage manufacturer in Colombia, extended fifteen job offers to MBA grads from IE in 2008 and planned to begin recruiting at INSEAD and the London Business School.[39]

This rapid globalization was accompanied, and perhaps hastened, by a slew of business school rankings. Like comprehensive university rankings, these began at the national level before expanding globally. *BusinessWeek*, for example, pioneered U.S. MBA rankings in 1988 and was later joined by *Forbes* and the *Wall Street Journal*. Now *BusinessWeek* has added to its offerings an annual list of "Best International B-Schools," while the *Economist* and the *Financial Times* have developed their own high-profile global business school rankings. The methodology of each ranking differs, but all include some measurement of alumni salaries, postgraduation career success, or both. One analysis found a fairly high correlation between almost all the MBA rankings.[40]

Like other rankings, the business school league tables have attracted critics and controversy. However, by providing a neutral yardstick that measures schools' effectiveness on key measures that matter to students and employers, the rankings have the power to confer instant legitimacy on relatively new players on the global B-school scene. China's CEIBS (China Europe International Business School), for instance, is only fifteen years old. But it has thrived in a short time and now touts its high rankings on its Web site: number eight worldwide in the 2009 *Financial Times* global MBA rankings, number four in the *Forbes* 2009 list of top non-U.S. business schools, number one in *BusinessWeek China*'s ranking, and so on.[41] By offering an external measure of CEIBS's success, these international business school rankings illustrate a point that economics columnist Robert Samuelson has made in the context of U.S. college rankings:[42] there is a strong case to be made that rankings have the potential to radically democratize the entrenched academic pecking order—on the global as well as on the national scene.

Rankings are also being used more generally by students or national governments as the equivalent of the Good Housekeeping Seal of Approval. They can give educational consumers a sense of which overseas institutions are likely to offer value for money. Similarly, they can inform governments about whether their own policies are well considered or their scholarship funds well spent. The Mongolian government has weighed a policy that would give study-abroad funding only to students admitted to a university that appears in one of the global rankings.[43] In the Netherlands, an immigration-reform proposal aimed at attracting more skilled migrants would restrict visas to all but graduates of universities ranked in the two top tiers of global league tables.

But if government quality-assurance efforts, consumer advice, and performance incentives for campus officials represent a largely benign aspect

of global rankings, another is the ignominy—and real-life consequences—
that can fall upon individuals and institutions that are viewed as not measuring up. The most oft-cited case of this phenomenon came in 2005 at
the University of Malaya (UM). One year earlier, the Malaysian university
drew accolades when it was ranked eighty-ninth in the world in the inaugural *Times Higher Education Supplement* rankings. So important an accomplishment was this for the university, and for a nation bent on creating
a knowledge economy, that the vice chancellor ordered banners reading
"UM a World's Top 100 University" and had them hung around that
city (and, Marginson notes, "on the edge of the campus facing the main
freeway to the airport where every foreign visitor to Malaysia would see
it"[44]).

The next year, however, the results of the *Times*' two reputational surveys were less favorable to the university. Compounding matters was the
discovery and correction of an error in the classification of foreign students
at UM, which served to further lower the university's rating. The result?
A drop from 89 to 169 in the THE survey and widespread calls for a
royal commission of inquiry into the unfortunate episode. "A Shocking
Global Slide," read one headline.[45] "Crisis in Malaysia's Public Universities?"[46] inquired another. Within a few months, the vice chancellor, who
had been vilified in the media, was effectively fired. "Though apparently
extreme, this reaction is not uncommon in university systems around the
world," writes World Bank higher education expert Jamil Salmi.[47] It has
certainly remained common in Malaysia. Just a few years later, when none
of the country's universities placed in the THE top 200 in 2008, Lim Kit
Siang, leader of the opposition Democratic Action Party, gave a speech to
party supporters, declaring that Malaysia "is losing out in the unrelenting
battle for international competitiveness," not only worldwide but vis-à-vis
regional competitors such as Thailand, Indonesia, and the Philippines.
He complained bitterly about the showing of the Universiti Sains Malaysia, which the government has singled out for cultivation as a world-class
institution, calling its 313th showing "sad and pathetic." The rankings,
the opposition leader concluded, "should be a wake-up call to the Higher
Education Minister and the cabinet of the advanced crisis of higher education in Malaysia."[48]

In Britain, too, analysts reacted with similar alarm, albeit in less heated
language, when the 2008 THE rankings showed a drop for many U.K.

universities. Both Oxford and Cambridge slipped slightly in the top ten pecking order, and overall twenty-two of the twenty-nine British universities in the top two hundred fell in the rankings. While Britain still had more highly ranked universities than in any nation outside the United States (which held thirty-seven of the top one hundred slots), the *Daily Telegraph* noted that universities from thirty-three different countries made it into the top two hundred, an increase from twenty-eight in 2007.[49] Though relatively modest, these shifts were enough to prompt a follow-up article headlined "Without Investment Our Top Universities Will Fall Behind Global Competition."[50]

Its author, Wendy Piatt, head of the Russell Group, a consortium of twenty elite research universities, noted that the United States invests more than twice what Great Britain does in higher education as a proportion of gross domestic product. What's more, she said, Chinese universities "have been steadily climbing up international league tables" and are on the verge of overtaking their British counterparts in faculty publication of research papers. Adding to the competitive environment, "closer to home, France and Germany are both pumping millions into their leading research universities," Piatt wrote. Her conclusion, perhaps unsurprisingly, was that notwithstanding concerns about the rankings' accuracy, their message should nevertheless be heeded as a sign that increased investment in U.K. universities is imperative.

While the range of responses to the global rankings from universities and policymakers shows their unmistakable influence, many detractors believe the rankings are unworthy of any kind of response. To begin with, there are the familiar and highly specific criticisms. These include, on the one hand, the frequently denounced bias toward science in the Shanghai rankings, coupled with the incentives the Shanghai approach gives universities to engage in questionable chasing of Nobel-winning professors whose work may or may not be of sufficiently recent vintage to add meaningfully to the institution's intellectual firepower. They comprise on the other hand, of course, the excessive reliance on peer reputation, low sample size, volatility, and English-speaking bias of the THE rankings.

But to some, the very notion of attempting to determine how an entire university stacks up against others is an exercise that has little meaning as an instrument of national policy. Ross Williams and Nina Van Dyke of the Melbourne Institute of Applied Economic and Social Research at the University of Melbourne argue that evaluating individual disciplines across universities makes more sense. After all, for many students and researchers making decisions about where to apply and study or work, and for government agencies seeking to fund excellent research, the quality of specific departments and disciplines is more important than the university's overall standing. Broad institutional rankings can make universities look worse—or better—than they really are. Their survey of a range of disciplines at thirty-nine Australian universities—arts and humanities, business and economics, education, engineering, law, medicine, and science—found that in twenty-three cases, a discipline at a particular institution was rated among the top one hundred in the world.

With universities in Australia and beyond under considerable pressure to place ever higher in the world rankings, Williams and Van Dyke argue that a focus on disciplines would, instead, encourage more specialization in fields in which a university may have a particular strength or comparative advantage. "At whole-of-institution level," they write, "it is not reasonable to expect, under current resourcing levels, more than three or four Australian universities to be in the top one hundred in the world, but it is feasible for many more Australian universities to be in the top one hundred in individual disciplines. . . . A system in which each Australian university was recognized internationally for some activity, including teaching, would be preferable to the current situation."[51] Indeed, beginning in February 2007, the designers of the Shanghai rankings began ranking universities by broad subject fields in addition to overall quality. Still, in many places, the obsession with making it to the top remains, however unrealistic the goal may be. Another Australian university official, Tony Sheil of Griffith University's Office for Research, argues that it would be prohibitively expensive for Australia and other small nations to make the kind of investments necessary to catapult a university into the top ten or twenty of the global research rankings, notwithstanding the expressed desire of several recent Australian federal education ministers to reach that goal. (The current minister has moved in a different direction, focusing on creating a world-class university system nationwide rather than on rising to the top of the rankings.)[52]

More broadly, just as many critics of the *U.S. News* rankings question the premise that institutions with widely varying missions can be meaningfully evaluated by outsiders, some academics protest the notion that global league tables capture the essence of institutional quality. While the aspiration to be world-class seems to be at the top of every university's to-do list, this argument goes, worldwide rankings are unavoidably a zero-sum game that implies excellence is found only at the heights of the league tables. As Franz Van Vught of the European Center for Strategic Management of Universities argued at an OECD conference on measuring quality in higher education, if just 3 percent of the world's 17,000 universities are world-class as measured by rankings, surely the rest cannot have utterly failed.[53]

France has been a particular hotbed of rankings discontent. Even as Prime Minister Nicolas Sarkozy has pushed to shake up the nation's moribund university system and create a lavishly funded group of world-class research universities, academics and some government officials have simultaneously expressed vocal discontent with global rankings. They complain among other things that the Shanghai rankings favor universities in English-speaking countries, don't take institutional size into account, and fail to measure the quality of teaching.[54] Moreover, some fear that student qualifications have been lost in the global rankings frenzy. Canto-Sperber of the École Normale Supérieure (ENS) argued before her Shanghai audience that ultra-selective colleges such as France's grandes écoles don't get rightful credit for the rigors students must undergo before they even begin their studies.

After graduation from lycee, she explained, the most brilliant students in France enroll in rigorous *classes préparatoires* before they can attempt entry to ENS. In these courses, "the competition between students is such that one who succeeds by the end of *classes préparatoires* would have typically studied for twelve to sixteen hours a day without holiday for two or three years." Among the graduates of these courses, she noted, "only the top few are allowed to enter the École Normale Supérieure," which stands as the most selective educational institution in France. Notwithstanding this intense selection process, ENS took the seventy-third slot in the Shanghai ratings in 2008. Institutions such as the University of Paris VI or the University of Paris XI were ranked higher despite, Canto-Sperber observed pointedly, having "completely nonexistent selection procedures (i.e., everyone who applies is admitted)." Ironically, other rankings that

take student qualifications into account—notably those produced by
U.S. News—are frequently denounced for focusing excessively on inputs
rather than outputs. Still, Cantor-Sperber insisted, "the quality of a university is based on its own procedures of student selection. Therefore, the
criterion of student selection has to be considered for the evaluation of
universities."

Given all this discontent, it is little wonder that some of those deeply
dismayed by the shortcomings of existing rankings have begun to develop
what are essentially counter-rankings. In India, where relatively few universities have merited inclusion in the global rankings, the University Grants
Commission in 2009 proposed its own ranking system, to be called the India Education Index, which would grade Indian institutions with respect
to their international peers.[55] In France, another prestigious grande école,
Mines Paris Tech, released its second Professional Rankings of World Universities in October 2008, leading to a memorably tautological headline in
the online publication *University World News*: "French Do Well in French
World Rankings." Perhaps inevitably, however, this alternative ranking
itself has been criticized for being one-dimensional: its sole criterion for
sorting the 350 institutions surveyed is the number of graduates serving as
CEO or the equivalent in companies listed in *Fortune* magazine's Fortune
Global 500. Using this measure, five French universities placed in the top
twenty alone, including two in the top ten. By contrast, just three French
universities appeared in the entire top one hundred Shanghai slots, and
only two were included in the top one hundred of the *Times Higher Education* league table.[56]

Despite Sarkozy's determination to place some French universities in
the world's top tier by 2012, France's disdain for the current rankings
(Valérie Pécresse, the nation's higher education minister, once said that
the problem with rankings was that they existed) has extended to efforts
to create a Europe-wide alternative. As France took over the presidency
of the EU, it convened a Paris conference in late 2008 to explore a range
of international comparative measures that participants hoped might do
better justice to the strengths in, say, teaching and innovation, that tend
to be underrecognized by existing measures. By the summer of 2009, the
European Union announced that it would begin developing a new "multidimensional global university ranking." Mostly focused on Europe, the
goal of the new assessment, still in the exploratory stage, is to move beyond

research in hard sciences to include humanities and social sciences, as well as teaching quality and "community outreach."

BETTER INFORMATION

Is there really a better way to rank universities? In addition to nationalist efforts like those of India and France, which invariably generate suspicions of chauvinistic intent, other attempts have been made to zero in on specialized aspects of the higher education enterprise that are overlooked by conventional rankings. In Spain, for instance, the "Webometrics Ranking of World Universities" was launched in 2004 to measure universities' Web-based activities—specifically the "volume, visibility, and impact of the Web pages published by universities."[57] Developed by the Laboratoria de Cybermetrics, a division of the National Research Council, Spain's largest public research body, these rankings place special emphasis on Web-based publication of scientific output, including refereed papers, conference contributions, theses, and reports, as well as courseware, digital libraries, databases, personal Web pages, and more.

The goal of the effort, which was first launched in 2004 and is now updated every six months, is to promote electronic publication by universities, and in particular to encourage university administrators to do more Web-based dissemination if their institution ranks poorly. While students shouldn't use these rankings as the sole criteria for choosing a university, the Webometrics creators say, a top position among the 17,000 higher education institutions worldwide[58] that are listed in the survey tells candidates that "the institution has a policy that encourages new technologies and has resources for their adoption." Despite this disclaimer, analysts such as Richard Holmes of the MARA Institute of Technology in Malaysia note that important aspects of a university's quality—teaching excellence or book publication, for instance—are not captured by this Web-centric indicator.

Another alternative measure that has attracted considerable attention in the past few years as a kinder, gentler form of evaluation comes from the Center for Higher Education Development (CHE), a German higher education reform think tank. In collaboration with a media organization (once *Stern*, later *Die Zeit*), the organization surveys 200,000 students and

15,000 professors at more than 250 universities,[59] mostly in Germany but also in Austria, Switzerland, the Netherlands, and recently Italy. The rankings include a range of quantitative measures, including student-professor ratio, average length of studies, failure rates, number of PhDs, and research productivity and funding; however, about two-thirds of its indicators are based on the survey questions. Students are asked about their experiences and overall satisfaction on their campus. Faculty are asked about their "insider's pick"—which three institutions in their own field they would recommend to their own son or daughter.

After all these data are collected, they are not weighted or in any way used to create an ordinal ranking of participating universities. That would be far too simplistic, say the survey founders. "There simply is no 'best higher education institution,' not in one subject and certainly not in all subjects," the organization's Web site declares. "For example, a university may indeed be a leader in the field of research, but the equipment it offers its students may be miserable, or it may be strong in German Studies, but poor in Economics and Business Administration. Instead of crowning some presumed overall winner, we offer a multidimensional ranking."[60] Along with avoiding comparisons between entire institutions, even within disciplines CHE stays away from numerical rankings and simply categorizes a given department as either in the top third, middle third, or bottom third compared to its peers. It also gives its rankings a strong element of consumer empowerment by permitting individual users to create their own combinations of the indicators they consider most important, and then order institutions accordingly.[61]

Still, while the CHE approach to rankings may appeal to certain constituencies, by design it sidesteps what may be a natural desire by policymakers and consumers alike to make judgments about which institutions are most effective overall—which ones are the *best*. Nor does CHE address the increasing interest in value-added assessment in higher education, which aims to assess how good a job universities do, not just in garnering research laurels—and Nobel laureates—but in passing on knowledge to their students.

One of the most closely watched experiments in ranking and assessment is attempting to do just that. This new initiative is known as AHELO, the Assessment of Higher Education Learning Outcomes. Its origins trace back to June 2006, when a group of OECD education ministers met in

Athens and concluded that as higher education expanded massively, it was important to do more to measure quality as well as quantity. The resulting project is premised on the notion that students and employers are seeking better information with which to make choices about either attending universities or hiring their graduates; that universities and professors need to know more about the strengths and weaknesses of different institutions; and that policymakers need a better sense of the impact of their decisions on university quality. The OECD's response has been to create an instrument intended to be valid "for all cultures and languages."[62] It is explicitly intended not to be a ranking in the Shanghai or *Times Higher Education* vein, but instead to focus on teaching and learning—not on inputs but on outputs and value added.

The initial design of the test focuses on four "strands" intended to reflect some of the crucial aspects of higher education. The first "generic skills" component attempts to measure students' abilities in such areas as analytical reasoning, written communication, ideas generation, and application of theory to practice. Such abilities are not explicitly linked to a particular course of study but are nevertheless vital characteristics of what students should be learning on campus. "The point is that the simple acquisition of knowledge is not enough to count as an education," as the OECD puts it.[63]

The model for this part of the OECD's new outcomes project is a test known as the Collegiate Learning Assessment, or CLA, which was developed in the United States by the Council for Aid to Education, an offshoot of RAND, the social science research organization. Since 2000 it has been used in hundreds of American colleges and universities to measure the kinds of skills all undergraduates should acquire, regardless of major. Researchers administer a computer-based exam, including essay questions, to a sample of students, typically a group of freshmen and a group of seniors. By controlling for the qualification of incoming students (as measured by their scores on the SAT or ACT), the CLA staff arrives at a value-added measure that attempts to show just how much students at a given university tend to improve their writing and analytical skills during their time on campus. Their research methodology has been controversial among some of their higher education colleagues, but the CLA's designers are highly regarded social scientists, and the question they attempt to answer—what do students really learn on campus?—has rarely been addressed in such a systematic way. For the AHELO project, the College Learning Assessment will be adapted to fit an international range of universities. As in the United States, the notion is to ask nonspecialized questions that undergraduates in any field of study can answer. The inaugural participants in this part of the new test will certainly test its cross-national aspirations: they include Finland, Korea, Mexico, and Norway.

The second component of the OECD's exam is designed to acknowledge that universities most often define their missions in terms of subject-specific knowledge, not generic skills. "Students and faculty would be astonished if an assessment left out the very reason they are in higher education," the OECD says. Thus, this strand tests what students have learned within their own disciplines. At the feasibility-study stage, the two areas tested will be engineering and economics, with the expectation that more disciplines will be added if the project goes to scale. AHELO's designers are quick to note that subject knowledge isn't just about understanding facts but about putting that content knowledge to use, "often in novel circumstances." Australia, Japan, and Sweden will take part in the inaugural round of engineering testing, while the economics tests will be administered in Italy, the Netherlands, Mexico, and the Flemish-speaking parts of Belgium. As OECD officials prepared to begin testing during the 2010–11 academic year, they announced a crucial development: the United States will take part in AHELO, with institutions in four states–Connecticut, Massachusetts, Missouri, and Pennsylvania–administering the generic skills test.

The third of AHELO's four sections rests on the notion that student learning outcomes have to be understood in context, from students' backgrounds to the characteristics of the universities they attend to what employers expect of them. To better understand such variables, this "context" section examines campus characteristics, such as total enrollment and male-female ratio; educational practices and quality, including student-faculty interaction, emphasis on hands-on learning, and level of academic rigor; what the OECD terms "psycho-social and cultural attributes," from what society expects of postsecondary institutions to students' career expectations; and various outcomes, both in behavior and attitudes, from degree completion and progress into the job market or graduate school to student satisfaction, self-confidence, and self-reported learning gains. Researchers will gather data for all these measures by examining public statistics, reviewing earlier research, and surveying students, professors, and university administrators. Eventually, they hope to develop alumni and employer surveys if and when a full-blown AHELO assessment is developed.

The fourth and final strand is intended to zero in on the value-added component of higher education, one that is increasingly scrutinized in the era of measurement and accountability. AHELO researchers pose an important question: When a top student enters a university and exits with similar levels of accomplishment, how much has the institution really done with the "raw material" that walked through its doors? By contrast, when a student enters with a B average and leaves campus with an A average, a case can be made that the university has performed a more valuable pedagogical role. "What a student brings to a degree programme and what he or she leaves with are a powerful indicator of teaching quality, availability of resources, and the capacity of students to learn," the OECD says. OECD researchers acknowledge that consumers of league tables care a lot about absolute measures of quality, not just relative growth. Nevertheless, they say, a comprehensive assessment such as AHELO should offer both "bottom line" as well as value-added measures to provide a full picture of how well universities are educating their students. Unlike the other three strands, however, the value-added measure is not yet being carried out even in an experimental way. Given the complexity of the task, researchers say, there is not enough time to develop an appropriate measurement tool during the initial AHELO study. Instead, they are considering possible methodologies, drawing on similar work being done by the OECD at the secondary school level.

Indeed, the implicit model for the OECD's new international effort is a respected assessment known as PISA—the Program for International Student Assessment—which was developed by the organization in 2000 and is administered to fifteen-year-olds in most OECD countries (and in some nonmember nations) to gauge the academic progress of students in one country vis-à-vis their peers in other industrialized nations. While it is not without critics, PISA provides an easily understandable gauge of global student achievement at the secondary school level. Indeed, as the AHELO project was getting under way, an OECD paper describing the new effort was titled "PISA for Higher Education." Despite the attention received by existing national and international university rankings, they may distort resource allocation and thus give short shrift to teaching and learning, the

October 2006 background memo observed. Instead, it declared, "a direct assessment of the learning outcomes of higher education could provide governments with a powerful instrument to judge the effectiveness and international competitiveness of their higher education institutions, systems and policies in the light of other countries' performance, in ways that better reflect the multiple aims and contributions of tertiary education to society."[64]

However, drawing a direct parallel to PISA has proven contentious. Given the controversy surrounding rankings, it is perhaps unsurprising that within a couple of years, OECD officials were insisting that the word not be applied to their still in gestation postsecondary effort. "AHELO is *not* PISA for higher education," declared Barbara Ischinger, director of OECD's education division, at the opening of a major OECD conference on assessing quality in higher education. In a similar vein, OECD officials maintain that their current efforts to test out the new measure in a range of nations (they will assess students at some ten postsecondary institutions in three or four countries for each of the four strands) should not be considered a pilot but merely a "feasibility" study. Any next steps, they say, will be determined only on the basis of the outcomes of their exploratory work. Still, OECD representatives acknowledge that the project is being conducted "with an eye to the possible creation of a full-scale AHELO upon its completion,"[65] and some of those involved in the process say it is a virtual certainty that it will go forward.

Together with the contentious PISA analogy, however, a related concern quickly surfaced. Influential American higher education officials initially expressed deep misgivings about the OECD's initial efforts, arguing that efforts to create a global postsecondary measurement and accountability system were inherently problematic, given the difficulty of finding a measurement instrument suitable for the wide variety of institutions involved in the effort. After all, huge controversy had already surrounded the Secretary of Education's Commission on the Future of Higher Education, which endorsed the use of outcome-measurement tools such as the Collegiate Learning Assessment, opposed by some university officials as overly simplistic. "The conversations in the last year have underscored for many folks both the importance of addressing issues of student learning outcomes and the difficulty of finding a common instrument for measuring them in the United States," Terry Hartle, a senior official at the American Council on Education, the umbrella lobbying group for U.S. colleges and universities, told *Inside Higher Ed.* "If we haven't been able to figure out how to do this in the United States, it's impossible for me to imagine a method or standard that would work equally well for Holyoke Community College, MIT, and the Sorbonne."[66]

But defenders of the new approach argue that while international comparisons may be challenging, there is nothing particularly new or objectionable about them. For instance, rankings expert Alex Usher, former head of the Canada office of the Educational Policy Institute, points to the example of the International Adult Literacy Survey, which is administered around the world, including in the United States, without incident. What's more, reiterates Andreas Schleicher, head of education research for the OECD and a key designer of the PISA testing regime, the breakthrough of AHELO is that it will shift the rankings conversation in a crucial new direction. "Rather than assuming that because a university spends more it must be better, or using other proxy measures of quality, we will look at learning outcomes," he says.[67] Initially, of course, the small number of universities taking part in the test in each country means that only national-level results are likely to be available. Ultimately, however, with sufficiently widespread participation, the OECD would be able to publish its own cross-national league tables—with the important difference, champions of the new approach say, that they would be based on results rather than on reputation. "We will not be reflecting a university's history, but asking: what is a global employer looking for?" Schleicher says. More important still, such measures have the potential to help students, governments, and universities themselves focus on more meaningful measures of quality when making educational decisions.

One prominent convert to the usefulness of ranking is Jamie Merisotis of the Lumina Foundation. When he first began investigating college rankings a few years back as then president of the Institute for Higher Education Policy in Washington, DC, he took the view, widely shared in the U.S. higher education community, that rankings are "fundamentally flawed" because of dubious methodology and a host of other shortcomings. But he has since come to be a leading proponent of two complementary views: that rankings are a fact of life, and that they serve a useful function. Thus, not only is resistance futile—not his exact words, to be sure—but a more productive approach is to improve the quality of educational data, among other factors used in league tables, in order to make rankings better.[68]

"The reason rankings are popular is that they actually serve a purpose," Merisotis says. Until the emergence of rankings, he argues, existing quality-assurance mechanisms left a glaring gap. In the United States, government regulations focused largely on such matters as whether a college or university met the minimum standards to be eligible for federal student aid. Accreditation has been a purely peer-based quality recognition process, with little or no transparency to the outside world. Rankings, he says, "are basically reflecting the market's desire for more information that the other two aren't bringing forward."

This insight applies not just to national rankings but to the burgeoning multicountry and global assessments as well. "What you're seeing is increasing recognition of the fact that people who have college educations are in a global employment market," Merisotis says. "Those individuals who are in that global employment market are being trained in a variety of institutions, for which we need to have a better understanding of which ones are good and which ones are less good."

Merisotis, who frequently joins international partners to convene global gatherings to discuss rankings, is cautiously optimistic that experiments by the OECD and others may produce more fine-tuned university assessments. "My view is that the state of the art right now is that there are no really good global rankings," he says. "But that doesn't mean there won't be." While AHELO may or may not succeed, he makes a persuasive case that the effort to collect data and assess learning outcomes across nations, languages, and cultures is invaluable. Merisotis is also a fan of a decade-old European assessment effort known as Tuning, a faculty-led process that attempts to focus universities on establishing clear learning expectations for students in every field. Indeed, the Lumina Foundation is now working with state and university officials in Indiana, Minnesota, and Utah on a yearlong effort to attempt Tuning reforms in U.S. institutions.

Still another indication of where rankings may go in the future can be seen in the European Union's new "multidimensional" assessment, with its emphasis not only on research but also on teaching quality and areas such as community outreach. The rankings are expected to focus on Europe but to have worldwide reach.[69] Rankings detractor Simon Marginson believes that the EU's new effort will "change the game by lifting the quality of holistic rankings" such as those produced by *Times Higher Education*. That said, he is still dismayed by the continuing problem of "arbitrary weightings" and other shortcomings of existing global rankings. He predicts that the Shanghai and *Times Higher* rankings won't go away, but that they are likely to be joined by a growing number of "custom-built" assessments that are disaggregated by field, employment rates, and the like. Thus, the department-by-department rankings that Marginson and others advocate will likely gain popularity even as universities, policymakers, and students continue to pay attention to the broad institutional rankings that have proven so controversial.

This cacophony of assessments, while likely at times to be hard to compare and contrast, is surely something to be embraced. For many years, relatively few external measures of university performance were available, particularly measures easily understood by consumers and policymakers. Rankings have emerged to fill that void. They are no doubt going to multiply and become more sophisticated as they mature. And they are no doubt going to remain a fixture on the higher education scene, emblematic of a world in which apples-to-apples, cross-border comparisons of educational quality are ever-more necessary.

In a relatively short period of time, a remarkably wide variety of rankings has spread and evolved around the world, from the national to the global, from reputation-based to research-based, from subject-specific to university-wide, from Web-oriented to multidimensional and unweighted, from the *Princeton Review*'s annual list of "top party schools" to the OECD's sophisticated amalgam of value-added approaches. The interest such efforts has attracted in far-flung locales is reflected in the meeting places periodically chosen by a geographically diverse group of global ranking experts, who have roamed from Washington DC to Berlin to Shanghai and then, in 2009, to Kazakhstan.

Still, rankings remain highly contentious nearly everywhere, from the United States to Europe to Asia and beyond. For some critics, the very enterprise of sorting colleges in rank order is suspect. Uwe Brandenburg, project manager at Germany's Center for Higher Education Development, quotes Einstein to make the point: "Not everything that can be counted, counts, and not everything that counts can be counted."[70]

Nevertheless, Brandenburg acknowledges that rankings can provide useful transparency so long as they are used in combination with other factors. A recent study of rankings in four countries, conducted by the Institute for Higher Education Policy, found that despite some potentially negative effects, such as encouraging a focus on elite research institutions, rankings had a useful impact on how universities make decisions, including more data-based assessment of success.

It is easy to see why, in a global market, students, universities, and governments have a growing need for better information about the comparative effectiveness of postsecondary institutions. But they need the right kind of information. And there are numerous barriers to providing it: many rankings are imperfect, to say the least, and refinements both large and small are badly needed. Even some of the most promising efforts, like the OECD's AHELO project, may prove hard to implement—and also have the central flaw of paying zero attention to research. While human capital is an important output of universities, so is the research on which so much innovation and economic growth is dependent. Striking the right balance in assessing universities will be very important: one could imagine a ranking that takes three parts Shanghai, adds five parts AHELO, then throws in two parts *Times Higher Education*, to create a mixture that is useful to students and policymakers alike.

As more sophisticated rankings are developed, what are the chances that they will be widely implemented? The United States is a good proving ground for this question: it is the nation where college rankings were pioneered and remain hugely influential and, at the same time, a country where rankings routinely encounter withering criticism and steep resistance from academics and university leaders. Even as better measures of student-learning outcomes are developed, then, barriers to their introduction at American colleges and universities will likely remain high. What should state and federal policymakers do to help develop better rankings or to ensure that universities cooperate?

At the federal level, probably nothing. In some nations—Kazakhstan, perhaps—universities would likely have little choice but to participate in rankings sponsored and mandated by the government. But in the United

States, with no tradition of centralized federal control of education, top-down efforts to mandate participation in either international or domestic assessments are unlikely to be successful. To be sure, for twenty-five years, the U.S. Higher Education Act—the standard-setter for accreditation rules, and thus the ultimate gatekeeper for billions in federal financial aid, has required colleges to report evidence of student academic achievement. However, efforts to satisfy this mandate through the accreditation system have taken what one analyst calls "a kaleidoscopic" variety of forms, and despite recent improvements, many have been ineffectual as instruments of accountability either within or outside universities.[71] Even rather tame suggestions that colleges should use uniform measures of student learning outcomes have met with alarm. The Spellings Commission's support for the CLA and NSSE was quickly, and perhaps mischievously, said to mean that it was advocating a federal No Child Left Behind Act for higher education—anathema to the academy and likely to be a political nonstarter.

States might have better luck introducing standardized measures of learning outcomes, and even using them for accountability purposes. After all, while U.S. higher education is remarkably diverse, high percentages of students are enrolled in state colleges and universities that are subject to the scrutiny, sometimes intense, of state lawmakers. Texas probably offers the best example of a successful state-mandated accountability system, which in many ways can be viewed as an extension of its widely imitated elementary and secondary accountability framework. Beginning with an executive order from Governor Rick Perry in 2004, the state has developed a comprehensive accountability system that requires state universities, among other things, to participate in the CLA and NSSE and to make the results public. Early results are positive, and if any additional state is likely to jump on the AHELO bandwagon, it would surely be Texas. Elsewhere, however, it is by no means clear that enough states share Texas's results-oriented education culture to allow for the meaningful national comparisons that are crucial to assessing universities' relative educational effectiveness.

It may well be that the best route toward widespread participation in the new generation of national and global rankings and assessments is the *Consumer Reports* model. No federal regulations or state laws require dishwasher manufacturers or automakers to submit their wares for testing and inspection by the widely consulted magazine. They do so anyway, knowing that the results will be pored over and referenced for years by potential customers, because the only thing worse than such comparative scrutiny would be no scrutiny at all. Indeed, in most of the nations where rankings have become increasingly pervasive and influential, universities face no government mandates to participate—they comply voluntarily with journalistic efforts such as those of Japan's *Ashahi Shimbun* or Canada's *Maclean's*. Similarly, most American universities do respond, albeit reluctantly, to the *U.S. News* survey.

But it will be more challenging to persuade them to participate widely in more sophisticated—and publicly available—measures of their educational effectiveness, either nationally or internationally. So far, U.S. universities have shown a greater appetite for self-assessment than for transparency. Most of the colleges that participate in the CLA and NSSE prefer to keep their results private, using them for "self-study" rather than to inform potential students, parents, taxpayers, and lawmakers about how much students are actually learning.

One promising effort that moves colleges toward increased openness is the Voluntary System of Accountability, or VSA, which grew out of the increased pressure the Spellings Commission put on the higher education world to assess student outcomes. A joint effort of the American Association of State Colleges and Universities and the Association of Public and Land-grant Universities, which together grant 70 percent of the bachelor's degrees awarded in the United States,[72] the VSA requires participating schools to choose one of several learning assessment tests. Following a period of experimentation, the results must be published, along with other data, such as graduation rates, in a College Portrait that is uniform across institutions. It remains to be seen how effective this initiative will be, and whether a critical mass of universities will sign up for a voluntary endeavor that risks highlighting their weaknesses in public. But it certainly moves universities in the right direction.

Indeed, a strong case can be made that highlighting weaknesses could actually have a salutary effect on many American universities. When the OECD's secondary school PISA test debuted in 2001, it showed that U.S. high school students were far behind many of their global counterparts. Finding out that America's K–12 education was lagging behind the rest of the developed world didn't hurt U.S. primary and secondary schools—it pushed them to make needed reforms. So far, U.S. colleges have little to fear from the currently available international rankings, which focus heavily on the research and reputation measures at which the long-established and top tier of American schools excel. But new rankings that shine a spotlight on student learning as well as research could deliver far less pleasant results, both for American universities and for others around the world that have never put much focus on classroom learning.

That doesn't mean U.S. institutions should follow the advice of many in American higher education and try to steer clear of assessments such as AHELO. Such a move would only preserve U.S. schools' international reputations in the short term; if the rest of the world cooperates with the OECD assessments, claims of American exceptionalism will look absurd. Furthermore, if the news AHELO brings about American higher education is worse than expected, the United States will be better off knowing it sooner rather than later. AHELO could be an instrument of much-needed change in the teaching side of American higher education, a useful way to get around the recalcitrance of those educational institutions that resist attempts at bringing some accountability to their multibillion-dollar enterprise. Even more broadly, as Merisotis argues, improved rankings can help universities innovate and thus maintain their standing in the face of intensified competition from upstart institutions. In undergraduate education, for instance, he suggests that a university that did away with the conventional credit system based on "seat time" in classrooms, moving instead toward measuring learning outcomes—the kind of content knowledge emphasized in the OECD's nascent AHELO assessment system— could quickly establish itself as an entrepreneurial front-runner in the global brain race.

Ultimately, it is unrealistic to imagine that complaining about rankings and lamenting their popularity will do anything to slow their growth and appeal. Moreover, despite their shortcomings, their proliferation is a healthy indicator of a well-functioning—and burgeoning—global education marketplace. That universities so often oppose rankings reflects, says Kevin Carey of the think tank Education Sector, "an aversion to competition and accountability that ill serves students and the public at large."[73] The real challenge will be how to improve rankings in order to give better guidance to students about university quality, and to provide more quality-driven incentives to universities that are eager to improve their national or international standing in the global academic race. If rankings ultimately spur universities to improve the quality of the research they produce, as well as the education their students receive, then the much-disparaged metrics will have succeeded, naysayers to the contrary, in providing their very own version of added educational value.

Chapter Five

For-Profits on the Move

As a seventeen-year-old high school senior in Baltimore in the early 1980s, Douglas Becker combined his interest in computers, his aspiration to be a doctor, and his entrepreneurial sensibility to start a company that could carry out his ideas for computerizing medical records. He was so intent on pursuing his plan that he twice deferred acceptance to Harvard (and ultimately never went to college at all). Within two years, his health care firm was purchased by Blue Cross/Blue Shield. Becker and three friends who were his partners took the proceeds and created a private equity firm. They quickly decided to focus on education investments, reasoning that the education sector had some resemblance to health care—notably in its potential to be improved by the transformational power of technology.

Before long, the group of investors had purchased a little-known tutoring firm called Sylvan Learning Centers, which offered a rudimentary version of computerized academic coaching. Becker became CEO of the firm in 1991. During his twelve-year tenure as head of the company, now known as Sylvan Learning Systems, it rode the wave of the testing and accountability movement sweeping the nation to serve 200,000 elementary and secondary students at more than 1,000 centers around North America. Because Sylvan relied heavily on moonlighting teachers as its academic coaches, Becker and his colleagues eventually realized that the 25,000 teachers the firm had hired made it the largest private employer of teachers in the United States. The recognition that teacher training was "a strategic imperative for us," Becker says,[1] led to the firm's first foray into the world of private sector higher education when, in 1997, Sylvan purchased Canter and Associates, a teacher-training company focused on distance learning that offered a fast-growing master's program in education.

Within a few years, Sylvan had a controlling interest in Walden University, another for-profit online university offering a range of career-oriented degrees. It also acquired a majority stake in the Universidad Europea de Madrid, a for-profit university in Spain. By 2003, postsecondary education was the source of two-thirds of the company's revenues, which approached $1 billion annually. It spun off its tutoring business into a publicly traded company called Educate, Inc., and renamed its existing company Laureate Education, positioning it to focus on the burgeoning market in for-profit postsecondary education in general—and global for-profit higher education in particular. The resulting firm is now a key player in the private sector version of global higher ed. Through the universities it owns, Laureate—now privately held—educates nearly half a million students in forty-three institutions in twenty countries around the world, from Mexico, Chile, and Brazil to France, the Netherlands, Cyprus, China, and Australia.

Becker himself has followed the company's global trajectory, moving his family from Baltimore to China to oversee several new acquisitions there, then going on to Paris to track Laureate's global business interests. The secret of Laureate's success, he says, is not that it has a global vision for what universities should teach and how they should teach it; quite the contrary. Unlike some Western nonprofit universities that have sought to spread overseas by setting up branch campuses, he says, "we never had a single model to export. We looked at every individual market. We asked, 'What does that market need?' And we said, 'Let's go give it to them.'"

A Vast New Market

Why did for-profit higher education become the kind of high-growth worldwide industry that would attract entrepreneurs like Becker? Because the globalization of traditional research universities has so far been largely an elite phenomenon. The for-profit sector, by contrast, has targeted a vast and vastly different student market: non-elite learners, often poorly served by existing institutions, who are eager to earn practical, career-oriented degrees. And for-profits have grown quickly in part because of their willingness to use technology far more aggressively than their more conventional university counterparts.

Growth in for-profit higher education is in part a function of growth in postsecondary education more generally. As of 2001, more than 90 million students around the world were enrolled in postsecondary institutions. Just two years later, that figure had passed 100 million (with much of that increase taking placing in China). And by 2006 the number had risen to some 115 million students. But this soaring enrollment, driven by growing middle-class populations with a healthy appetite for higher education, could not easily have taken place in the public sector alone because of lagging government spending on postsecondary education in many countries. That is why the new global demand in turn created a vast private higher education market, with a value estimated by the World Bank's International Finance Corporation at about $400 billion worldwide in 2006.[2]

For-profit higher education has grown especially quickly in Asia and Latin America. A leading expert on private sector higher education globalization cites a range of statistics that demonstrate the trend. Ron Perkinson is a New Zealander who was formerly senior education specialist with the World Bank's International Finance Corporation and senior vice president of Whitney International University System, one of the new U.S.-run for-profit providers moving into international markets. He notes that in the eight Asian countries with the largest populations, student enrollment from 1991 to 2001 grew by 260 percent. "Most of this growth was absorbed by the private sector," he writes. In Indonesia, for example, state universities are vastly oversubscribed: in 2004, 344,000 students applied for about 80,000 slots. Growing numbers of Indonesian students leave the country to study overseas each year. And domestic enrollment is skewed toward private sector institutions, which enrolled 68 percent of students—2.1 million—in 2004, compared to 900,000 students enrolled in public universities. Elsewhere, for-profit higher education makes up an extremely high percentage of enrollment: 80 percent in South Korea; 77 percent in Japan; 75 percent in India and Brazil; 68 percent in the Philippines, Indonesia, and Columbia; and 63 percent in Belgium. The percentage is substantial in Mexico and in the United States as well, at 33 and 32 percent, respectively.[3]

The majority of for-profit postsecondary institutions are domestically owned and operated. But a group of new corporate players, most based in the United States, have seized on the potential of for-profit universities, acquiring a growing number of institutions that have the capacity for even greater growth. Laureate is certainly not alone on this terrain. Other participants in the new market include Whitney International, created by Texas entrepreneur Randy Best; Apollo Global, formed by the Apollo Group, the parent company of the hugely successfully University of Phoenix; Kaplan, Inc., the fast-expanding education provider; and DeVry Inc., the parent company of DeVry University, which specializes in business and management degrees.

Whitney International, for instance, is a relatively new entrant that has controlling interests in Brazil's University Center Jorge Amado, Panama's Isthmus University, and two Colombian community colleges. It is also creating alliances with a number of established Latin American universities, including Argentina's Twenty-first-Century Managerial University and Colombia's Grancolombiano Polytechnic. It relies heavily on moderately priced distance-learning programs and is seeking to partner with for-profit institutions—most considered low- to middle-tier—that offer practical degree programs at the associate and bachelor's level, including business, engineering, and marketing. The company enrolled some 40,000 students in distance-learning classes in Latin America in 2008, a figure it hoped to double the following year. And beyond Latin America, it plans to expand into India and other Asian nations. "With a bit of technology and affordable tuition, we're reaching thousands of people," Whitney's chief technology officer told the *Chronicle of Higher Education*.[4]

International education now provides a significant source of revenues for companies better known for other activities. Kaplan, Inc., became a giant in the U.S. test preparation business, making the company a huge financial success (so much so that its parent firm, the Washington Post Company, has been able to stay profitable even as its flagship newspaper suffers from the same woes as the rest of the media industry). Like Laureate, however, Kaplan made a significant move into higher education, with test preparation now accounting for less than a quarter of its business. Its major activity is now postsecondary education: in the United States, the company offers mostly online certificates and degrees in practical fields such as nursing, criminal justice, and information technology. Overseas, it runs a variety of higher ed ventures, often so-called pathway programs that serve students in assorted non-Western countries who wish to study in the West. These programs are typically one-year courses that cover everything from English-language training and core academic skills to instruction in how Western universities work. Such preparation is sometimes required as a condition of admissions by British or Australian universities. Kaplan doesn't only offer a year of college prep, however. Some of its campuses have partnerships with Western universities that allow students to begin in China, under Kaplan auspices, and then go on to complete their coursework at, say, Northeastern University, the University of Adelaide, or Sheffield University in Britain.

Another giant on the American for-profit higher education scene, the Apollo Group, sees big growth prospects overseas. Apollo, the parent company of the University of Phoenix, which created a thriving business catering to working adults with mostly online courses, waited for some time to dive into the international for-profit market. It did so with a splash, however, announcing a joint venture with the Carlyle Group in October 2007. The two partners agreed to pledge $800 million and $200 million, respectively, to the newly formed Apollo Global, which set its sights in particular on serving the "attractive demographics" of Latin America and Asia.[5] The following year, the new venture went on to acquire the Universidad de Artes Ciencias y Comunicación, a Chilean arts and sciences university known as UNIACC, and to purchase a majority stake in the Universidad Latinoamericana, a private university in Mexico City specializing in dentistry, medicine, and communications programs that had previously been part-owned by Carlyle. By the spring of 2009, Apollo Global was in talks to acquire a British higher education company, BPP Professional Education, which was the first for-profit institution to offer degrees in Britain.[6]

Apparently not wishing to be left behind in the rush to seek international business, one of the biggest publicly held for-profit higher education companies, DeVry Inc., is also entering the fray. The firm has already been successful enough in the United States to win over onetime skeptic Harold Shapiro, former president of Princeton and the University of Michigan, who now chairs DeVry's board.[7] Next, in March 2009, DeVry, which owns such U.S. institutions as DeVry University, Ross University, and Chamberlain College of Nursing, announced its first major overseas foray—the purchase of a majority stake in Fanor, a firm that provides private postsecondary education in northeastern Brazil. The agreement called for DeVry to pay $23.5 million in cash for Fanor and to assume the company's debt in exchange for a 69.3 percent stake in the company. The three colleges owned by Fanor serve more than 10,000 students in some twenty-eight undergraduate programs in business, law, and engineering.[8] This vocational focus is in keeping with the U.S. operations of DeVry, which focuses on professional education in technology, business, and management, delivered in undergraduate, graduate, and lifelong learning programs aimed at working adults.

The international for-profit education market is certainly not restricted to U.S. companies. Singapore-based Raffles Education has campuses in Australia, India, Malaysia, and Hong Kong. The Estacia University Group in Brazil invested in a Paraguay campus. Nyenrode Business Universiteit, an elite for-profit business school in the Netherlands, opened a branch campus in Nigeria.[9] But the largest and higher-profile new entrants in the cross-border for-profit university market are American firms. And of those, by far the biggest is Laureate, which seems poised to build significantly on its already dramatic success.

Laureate already has more than 150 campuses in North America, Latin America, Europe, and Asia. It offers a multitude of degrees in engineering, education, business, health care, hospitality, and information technology. The company experienced 30 percent growth annually for six years running, with $2 billion a year in revenues.[10] CEO Becker projects that demand for higher education among eighteen- to twenty-four-year-olds will continue to grow by 10 percent a year. And he notes that private, for-profit operators are no longer content simply to acquire open secretarial schools and other vocational programs; now they are beginning to operate mainstream research and medical institutions as well—both of which Laureate has done. Indeed, in July 2008, Laureate announced that it had acquired several large private universities in Mexico and Costa Rica, one of which includes a medical school (overall Laureate now runs fifteen medical schools).[11] And in Chile, according to Becker, Laureate's institutions are the largest private recipients of federal research funds.[12]

While Laureate runs postsecondary institutions worldwide—including well-regarded hotel-management schools in Switzerland and Spain—the core of its operations are in Latin America. Becker cites two Laureate-owned universities in the region as particularly good examples of the company's approach. One is the Universidad del Valle de México, or UVM, a well-regarded university founded in 1960 that educates some 90,000 undergraduate and graduate students on thirty-five campuses. Becker calls the university a "mid-tier" institution that caters to Mexico's expanding middle class. He is proud that in a *Reader's Digest* survey UVM placed in the top ten for six years in a row, ranking seventh in 2009. He is prouder still, however, of the fact that all the higher-ranked institutions were elite universities—either public institutions that cost little or nothing but reject most applicants, or private universities that charge two or three times UVM's annual tuition (which stood at around $4,100 in 2009).[13] Using language that echoes almost precisely the rhetoric used in U.S. higher education policy debates, he argues that through institutions such as UVM, Laureate delivers "recognized quality education while adhering to a mission of access and affordability."[14]

That the rising global for-profit sector typically focuses on universities offering programs in health care, nursing, business, and the like is no accident. Increasing numbers of university students are nontraditional age: close to 40 percent of U.S. undergrads and 30 percent of Canadian undergrads are over twenty-five years old, while more than 20 percent of first-year university students in Australia, New Zealand, Denmark, Norway, and Sweden were over twenty-seven in 2000, according to OECD figures. That demographic shift, toward what is usually known as "lifelong learning," has required universities to rethink the mix of educational offerings they provide to cater to the needs of different kinds of students, many of whom are older and seek part-time coursework. That has led them to consider not only the formal education they have traditionally provided but also on-the-job vocational training, as well as distance learning that students can complete at home.[15]

At the same time, Perkinson reports, demand for technical and vocational education and training has risen substantially with, among other developments, the massive growth of the information technology (IT) industry. For example, some European and U.S. firms have reported shortages in IT jobs, a development that—combined with other factors—has led many universities to include vocational programs in their mix of offerings. It has also, of course, provided huge new opportunities for for-profit institutions to offer classes, both in and outside university settings, that are typically less expensive and shorter in length than regular college courses. India's IT training firm APTECH, for instance, has some 3,000 training centers in 52 countries.[16] For similar reasons, plenty of international activity can be found in the corporate-training sector as well. Cisco Systems has a "Networking Academy" that provides practical IT courses to 600,000 students in more than 160 countries. In Morocco, enrollment rose 47 percent from 2007 to 2008 alone, with women making up nearly one-third of students.[17]

That market demand is so career-oriented explains why international for-profit universities rarely do more than dabble in research. Despite conducting some applied research projects—in part because this kind of work can be important to the job satisfaction of faculty members—Becker says pushing scientific frontiers will never be part of Laureate's mission. "We will never do basic research," he says. "We need to pick our niches." That is one of several defining characteristics of the flourishing private university market overseas, he adds. While he takes pains to note that his institutions are universities, not trade schools, Becker says that in general, "the private sector will focus on employment-oriented outcomes for students who can afford to pay. The public sector will focus on three things: research, the absolute elite best students, and the students who aren't great students and can't afford to go to private universities."

However, while the growth of for-profit universities has led to criticisms that they provide education for the privileged elite, the reality is far more complicated. In some ways, the growth of private institutions, which cater to a level of demand that public universities are often unable to meet, overturns stereotypes about which kinds of students are served by each type of institution. While good data are hard to obtain, many students who would not otherwise have access to higher education receive important skills from private institutions, argues Daniel Levy, a professor at the University of Albany (SUNY) and director of the Program for Research on Private Higher Education. "A lot of the private institutions are what I call 'demand-absorbing institutions'—they are attracting a lot of people who couldn't make it in the public sector."[18]

While Americans tend to associate private (nonprofit) universities with elite education (even though most U.S. private universities are not elite), in the rest of the world almost all elites are public. With fiercely competitive admissions exams, often the children of the wealthy are best able to obtain the preparation necessary to get in. In a country such as Brazil, with its deep class divides, Levy says a typical pattern would be for exclusive public universities to admit affluent students who have attended private primary and secondary schools before receiving taxpayer-subsidized postsecondary education. Lower- and middle-income students tend to be squeezed out: "At stage one, they weren't from privileged backgrounds," Levy says, while at stage two, "they weren't strong enough academically." All this means that domestic opportunities for some students are limited, thus opening the door for the Apollos, Kaplans, Laureates, and more.

While global for-profit universities certainly face barriers, they have investors convinced that they represent a major financial opportunity notwithstanding gloomy economic times. Brooke Coburn, managing director at the Carlyle Group and head of the blue chip investing firm's U.S. Growth Capital Team, lays out a detailed case for his company's interest in private sector education in general and its decision to enter a joint venture with Apollo Global in particular. Carlyle invests in for-profit companies, with Coburn's fund focusing on "long-term investment in growth sectors where you have the potential to meaningfully expand companies over five to ten years."[19] Carlyle makes particular efforts to help the companies in which it invests expand internationally. For more than a decade, Coburn's fund has been active in the global education sector, which he views as an area where "opportunities are very significant from an investor's point of view."

Why are those opportunities so great? First, massive funds are spent on education. Coburn notes that in most countries around the world, education "is a big-four or big-five spending item" coming not far behind health care. Moreover, the importance of developing human capital is increasingly clear on a practical level. "There's a near-perfect correlation between educational level and earnings potential, so it's one where, from the consumer's standpoint, there's a very high return on investment." In addition, he sees growth potential for the for-profit sector because of the capacity limits that have often characterized postsecondary systems in nations where university education has been geared at the elite rather than the masses.

Finally, drawing another health care parallel, Coburn says the introduction of technology has improved efficiency a lot, whereas "education is still relatively nascent in terms of technology adoption." As an example of the room that exists for growth, he points to Blackboard, Inc., an education-technology firm in which Carlyle invested more than ten years ago. In the past decade, Blackboard has grown a hundredfold, from a small firm to the world's largest provider of instructional software for postsecondary institutions. Most of Blackboard's business is in the United States, but it has expanded overseas as well.

While Carlyle rarely forms joint ventures with corporations, it did so with Apollo because "there was a very symbolic fit between what they do well and what we do well," Coburn says. The investment firm brings capital, of course, plus an international presence that is rare among private equity firms, long-standing interest in education, and extensive experience making acquisitions. For its part, Apollo has developed a flourishing domestic business but hadn't previously done much to expand internationally. The online-learning giant stands out from many other companies, Coburn believes, because of its course delivery mechanisms, its student support structure, the breadth of its curriculum, and operational strength so great that it has call center staff around the world who speak more than thirty different languages. (The company's programs reach more than 130 countries.)

Carlyle is happy with the joint venture so far, but it is too early to tell whether it will be a success either financially or in terms of student learning outcomes, enrollment, and job placement, Coburn says. "We'll answer that question in five years." While rival Laureate remains by far the largest for-profit operator internationally, the company's overall size is considerably smaller than Apollo's. And there is apparently plenty of room to grow. "Cornering the education market is a little bit like cornering the health care market—it can't be done," Coburn says. "This sector is so large that it could support fifty or one hundred companies the size of Apollo worldwide."

He sees Apollo's particular strengths—notably the centralized operations it has perfected at the University of Phoenix—as positioning the company especially well for global expansion. "There is a lot of leverage and efficiency to be gained from having multinational operators." Apollo's course-delivery systems, from technology infrastructure (computer servers and software, call centers, and so on) to telephone advisers who walk students through the matriculation process and advise them about financial aid, are well established, scalable, and give the company distinct advantages over its competitors, Coburn maintains. "These technology platforms and the concept of scalability is something that's foreign to many institutions."

The goal of eventually going to scale, of course, is to serve the significant numbers of adult learners to whom mainstream universities have not traditionally catered. "Ultimately, is Apollo Global going to be competitive with Harvard and INSEAD [the Fontainebleau- and Singapore-based international business school] and other elite institutions around the world? No. But that's not the objective," Coburn says. "The objective is to focus on the fat section of the demographic curve where there is an unmet need, and where elite institutions don't have the capacity, or it's not within their strategic objectives to meet the needs of those students."

PLUGGED-IN LEARNING

With the expansion of the global for-profits, those needs are being catered to with distinctly new forms of instruction. Hand in hand with the rise of for-profit education, technology is increasingly being used to reach students both within individual nations and across borders. Overall, the growth of online postsecondary education around the world has been enormous—it makes up some 15 percent of all higher education globally. That, says Perkinson, makes it "the fastest growing subsector in education today."[20] While some students take purely online classes, the most common arrangement is for students to combine some face-to-face classroom instruction with distance learning, an approach sometimes known as click-and-brick or "blended delivery." As of 2004, in China alone there were about 2 million postsecondary distance-learning students, with about a million in Latin American nations and another million in Europe. Half the students enrolled in Australian universities from Hong Kong and Singapore are doing so through distance-learning programs, while about one-third of all postsecondary courses in Russia are being taken online.[21] In the United States, the 400,000-student University of Phoenix is now the largest private university, enrolling about three-quarters of its students in distance-learning courses. Overall U.S. enrollment in individual online courses jumped from under 1.9 million students in 2004 to 3.5 million in 2009. Even when the student count is limited to those enrolled in fully online programs, the numbers are substantial: the research and consulting firm Eduventures estimates that 2 million Americans studied wholly online in 2009, up from 1 million in 2004.[22]

Most of this growth in Web-based education has taken place in the private sector. "For-profits are the logical purveyors of distance learning," according to William Tierney, director of the University of Southern California's Center for Higher Education Policy Analysis.[23] While elite institutions such as MIT and Yale have attracted considerable attention for their "open courseware" offerings that provide either their entire curriculum (MIT) or selected courses (Yale) free to students willing to study online, for-profit firms, unsurprisingly, have targeted paying customers seeking practical courses. And they have quickly done so at scale. In Mexico, for instance, Tecnológico de Monterrey, one of the largest private universities in Latin America, has thoroughly integrated online courses into its programming. About 83,000 of the university's 101,000 students take one or more of their classes online through its affiliated Universidad Virtual.[24] And more than 5,000 of its students live outside of Mexico, taking a mixture of online and campus-based classes in other Latin American nations.

The possibilities that this kind of learning can open up—as well as some of the uncertainties—are apparent in the *Chronicle of Higher Education*'s portrait of a Whitney University venture in one small town in Colombia.[25] In Anapoima, two hours from Bogota, construction of a five-foot satellite dish at a local school has opened up new vistas for residents such as Jhon Harold Peña, who works in the stockroom at a nearby country club, and his wife, Marta Castiblanco, who cleans guest rooms there. The two want to improve their family's life—they have three children—but they have never before had the chance to study. Now Castiblanco, who wants to be a tour guide, is studying tourism. Pena, who would like to run his own auto-parts business, takes classes in financial management. Both study via weekly online classes beamed to their town from the campus of Grancolombiano Polytechnic in Bogota, which runs the classes in Anapoima as well as at four other distance-learning sites (dozens more are in the works). Many of their classmates never knew how to use e-mail or surf the Web before taking the class.

Technology apart, the setting in which these students pursue their education is distinctly low-budget. In one business administration course, students sit in a ramshackle metal-roofed classroom and take notes as a lecture—delivered via satellite—is shown on a screen. A proctor e-mails their questions to Bogota, where professors can sometimes respond right away. Another group of students studies in a small computer lab, while a third studies at picnic tables lit only by a few bulbs. Still, the ability to study close to home is a must for many students. "Bogota is too far," says Jimmy Benavidas, who is studying for a business degree. "I couldn't afford to live there, plus I'd never see my family."

Whitney University says its online partnership with Grancolombiano is bringing higher education to disadvantaged students—often adults—who are typically unable to access traditional universities. The rector of Grancolombiano says he wanted "a new education model that didn't just serve the privileged few." Whitney, of course, wants to make money—in part by linking its virtual classes with university brand names that are known in the region. At Grancolombiano, the university develops the online curriculum, while Whitney International's end of the deal includes building a modest television studio, connecting the university to its Panama-based South American satellite network, setting up remote-learning sites, adapting existing course materials for online use, and training professors to lecture from the studio.

The adaptation process isn't always easy. At first "I was nervous as heck," says mathematics professor Nidia Mercedes James, who had never before lectured to a camera in a TV studio (students get a combination of live and prerecorded lessons). But she is now becoming used to the new medium and says she enjoys the online forums that let her interact daily with some of her 250 students. Students studying long-distance, she says, are especially in need of feedback. "They aren't here on campus, so they need the extra motivation," she told the *Chronicle*.

While students certainly benefit from personal interaction, receiving such attention in a distance-learning environment is inevitably harder. Many are nonetheless willing to make the trade-off because of the enormous flexibility that online study provides. Around the world, the convenience of distance learning for working students is a major selling point for the international for-profits. In Australia, for instance, a division of Kaplan, Inc., known as Kaplan Professional offers specialized graduate-level degrees and certificates in applied finance—asset and liability management, equity analysis, sales and marketing for financial institutions, and the like. The company's marketing materials play up the practical nature of the coursework, the personal guidance provided by a student adviser, and the flexible scheduling made possible by online learning options. Students can choose from a menu of "delivery modes"—distance learning, the more personal touch of face-to-face instruction, or a combination of the two.

A brochure for the courses, which were previously delivered by the Securities Institute of Australia and the Financial Services Institute of Australasia, touts the benefits for self-paced learners of "comprehensive course notes, downloadable lectures, electronic assignment submission and online access to experts and learning tools [that] enable you to study when and where you choose, anywhere in the world." In the same vein, a first-person testimonial from Luke Bates, an analyst with the global accounting firm KPMG, backs up the point. "The course gave me the flexibility to be mobile without my studies being affected. I started in Sydney, spent six months in Perth and then finished in Adelaide," he says. The pamphlet also quotes Bates praising e-learning tools that allowed him to build professional networks with fellow students, across Australia and overseas, "with whom I would otherwise have had no interaction."

That Internet technology holds special appeal for for-profit educational firms is in many ways unsurprising, given the long tradition of private sector leadership in long-distance education. As far back as 1840, when the penny post was introduced in Britain, a correspondence course in shorthand was offered by Isaac Pitman. Correspondence courses became a veritable industry—the online learning of its time—offering much of the same flexibility as today's distance-ed classes and also dominated by private providers. For a time, public sector universities offered various forms of distance learning, but today the for-profit sector is again at the forefront of the trend. As global higher education experts Sir John Daniel, Asha Kanwar, and Stamenka Uvalic-Trumbic explain, online learning makes particular sense for the private sector because of the way its costs are structured: relatively high investment on the front end, offset by substantially lower marginal costs as more and more students are signed up.[26]

"For-profit institutions' access to capital markets makes them uniquely suited to make those investments," they write. Moreover, they argue, for-profit firms offering distance learning also benefit from two concurrent trends—the availability of freely shared course material, known as open educational resources, together with online learning–management systems easily available to anyone. Still, they fret that cross-border distance-learning programs, given their market-driven nature, too often focus on business and information technology at the expense of liberal education. They also worry that programs designed in one nation to be offered to students in another "may incorporate no recognition of social, cultural, and ethnic differences." Maybe so. But one clear lesson of the surge in demand for cross-border education, both online and in brick-and-mortar classrooms, is that students and their families are less interested in cultural sensitivity than in securing the opportunities—and often the practical skills—associated with universities and training programs that are sometimes to be found most easily at institutions based in other countries.

Indeed, the version of branch campuses established by for-profits underscores the point. A number of programs operated by for-profit universities could be viewed as counterparts to the satellite campuses, established by mainstream universities, that have swept the Middle East and Asia. The two have in common the quest for new revenues, particularly in Asian countries (although some elite Western universities insist that internationalization, rather than tuition dollars, is their primary motivation). One notable difference, however, is the for-profits' unusual hybrid credit-transfer arrangements. These permit students to begin part of a degree program at a for-profit institution in their home country, then travel abroad to earn a degree in another nation, often at a state university. In India, for instance, students can begin studying information technology at APTECH (the private firm with worldwide training centers), then after two years go on to complete a degree at the University of Sunderland in the United Kingdom or Southern Cross University in Australia.[27]

The model bears similarities to the one offered by Kaplan in partnership with a consortium of nine British universities, as well as institutions in Australia and Singapore, that allows students in, say, China and Vietnam to combine coursework from Kaplan and the institution that will grant their degree. This arrangement might involve one year at home followed by three overseas, or two years each at Kaplan and the foreign university. "If you look at a place like China, with a rising middle class that's expanding, many families could afford to send their child to a really good-quality university program," says Mark Harrad, Kaplan's vice president for communications. "But they're unable to gain access to that because there are so few spaces. And my understanding is that there's a big gap between high-quality programs and lower-quality technical programs. So the opportunity to go to the University of Sheffield in the U.K. is a very good opportunity for them."[28]

In some places—Shanghai, for instance—students who wish to receive a degree from an overseas institution while staying in their home country can study for all four years at a campus either created by or operated by Kaplan, which essentially acts as a subcontractor for the foreign university. This doesn't mean a watering down of standards, company officials insist. "There's an extraordinary amount of quality assurance put into the delivery of these educational programs by the overseas universities," says Gerald Rosberg, a Kaplan senior vice president who is the architect of many of the company's global partnerships. "The partner universities want this done to their satisfaction, in terms of not only articulating the curriculum and creating the examinations students have to take, but often also moderating the exams—they actually read the students' exams." In certain cases, the degree-granting universities send their own faculty to teach courses to third- and fourth-year students at the overseas campus.[29]

Even as it forges alliances with mainstream universities, blurring the distinction between for-profit and nonprofit, domestic and overseas campuses, the next frontier for Kaplan will be to establish its own full-fledged educational programs around the world. "We're going to be delivering higher education programs that are entirely our own, that don't come with degrees from conventional universities," Rosberg says. The firm's higher-ed division is unapologetic about the kind of education it provides, he adds, bristling at the notion that Kaplan offers simply a stripped-down, less expensive, and lower-quality version of what traditional institutions offer. "We view it as equal or better, with a clear focus on outcomes, lots of testing, and very creative use of technology. What we are very eager to do is take all those capabilities that we believe have worked so successfully for students in the U.S. and make them work for overseas students. They won't get big brand names, but they'll get a better educational experience."

As profit-making universities expand worldwide, finding the right balance between a global and a local presence can be a delicate matter. At least one major player—Laureate—makes a point of portraying itself not as a McDonald's-like multinational conglomerate, spreading a single product and brand identity around the world, but rather as a culturally aware parent company of a network of distinctive local institutions. "We never talk about Laureate International University. We talk about Laureate International Universit*ies*," says Joseph Duffey, senior vice president of Laureate and a former president of the University of Massachusetts system and of American University. He contrasted this approach with Apollo's, which he said focused first on creating a model in the United States, then on exporting the same model overseas.[30] For his part, Jeff Langenbach, a former investment banker and now president of Apollo Global, disputes that characterization. It is true that the University of Phoenix was at one time marketing its core brand-name services to students around the world, he says. Now, however, with the formation of Apollo Global, the company's strategy is twofold: targeting the University of Phoenix's offerings at the U.S. market, including servicemen and women on American military installations, while using local brands, not the Phoenix or Apollo name, for Apollo's overseas university acquisitions. These universities will, however, be linked globally by technology, and, unlike Laureate's mostly on-the-ground classroom instruction, they will be largely online, permitting shared use of back office functions among campuses.[31]

If companies such as Laureate and Phoenix are not cross-border purveyors of a particular curriculum and brand-name educational experience, in what sense can their operations truly be considered part of the globalization trend in higher education? Becker answers this question by first underlining the "huge competitive advantage" Laureate brings to its spreading empire by applying its business model to institutions around the world. "These individual universities are made strong by welding them into a global network," he says. Laureate's market-based "best practices" include everything from how classroom capacity and scheduling are handled to the use of technology to design and build campuses (the company built 9 of its 150 campuses from scratch and renovated many more of the institutions it acquired).[32] "These things are incredibly powerful, but students may never see them," Becker says.

All this contrasts significantly with the international activities of nonprofit universities, he stresses. "The mind-set of business is accountability, measurement, and analysis. And there's not a lot of that in the international [nonprofit postsecondary] markets. A lot of that is in the private sector." When Cornell opens a branch of its medical school in Qatar, he continues, "they're not there to bring state-of-the-art analytics and a commercial sense of accountability, because that's just not what traditional nonprofit institutions do—that would not be their strength. But what would be their strength is academic rigor, a tremendous reputation and brand awareness, and [awarding] a U.S. degree."

As for the growing global student mobility that has been such a striking feature of the nonprofit sector, Becker sees it as largely irrelevant to for-profits. "Some people think having a few wealthy people traveling around the world really creates globalization. What is that really going to do for students in Mexico and Shanghai who can't afford to go overseas?" Becker says that the privately held company earns at most 35 to 40 percent of its revenues from Europe and the United States combined. By contrast, it earns about 60 percent of its revenues in Latin America and is investing heavily in Asia. In these emerging markets, overseas study is a pipe dream for the kinds of students Laureate targets, he says. While Laureate offers its students in Mexico the opportunity to study at its university in Madrid, and at the same tuition they pay at their home universities, few are able to take advantage of the company's global network simply because travel and living costs are too high.

By contrast, Becker does see international synergies in the ability of Laureate-owned universities to share faculty know-how and curriculum. A professor at one of the company's Mexico campuses might be trained by a professor from China or the United States or Spain, for instance. Similarly, there is cross-pollination between Laureate's showcase programs and other universities. Students at one of the firm's Mexican universities can study the same curriculum offered by the two elite hotel-management schools Laureate runs in Switzerland.

Still another way of understanding the participation of for-profit universities in globalization is as providers of human capital. "There is some global culture, but the primary focus of the privates is responding to the localized postsecondary learning needs of the population," says Gerald Heeger of Whitney International.[33] Private universities are less likely than elite nonprofits to train students to be global businesspeople, he says. But they are very likely to educate, say, accountants who must know how to help local businesses confirm to increasingly standardized international accounting rules, "even if they never leave their hometown of Cordoba, Argentina." Thus, for-profits train local human capital for local and regional businesses, which in turn take part in the global economy.

REGULATING QUALITY

For all the successes of the global for-profits and their rapid spread to new markets around the world, they face huge skepticism from their more traditional nonprofit counterparts—and sometimes from outside analysts and government regulators as well. The key question mark for many critics is quality. In Colombia, for instance, Whitney International's alliances with several for-profit universities have drawn concern. "Very little is known about Whitney or its partner universities," says Ana Lucia Gazzola, who directs UNESCO's International Institute for Higher Education in Latin America. "I strongly suspect that what we are seeing here is a commercial service operating at the margins of the education system, with hardly any oversight."[34] Daniel, Kanwar, and Uvalic-Trumbic are even more emphatic about the quality shortcomings of some private providers. In India, for instance, while international for-profit institutions are needed to expand access, many have "problematic" quality, they write. "Even when the foreign providers are universities, they are not in the premier league and have mediocre reputations in their own countries."

Some criticism of the for-profits is grounded in legitimate concerns about their shortcomings. At the same time, some seems to be based on fundamental philosophical disagreements about the legitimacy of profit-seeking entities entering the postsecondary market in the first place. Higher education is widely viewed as a public good—one with such widespread benefits to a nation, its citizens, and its economy, that it should be viewed, and funded, as any public service would be. Hence, the suspicion of the Whitneys, Apollos, Laureates, and Kaplans of the world. "I think a large part of it is cultural," says Levy of the University of Albany (SUNY). "It's [also] historical. Higher education in most of the world, outside the United States, has been a public enterprise—publicly funded, with public across-the-board rules."[35] With that university form so well established, he says, any new entrant would inevitably face wariness and challenges. For-profits typically shy away from expensive areas of study and from conventional scholarly research, he notes, operating with significantly lower costs per student than their inefficient public sector counterparts. This has the effect of increasing access to underserved student populations—but also fuels a continuing debate about whether greater efficiency comes at the price of substandard quality.[36]

Still, even some observers who share a degree of skepticism about the quality of for-profits argue that what they have to offer must be understood in the context of the markets in which they compete—all the more so in the case of for-profits expanding into foreign countries. Jason Lane, an assistant professor of education at SUNY–Albany who studies the global for-profit sector, argues that cross-border higher education providers come with a certain level of built-in quality assurance because of the reputations they bring with them from their home countries. In places like Malaysia, which has a large for-profit postsecondary sector, foreign providers may well provide educational quality superior to that of the often-problematic domestic for-profits. Moreover, an argument can be made that foreign-owned for-profit universities have a clear self-interest in policing their own quality standards. "They want to make sure they maintain a positive image," says Lane. "They have a product to sell."[37]

Indeed, the international for-profits take the view that it is domestic universities of all stripes, rather than their globally minded counterparts, with which they must contend for market share. "Our competitors are not the Apollos or the Kaplans," insists Laureate's Duffey. "Our competitors are the other universities in the countries where we operate, both public and for-profit." That view is certainly held, at times with alarm, by many of the conventional universities in countries that have seen a substantial and growing presence of for-profit providers. In September 2008, Universities U.K., a group representing British university heads, issued a report warning that U.S. firms such as Kaplan and Apollo are aggressively expanding into the United Kingdom, Western Europe, and beyond, sometimes working in partnership with state universities—and sometimes purchasing them outright. That means British universities may lose both students and money, the study concluded. Kaplan "is Hoovering up institutions in the UK and Australia," said the report's author, Roger King, a longtime higher education scholar and visiting professor at the Open University's Centre for Higher Education Research and Information.[38]

King pointed to cases where regulators cracked down on for-profits for "over-aggressive and inappropriate student recruitment and retention practices," suggesting that these indicate how much pressure for growing revenues exists in the for-profit sector. Sally Hunt, the general secretary of the University and College Union, put it even more bluntly: "If we move towards more private involvement in higher education, then successful universities of the future will be the ones who can flog cheap courses for the most cash." Others, however, said the entrance of for-profits expanded student choice and usefully catered to the needs of employers. "How much should we all be worrying if it encourages us to further sharpen up the quality of higher education provided to the benefit of our students?" said Alice Hynes, CEO of GUILDHE, an organization representing newer and more specialized postsecondary institutions.[39]

Perhaps unsurprisingly, political ideology plays a decisive role in whether cross-national for-profits are granted access to a new global market. While Laureate has had notable success in Latin America, a secondary presence in Europe, and plans to expand to Asia, it has been frustrated in its efforts to enter the massive and potentially lucrative Indian market, according to Levy. The firm thought it could gain permission to operate in India but was then told no. Indian neoliberals favored Laureate's entry, Levy says, but the country's powerful socialists vetoed the plan.

This kind of antipathy toward new private sector players seems to rest on a fundamental conviction that education is a public good, just like national defense or perhaps health care. In this view, there is something inherently distasteful about private provision of something that is close to a fundamental human right and ought therefore to be provided by the state. It is true, write Daniel, Kanwar, and Uvalic-Trumbic, that higher education is a public good. "Having a fire brigade at hand if your house catches fire is a more obviously useful public service than having accessible higher education, but the proportion of people with higher education correlates well with a society's state of economic and civic development." However, because of the personal economic rewards that accrue to those with greater education, it is simultaneously a private good, "with direct benefits to those who participate."[40]

The latter argument has not made significant inroads in many nations, however. The philosophy that there is something dubiously mercantile and crass about for-profit higher education is reflected in the laws passed in countries such as Mexico and Chile that require all private postsecondary providers to be nonprofit. Operators such as Laureate have found a variety of creative means around such provisions, however. Douglas Becker of Laureate says the company sometimes receives contracts with nonprofits to run universities, or is able to operate as a nonprofit itself in countries such as Mexico, where certain kinds of nonprofits can nevertheless have shareholders and declare dividends. ("We operate in the cultural and regulatory context of each country," a Laureate spokeswoman says.) More important, Laureate officials argue, distinguishing between for-profit and nonprofit universities is often difficult. Some nonprofits are run by families that have built up significant wealth through university real estate holdings, and some have for-profit business units. Moreover, they say, their money-making universities engage in plenty of altruistic activities, from providing shelters to refugees from severe flooding in Villa Hermosa, Mexico, in 2007 to offering free medical care to patients being treated by students at Laureate-owned medical schools.

In the vast majority of cases, Duffey suggests, the for-profit versus non-profit distinction is moot in the communities where Laureate operates. "Let me describe a conversation I've had about a dozen times on the fringes of Mexico City or in nearby cities. I look the place over, sit down with the city fathers, and say, 'Do you have young people who are eager for a university education? Could you get more investment in your community with more trained workers? Oh, and by the way, I saw an abandoned monastery on my way here. Suppose we put a university branch there? Would you like to have a career-oriented higher education institution here that would pay taxes on its earnings?'" This isn't a hard sell, Duffey says. "Nobody else has come in and offered to set up a university." Little surprise, then, that there are now a dozen branches of Laureate's UVM around Mexico City.

Laureate's example is evidence that official policies may have little bearing on the ability of the for-profits to spread and thrive. The University of Albany's Levy cautions against falling into the trap of equating government policy or national attitudes with the level of student demand necessary to sustain a successful postsecondary enterprise. "It is not a requirement that most of the country like you. You need to attract enough students, and maybe enough capital. But for most people to have a visceral reaction that's negative doesn't mean the private can't thrive—so long as the regulatory regime is liberal."

The regulatory regime, of course, falls precisely at the intersection of the current operations of for-profits, critics' concerns about their quality and viability, and their prospects for further growth. How can the promise for-profits offer of access and equity be squared with the need to ensure basic standards? Higher education should not be treated as a government monopoly, Daniel, Kanwar, and Uvalic-Trumbic argue persuasively, particularly in circumstances when state-run universities are not able to meet the needs of a nation's citizens. "So a choice must be made between inadequate provision of higher education by a public-sector monopoly," they write, "or meeting the demand by a combination of public and private for-profit institutions." That said, they say that a role for government oversight is inevitable: "Government is most effective when it monitors and regulates the provision of public services by others, rather than controlling those services directly."

But given that for-profits are spreading rapidly and that regulation is inevitable, what form should it take? This is a hot topic in the higher education and international development communities. Regulatory barriers to for-profits can be huge. Uncertain and inconsistent oversight criteria; quotas for students from certain backgrounds, as in India; rules prohibiting foreign ownership of private institutions; and limits on fees and for-profit status are just some of the obstacles with which the for-profit sector must contend. In Vietnam, guidelines from the Ministry of Education and Training require that, in addition to their regular coursework, students "must study and obtain a full diploma in Marxist-Lenin philosophy, Marxist-Lenin political economy, scientific socialism, history of the Communist party of Vietnam, and ideology of Ho Chi Minh."[41]

Such regulations are a significant impediment to companies that want to enter and operate in new markets. "Regulatory risk is one of the few things that can put you out of business," says Brooke Coburn of the Carlyle Group. The company is far less likely to enter a country such as India, with its highly restrictive regulatory environment, he says, than China, which welcomes capital and expertise from abroad, or Chile, which he calls "one of the most progressive markets in the world from a regulatory standpoint." Governments with severe postsecondary capacity problems, others concur, are thwarting innovation and hurting their own citizens by "putting up barriers" to new entrants, in the words of Sir Graeme Davies, vice chancellor of the University of London.[42]

Interestingly, however, at a May 2008 meeting on innovation in private higher education, sponsored by the World Bank's International Finance Corporation, two leading representatives of the for-profit sector, Doug Becker of Laureate and Jorge Klor de Alva, a senior vice president at the Apollo Group, both expressed support for greater regulation as a means of keeping out fly-by-night providers. "My biggest hope is that governments will set high standards," Becker said. "The people really in it for the quick buck—they're not helping the industry."[43] Agreed Klor de Alva: "We have to make it very difficult for shoddy providers." (Perhaps not coincidentally, a higher bar for all for-profits would likely cement the dominance of the market leaders.)[44]

The two approaches are by no means mutually exclusive, of course: it seems possible to imagine a general policy of relatively easy entry for for-profit universities, combined with careful oversight designed to guard against either academic or financial fraud. Still, even finding this golden mean may be harder than it seems. Daniel Levy suggests that regulators avoid taking a one-size-fits-all approach to institutions that vary enormously—and that lower-status universities warrant respectful treatment. "I don't think there is an ideal regulatory framework," he says. "If there is for my setting, there might not be for someone else's." Governments ought to tread cautiously when it comes to university oversight, he says. "While I believe fervently in regulation, and it's certainly necessary for private institutions, ideally it should be done with a sense of modesty and humility. There will be lots of mistakes made, lots of unanticipated consequences—some negative, some positive."[45]

Whatever obstacles regulation may bring, for-profit providers remain bullish on their prospects in the years to come. One likely source of expansion, according to Kaplan's Rosberg, is continued growth in partnerships between public universities and for-profit providers, such as Kaplan's "pathways" college-prep programs, in which conventional universities hire for-profits to provide a range of services that were previously handled on campus. "Student recruitment, English-language training, and teaching the basic first part of the curriculum can really be done more efficiently and effectively by for-profits—and there are more and more examples around the world of this happening," Rosberg says. At this point, these arrangements are far more common in the United Kingdom and Australia than in the United States, however. "At some universities the faculty senates are very uneasy about outsourcing—the whole word 'outsourced' is anathema to them." Nevertheless, he predicts confidently, "it's going to come here just as it has at other Western universities."

Rosberg acknowledges that for-profit universities face obstacles to overseas expansion, notably the difficulty of competing with traditional universities that are so heavily subsidized that students pay only nominal tuition. But he is convinced that the entrepreneurial approach pioneered by for-profits, first in the United States and now internationally, will give them a larger and more important place in the higher education systems of many nations. "We're challenging some of the assumptions on which the traditional education world is based," Rosberg says. For-profits are typically better than traditional universities at focusing on part-time students and working adults who want studies that will further their careers, he says. Their mantra is outcomes-based instruction in which student progress is measured regularly. And they have become adept at using a blended learning environment that combines classroom and online instruction.

"One of the tensions that exists all over the world," Rosberg says, "as countries are looking at what to do in the higher education sector and whom to admit from overseas, is prestige. For many students, prestige is very important. However, many of these same students will come to realize they cannot get into elite institutions without conversion programs that prepare them for Western universities. For other students, prestige is less important than access to schools that provide retraining programs, skill enhancement, and the academic fundamentals necessary to win acceptance into Western universities. When you look around the world to see who knows how to do that, the answer is that it's again America's for-profits."

Certainly, nobody expects vocationally oriented for-profits to push aside the global research institutions that are vying for global predominance. But the for-profits make a respectable case that, notwithstanding their differing mission and status, they are likely to have a place at the table. As long as the middle class continues to grow in the developing world, demand for postsecondary education continues to outpace supply, and government provision of public higher education lags behind the public's needs, customers will flock to global players such as Laureate, Kaplan, and Apollo, and to their non-brand-name counterparts. While this form of globalization is certainly not identical to the kind sweeping more conventional nonprofit universities, it nevertheless holds significant promise as a form of global educational influence that reaches a completely different segment of the population and builds the human capital that is so vital for global economic growth. To make the inevitable comparison, in the decades since multinational corporations began to dominate industry after industry, their proliferation has dismayed critics but has also brought huge benefits to the global economy. Similarly, in the realm of education, the multinational for-profit firm could turn out to be the vehicle best suited for providing broad-scale access to practical higher education, benefiting students who might otherwise have far fewer opportunities.

Chapter Six

Free Trade in Minds

What does it mean that students now move around the globe in unprecedented numbers? That academic migration is beginning to shift, so that students are not only heading to traditional magnets such as the United States and Great Britain but also to new hot spots such as Australia and Singapore? How should we understand a world in which well-established Western universities begin to extend their "brands"—just like successful corporations—to faraway nations in the Middle East and Asia? What is the meaning of the push by countries from China and South Korea to France and Germany to establish (or reestablish) their university systems as among the best in the world, importing the Western research university model, and often Western academics, to make this happen? Why should for-profit institutions born in the West increasingly find their biggest new markets in the developing world? What accounts for the extraordinary growth of global university rankings?

The answer to all of these questions, in one way or another, is that higher education has become a form of international trade. With ever-fewer restrictions on the circulation of students, professors, and ideas around the globe, this intellectual commerce could be called free trade in minds. Like businesses that are able, through the forces of globalization, to find the best goods or services at the lowest prices throughout the world, those seeking to teach, study, conduct research, and publish are able to take advantage of a massive worldwide market. This market is particularly visible in the elite stratum of higher education. While information is often imperfect—witness the ongoing debate about the specific methodology and fundamental legitimacy of global college rankings—top students and top universities have fairly sophisticated mechanisms for finding one another. South Africa's Claire Booyjzsen, after all, began her search for a graduate chemistry program after consulting global league tables and ultimately enrolled at the University of Warwick. Even among non-elite students, such as those eager for a Western degree of any kind, or who are seeking a vocational diploma, the availability of cross-border options in either direction has transformed the number and kind of academic choices available, creating a more level market than ever before.

Indeed, one of the striking characteristics of the global academic marketplace is the extent to which students, professors, and university administrators are acting less and less like parochial scholars and more like citizens of the world. Where study overseas might once have been seen as a "broadening" experience for the upper classes, it is becoming both more common—recall the 41 percent increase from 1999 to 2006 in the number of students studying internationally—and more strategically considered. For a certain group of students, the choice to leave home to earn a degree in another country is less a matter of seeking new cultural or linguistic experiences than simply of finding the best available scholarly brand.

This global brand mentality was captured in a 2008 survey by the British market research firm i-graduate, which polled international students from 221 countries studying at seventy-one British universities. "These students are not choosing between the U.K. or the U.S.," said Simon Bush, the firm's head of analysis and research. "They are choosing between Yale and Cambridge." One of the students surveyed, for instance, a thirty-seven-year-old Nigerian named Ibrahim Umar, considered universities in New York, Virginia, Oslo, and Leicester before settling on the British institution when his research indicated it had the strongest teaching faculty. "I didn't make my choice on the lifestyle in the UK," he told the *Guardian*. "I hadn't considered that."[1]

The pull of elite universities is, to be sure, nothing new. In his 2008 book *Superclass: The Global Power Elite and the World They Are Making*, international consultant and former government official David Rothkopf notes that academic networks around the world play an important early role in molding the corporate power elite. "Because schools like Oxford, Cambridge, France's École Polytechnique, the Indian Institute of Technology, and the University of Tokyo all perform a similar function," along with places such as Harvard Business School, he writes, "cadres of leaders emerge into the world with important linkages even before other layers of ties begin to form."[2]

It is probably no surprise, then, that when Rothkopf compiled a list of more than 6,000 members of the "superclass" around the world—including leaders of corporations, banks and investment firms, governments, the military, the media, and religious groups—he found that attending a top-tier university corresponded highly with membership in his exclusive group. After drawing a "globally and sectorally representative sample" of 300 randomly selected members of his list, Rothkopf and his colleagues found that close to 3 in 10 attended one of twenty elite universities—with Stanford, Harvard, and the University of Chicago most highly represented. Unsurprising, too, is Rothkopf's finding that superclass members from the developing world are much more likely than their homeland peers to attend a university in the developed West: "Over 41 percent of superclass members from developing countries did so," he writes.[3]

This association between global higher education and what Rothkopf terms a worldwide power elite might seem troubling at first glance. Some analysts fret that these global citizens could become student versions of the late political scientist Samuel Huntington's "Davos Man," having more in common with one another than with their compatriots and losing valuable ties—intellectual, social, emotional—to their home countries. At the other end of the spectrum, in developing nations where university access is severely limited, will large swaths of the populations simply be left out of the global education revolution?

These are legitimate concerns. But it isn't clear how one would measure the growth of any alleged rootlessness—or why students cannot simultaneously be comfortably cosmopolitan and committed citizens of their own nations. And there is reason to believe that educational mobility for less advantaged students will increase, slowly but steadily, both because of study-abroad programs targeted at nontraditional students and because of the gradual lowering of political, economic, and cultural barriers to overseas study. The emerging face of educational globalization is one marked more and more by fluidity, mobility, and meritocracy. All of these developments, over time, can be expected to undermine rather than reinforce elites based on inherited privilege and political pull. This is an imperfect process, to be sure, sometimes slow even in optimal circumstances, and hardly operational at all where barriers are simply too high for the time being. Nevertheless, there are ample signs that the same educational forces that Rothkopf sees as creating an interlocking directorate of global power brokers are also at work for a broad range of students seeking worldwide opportunities.

One prerequisite for global citizenry among students is the acceptance of academic credentials across national borders. Peggy Blumenthal of the Institute of International Education says that is increasingly the case. "It used be that it was assumed that you had to have the credential from your own country's leading institution if you were going to be a success." This remains true in some places—particularly in Japan, and even to some extent in the United States, where employers don't necessarily understand whether a degree from a top college in another country has value and prestige equivalent to one from an elite American university. But, Blumenthal continues, "in all the rest of the world, increasingly having a credential from a leading university anywhere in the world adds value, not subtracts value, from your resume."[4]

A second prerequisite, of course, is meritocracy. It is one thing for university degrees to be accepted across borders, but another for potential employers or graduate schools to have some confidence that those degrees (and admission to those universities) were earned on the basis of academic accomplishment. The merit principle became a defining feature of the American university system following World War II. This was true not only in the large public institutions attended by most students, but also at the Ivy League and other elite schools that had long shaped the nation's image of what constituted a top-tier university education. In these exclusive institutions, the 1960s and 1970s saw the sharp erosion, albeit not the elimination, of admissions decisions based on family connections, wealth, and ties to blue-blood prep schools. These universities based admissions instead on a subjective but rigorous mixture of academic prowess and extracurricular talent. Other nations have in many cases adopted similar competitive principles, either by long-standing tradition (China's imperial civil service exams are believed to have begun in the sixth century and lasted for 1,300 years),[5] in response to the imperatives of newly adopted republican principles (France's ultra-selective grandes écoles were started just after the Revolution),[6] or in a postcolonial effort to create high-quality indigenous universities, as with India's creation of the Indian Institutes of Technology.

In a world of globalized postsecondary institutions—and globalized employers—the growing institutionalization of the merit principle has created a talent pool and a set of academic and job opportunities that would once have been hard to imagine. A conversation with Vivek Upadhyay, a student in his final year at the IIT–Bombay, provides a useful illustration of this new global meritocracy. Upadhyay's university is located on lush, somewhat dilapidated grounds in the northern suburbs of India's massive commercial center. The IIT–Bombay is a place where cows can be found wandering the same dusty pathways trod by some of the best undergraduates in the nation, along with visitors like Larry Davis, chairman of the University of Maryland, College Park's well-regarded computer science department, who travels regularly to India to recruit top students for his graduate program.

Upadhyay, the son of a homemaker and an engineer for India's Eastern Railways, came to the sought-after university from Calcutta. A top student, he decided in the ninth grade to sit for the infamously competitive IIT-JEE—the Joint Entrance Exam students must pass to gain entrance to one of India's seven IITs (new IITs were hastily added to the system in 2008, amid much controversy). With his family firmly behind him ("there was considerable—I won't say pressure—encouragement," he says),[7] Upadhyay spent considerable time during his last two years of high school preparing for the big test. Others go still further, leaving home for one or two years to attend one of the burgeoning number of coaching centers, where students typically live in hostels and spend every waking hour learning the ins and outs of the exam. Upadhyay ultimately carried off the remarkable feat of placing 21st out of some 200,000 test takers in the nation (the number of applicants has grown still larger since then). With all options open to him, he choose IIT–Bombay, where he encountered some "amazing people"—brilliant classmates and kindred spirits who shared his love of crosswords, anagrams, and debating. At the same time, he was dismayed to find many classmates so burned out by the rigors of preparing for the IIT that they paid little attention to their classes, skipping lectures and wasting time playing online games and downloading movies and television shows from the Internet. These students know that India's booming economy ensures strong job prospects even with a mediocre academic record.

There are certainly ways in which even the famed IITs (and their business counterparts, the Indian Institutes of Management, or IIMs) deviate considerably from the merit principle. Most notable are the extensive quotas for admissions and faculty hiring—the academic counterpart to those found throughout India's civil service. These "reservations" take account of the nation's entrenched history of caste prejudice by giving strong preferences to students and professors from "backward castes" and to those who are members of certain minority groups. As in the United States, IIT preferences have given rise to charges that they hurt those they are designed to help when underprepared students are thrust into highly competitive classrooms, and also that some relatively privileged members of targeted castes receive preferences intended for the truly disadvantaged.

Still, the reservation system is viewed by many, including Upadhyay, as a "necessary evil." And overall, the exam-based IIT admissions system and the institutes' semiautonomous governance make the IITs a relative beacon of meritocracy and excellence in an Indian higher education system marred by petty corruption and mediocrity. Unquestionably, for a student like Upadhyay, who became the editor of the IIT–Bombay student newspaper, making it to the vaunted university opened numerous doors of opportunity. Growing up, he says, traveling overseas was "only a dream"—something that would have to wait until he was much older and financially secure. But as an IIT computer science undergrad, he landed a summer research internship at ETH, Switzerland's elite federal institute of technology, where he realized that he wasn't cut out to become an academic. The next summer, he took an internship in Hong Kong at UBS, the global financial services firm, where he was offered a job upon graduation (and, after a stint in Hong Kong, was later transferred to London). The IIT, where global firms like Boston Consulting and McKinsey make regular recruiting trips to snatch up India's best and brightest, gave him an "amazing platform" he says.

The merit principle is also on vivid—and intense—display in China, where some 10 million students per year sit for National College Entrance Exam, known as the *gaokao*, or "difficult test." This exam, in the words of *Slate* magazine, "is China's SAT—if the SAT lasted two days, covered everything learned since kindergarten, and had the power to determine one's entire professional trajectory."[8] As with the JEE in India, students spend years preparing for the gaokao, which can provide the keys to upward mobility in a land where test scores are king.

This is all in marked contrast to American universities, where the SAT has become the subject of massive debate. First introduced as a means of leveling the academic playing field—permitting Harvard, as Nicholas Lemann explains in *The Big Test*,[9] to identify worthy midwestern scholarship boys with high innate abilities who hadn't had the advantages of an eastern prep school education—the exam later came to be viewed by critics as perpetuating privilege, restricting rather than expanding opportunity. To be sure, the SAT remains in widespread use, in part because many college admissions officers say they need some kind of universal yardstick in an age of massive grade inflation. But some colleges have made the exam optional for applicants, and everywhere the test continues under a cloud of mild suspicion, as elite universities in particular seek to evaluate applicants on a range of subjective "holistic measures" that include personal essays, leadership prowess, athletic success, and other extracurricular strengths.

Not so in China. While a few elite schools are experimenting with interviews and letters of recommendation, the gaokao is frequently the only measure used for university admissions, which have become increasingly important as the nation's breakneck economic growth creates massive demand for university education. The 10 million Chinese high school students who took the test in 2008 were all scrambling for just 5.7 million or so seats on the nation's college campuses. Students' results matter enormously not just for whether they obtain admission but also for where they are placed. The scores required for admission to elite universities such as Tsinghua, often termed "the MIT of China," are sky-high, whereas less renowned regional institutions set the bar significantly lower.

As in India, numerous concessions to realpolitik have made the Chinese exam less than a pristine model of egalitarianism. For one thing, while the exam is theoretically the same around the nation, in practice each province administers a modified version, some of which are easier than others. Also, as Manuela Zoninsein explains in *Slate*, universities set quotas intended to ensure some representation of ethnic minorities, students from the poorest provinces, and applicants from near their campuses. Probably the most substantive critique of how the exam is used is that it reinforces a culture of rote learning at precisely the time that many Asian nations are eager to foster greater creativity, which many view as the secret of the economic success of Western industrialized nations. Moreover, poor test takers may find their prospects unfairly limited.

Despite all these shortcomings, however, the tests do perform an invaluable function—permitting those with no particular connections or family wherewithal to catapult themselves into the educated classes, and sometimes into the very top institutions. While the rigid test prep regime may not spur creativity, Zoninsein explains, "for the world's most populous country, the gaokao provided an objective yardstick by which to measure academic success. In theory at least, students' social and economic statuses don't matter." Thus, one student told Zoninsein, the all-or-nothing exam "allows someone very poor the opportunity to rise out of poverty. . . . It's not perfect, but it's the fairest system." One example of the possibilities created by such a system is Michael Yu, the son of illiterate farmers, who took the gaokao three times before gaining admission to an English-language program at Peking University. He went on to found New Oriental, an educational services firm with a market capitalization of $2.6 billion—whose offerings include, among others, gaokao test prep. More broadly, just as Upadhyay was vaulted onto a global fast track by his academic success in India, so Chinese students have the possibility of making it to, say, Tsinghua or its crosstown rival Peking University, then on to a major multinational firm.

Indeed, as the merit principle increasingly crosses national boundaries, academic success in one nation can be a route to elite universities in another. Top American universities now regularly travel to China to find outstanding students who might not otherwise think to apply to distant and expensive institutions. In 2008, during a newly inaugurated high school mathematics contest named for Harvard math professor Shing-Tung Yau, admissions officers from Harvard, Brown, and Stanford talked to some of China's most promising young people in hopes of luring them to their sought-after campuses. They spoke of students' prospects of conducting research, of the advantages of U.S.-style liberal arts education (an approach to postsecondary studies that is still rare in most of the world), of life in the dorms, and—of course—of the likelihood of winning generous scholarships. Harvard's legendary admissions dean, William Fitzsimmons, sounded the same theme when he visited Beijing No. 4 High School, part of a busy agenda of meetings with Chinese students, party officials, and

VIPs. "We know there are very good students from China not applying now. I hope to get them in the pool to compete," he said, while also reassuring students and parents that meritocracy would prevail in the admissions process. "There are no quotas, no limits on the number of Chinese students we might take."[10]

That message of opportunity resonated well with students, including at the math competition. Admission to Harvard "might change my life, my whole life, I think," said one sixteen-year-old student who ranks in the top 10 of his high school class of 750 and would seem to fit in quite well with the breathtakingly accomplished superachievers who clamor to enter America's elite campuses. He serves as student body president, heads the Model United Nations Team, belongs to the literary club, and plays badminton and soccer. A frequent visitor to Harvard's Web site, he extolled not only the top-ranked university's physical appearance—"Harvard is so beautiful compared to the campuses of Chinese universities"—but also the innovation-oriented Western pedagogy he expected to find there. "I want to go because it is said that schools in the United States inspire you to think, instead of just teaching you what to do."[11]

Academic Protectionism

But even with growing indications that academic meritocracy and scholarly mobility have huge benefits, both for students leaving their home countries and for the institutions and countries that receive them, there remains considerable resistance around the world both to the merit principle and to free movement of students and professors. In some instances, this opposition takes the form of outright barriers to the movement of academic migrants or of foreign campuses that seek to establish new outposts. In others it manifests itself not in such direct restrictions but in misplaced alarmism about foreign competition. This unwarranted panic has the potential to create new barriers to academic mobility because it misleads policymakers and the public about the real benefits of free trade in minds.

In many ways, academic protectionism is the knowledge-economy counterpart to the understandable but misguided cries for protection from foreign competition that have periodically been heard from the textile industry, steel manufacturers, and other industrial sectors that have sought government quotas and tariffs under pressure from higher-quality, lower-priced foreign imports. If foreign trade in goods is threatening, little wonder that some feel the same way about foreign trade in intellectual capital. This fear isn't new, of course. Recall that as early as the fourteenth century, concerns about brain drain led some European nations to pass laws that discouraged overseas study by excluding those who had attended foreign universities from public office. Today, variations on this theme are legion.[12] The phenomenon occurs around the world, but some nations—India, for example—are far worse than others.

Despite its reverence for education, its turbocharged economy, a vast population hungry for knowledge, and a postsecondary system that is typically mediocre or worse, India has repeatedly sought to keep out foreign universities and, in some cases, foreign researchers. At times, the barriers have been explicitly political and cultural in nature. In 1973, officials announced that India would limit the number of American scholars permitted to visit the country to twenty each year. At the same time, they set strict limits on the kind of research that these outsiders could conduct. To take one example, the government nixed a planned research project on the changing role of women in Central India on the grounds that U.S. scholars were studying Indian people as objects of curiosity, "as if under a microscope," and thus engaging in a form of "academic colonialism."[13]

Thirty-five years later, with foreign universities clamoring to establish branches in India to cater to enormous student demand, the country was until recently no more open to overtures from beyond its borders. While India's economy boomed and the government threw open the nation's doors to corporations such as Coca-Cola and General Motors (this was before the worldwide financial crisis, of course), the government continued to make it impossible for foreign universities to establish degree programs. "In India: No Foreign Colleges Need Apply," read the headline in the *Chronicle of Higher Education*.[14] Thus, even as total foreign direct investment reached $16 billion in 2007 and delegations of college presidents and senior administrators from the likes of Stanford; the University of California, Berkeley; Cornell; and Columbia regularly visited India to assess prospects of catering to its underserved and potentially lucrative market, academic protectionism persists.

Some university administrators and legislators support legislation to open up the scholarly market, but thus far their proposals have stalled because of opposition from Communist political parties and academics who are suspicious of foreign universities' quest for profits, wary of low-quality institutions entering the Indian market with insufficient regulation, and concerned that foreign institutions would charge exorbitant tuition, making their campuses accessible only to the wealthy. "We don't want them here," Nilotpal Basu told the *Chronicle*. Basu is a member of the Marxist Communist Party of India. "It's a very miniscule portion of society and students who will really benefit." Such critics prefer to see the government pour more money into India's own beleaguered universities.

But proponents of a more open market argue that inequality is hardly likely to be heightened by letting in foreign universities, since huge numbers of students, and tuition fees, already leave the country each year—costing India some $4 billion annually according to an analysis by the Centre for Policy Research, an Indian think tank. "You are already sending huge amounts of money abroad," argues Pratap Bhanu Mehta, the group's president. "The only thing that could slow the flow is creating more opportunities in India."[15]

Such changes may be in the offing if India's recently appointed higher education minister has his way. Kapil Sibal, who took office in May 2009, is a strong advocate of opening up India's higher education market. He is confident that a long-delayed bill doing just that will pass in the first half of 2010.[16] But opposition continues, and Sibal, a Harvard Law School graduate, has sent mixed signals about whether foreign universities will have to abide by India's caste-based quotas for student admissions and faculty hiring—a restriction that would be a huge disincentive for any foreign university considering an Indian presence.

Even at the upper echelons of India's education system, the impulse to turn back from the new age of talent-based mobility periodically reasserts itself. In June 2008, then president of IIT–Bombay Ashok Misra announced that undergraduates could receive academic credit for their mandatory internships only if they worked for Indian companies or research institutions. "This move should help the students and the country," he declared.[17] But the new policy was hugely controversial among students, both for those seeking business internships and for those hoping to get a taste of academic research. "It has always proved difficult to find intern positions in Indian companies," says Upadhyay, who himself found two overseas internships before the new rules took effect. On the academic front, undergraduates with the ambition of earning a doctorate from a top-tier American university would often obtain research positions in Europe, he said, allowing them to get hands-on experience and also to prove their abilities and get a crucial recommendation for graduate work. "The bane of this ban is clear," he wrote in an e-mail message. "The boon is yet to be seen."[18]

India's suspicion of academic free trade doesn't stop at home. The government also targeted the efforts of its private universities to expand overseas. Because of the nation's massive faculty shortage—a function, among other things, of salaries that are pathetically low compared to those many professors can earn in the private sector—the government announced in 2009 that it would ban private institutions from employing Indian professors when setting up overseas branches. While permitting the Tamil Nadu–based Sri Ramchandra Medical College and Research Institute to establish an offshore campus in Mauritius, government officials outlined a series of restrictive new regulations.[19] Out of ostensible concern for maintaining high quality at domestic private campuses, the government hammered home its distaste for foreign expansion through a series of other edicts: requiring private universities to seek government permission to offer any course at a foreign campus that isn't offered at a campus on Indian soil; prohibiting these universities from cross-subsidizing offshore campuses with profits earned from their domestic branches; and conferring second-class status on private degrees earned outside the country. These degrees would not be considered identical to those earned on the home campus (unlike the degrees conferred by U.S. universities in Qatar's Education City, for instance, which are indistinguishable from those earned on U.S. soil). Medical graduates of a private Indian university's overseas campus, for instance, would not be allowed to practice in India without passing required screening tests.[20]

Such measures have costs, of course. For years physicians who had undergraduate degrees from Indian universities but had earned medical degrees abroad were forbidden from practicing in India. By 2008, however, India developed a severe shortage of doctors—it had only one doctor practicing Western medicine for every 1,634 citizens—leading the Ministry of Health and Family Welfare to announce that it was overturning the ban for graduates of medical schools in the United States, Canada, Australia, Great Britain, and New Zealand. The ministry said it hoped the policy change would induce the large number of Indian citizens with foreign medical degrees now living outside the country to return home to practice.[21]

Medical education and employment have also been the target of restrictive measures in Great Britain and Austria. In 2006, Austrian officials imposed quotas on the nation's schools of medicine and dentistry, reserving 75 percent of seats for Austrian secondary school graduates and limiting students from other European Union countries to 20 percent of the remaining seats, with just 5 percent allocated for international students from other countries. The rules, akin to similar restrictions established the previous year in Belgium, were imposed on the grounds that an influx of foreign students at Austrian professional schools, particularly from Germany, could threaten the stability of the nation's health care system if those students eventually returned home. The European Commission initially denounced the restrictions, calling them "indirect discrimination on the grounds of nationality"—something prohibited by commission rules. But it backed off a legal challenge, allowing both Austria and Belgium five years to provide data to support their claims that the restrictions are needed.

In a similar vein, in February 2009 the United Kingdom introduced new immigration rules that limit foreign medical graduates' access to postgraduate medical training. The restrictions came in response to an oversupply of doctors that had made it difficult for British medical graduates to find places in specialty training after completing their studies. "Doctors from overseas have played an invaluable role in the NHS [National Health Service] for many years and will continue to do so. They have helped us fill key shortage areas such as psychiatry, obstetrics and gynecology, and pediatrics," said Alan Johnson, Britain's health secretary. "But as the number of UK medical school graduates expands, there should be less need to rely on overseas doctors for these specialties." He declared that Britain was moving to a policy of "self-sufficiency." If a large number of applicants from outside the European Union prevents British medical graduates from accessing specialist training, he said, "then it is only right that we consider what needs to be done." Under the new rules, international doctors would still be able to practice with the National Health Service and would still be eligible to enter training program for specialties in which shortages exist.[22]

While some efforts to restrict the entry of overseas students and universities can at least be rationalized on the grounds of quality control or protecting domestic jobs, other efforts to protect a nation's academic patrimony verge on the absurd. In January 2008, an American researcher working in Germany at the Max Planck Institute for Chemical Ecology in Jena found himself unexpectedly called in for questioning by police. Ian Thomas Baldwin's crime? Referring to himself as "Dr." on his business card, a reference to the PhD he holds from Cornell University. A law on the books since the 1930s prevents anybody whose doctorate or medical degree was earned outside Germany from using the title "doktor." A 2001 law updated the status to permit European Union degree holders to use the honorific, but all others who fall afoul of the rules can still be prosecuted for "title abuse."

Along with Baldwin, a molecular ecologist, a number of other Americans have faced criminal investigations, with conviction carrying a potential penalty of up to a year in jail. Among them: an astrophysicist who is a member of the German Academy of Sciences and holds a doctorate from the California Institute of Technology. "It's totally absurd," Baldwin said. "Coming from the States, I had assumed that when you get a letter from the criminal police, you've either murdered someone or embezzled something." For their part, many German higher education officials have condemned the rules—which hardly help the country's effort to attract top researchers from the United States and elsewhere.[23] Still, even the reform initiative they championed—which was approved in principle in March 2008—extends the right to be addressed as "Dr." only to holders of doctorates from some two hundred American universities accredited by the Carnegie Foundation for the Advancement of Teaching and from a limited number of universities in Australia, Israel, Japan, Canada and Russia.[24]

Other restrictions stem from far more serious motivations, notably the need to protect national security in an age when terrorism is a sobering fact of life. In the United States, the post 9/11 era ushered in a fierce debate about the balance between security and access when scrutinizing student visa requests. Careful examination of applications made by would-be students from overseas—particularly from countries in the Middle East and from nations such as India, Pakistan, and China—led to massive delays in visa issuance and a drop in the number of international students at both the graduate and undergraduate level. Given that the restrictions stemmed from legitimate and serious concerns, calling them protectionist in motivation would be unfair. Nevertheless, the higher education establishment argued vehemently that the new controls were excessive and unwarranted in many cases, and that the nation's ability to attract the best and brightest from around the globe was being seriously compromised.

A similar battle took place over the activities of foreign students who had already entered the United States. In July of 2005, the Department of Defense proposed new rules that would have greatly restricted the research activities of international students: those working on defense contracts would have been required to wear special badges and to work in segregated areas of research labs, for instance. The move came in response to a report from the department's inspector general that found certain contractors were giving foreigners unauthorized access to technologies that, while unclassified, were sensitive enough that they would have been subject to export restrictions. But several academic groups, including the Association of American Universities, protested that the rules were too onerous. First, they argued, the proposed regulations would cost universities millions of dollars in compliance costs. Second, they would do even greater damage by discouraging foreigners, with their critically needed scientific expertise, from coming to U.S. labs in the first place. In the end, the Defense Department backed down. One year after the rules were proposed, the department announced that it would not implement them, citing both academic and business opposition. "National security, as it relates to research and development, involves a balancing act," the department said. "The first proposed rule was overly prescriptive."[25]

The student visa controversy followed a comparable trajectory at first. After several years of vigilance that critics saw as excessive, the visa process was streamlined considerably—in many cases processing times for first-time visa and renewals declined to about two weeks. Not surprisingly, international student numbers rebounded and, given continued high demand, eventually increased. However, by 2009 visa delays became common again, particularly for graduate and postdoctoral students in science and engineering, who form the backbone of many university-based research laboratories and thus serve as key players in the U.S. drive for scientific and technical innovation. A State Department official said the delays were attributable in part to personnel shortages and to conditions laid out in reciprocal agreements between nations. But the official also underscored the need to look "very closely" at applicants from potentially problematic countries who are interested in research fields that relate to national security. Still, the overall level of delay has become worrisome to the U.S. scientific community, particularly given that the global academic marketplace could deprive American universities of the best candidates. A 2008 report by the National Academy of Sciences, "Beyond 'Fortress America,'" argued that when the United States erects barriers to international students, "foreign universities are well positioned to extend competing offers." John Marburger, science adviser to President George W. Bush, agreed: "We need to be careful about our openness to the world."[26]

Robert Dingwall, director of the Institute for Science and Society at the University of Nottingham, relayed a similar message at a 2008 meeting of the Symposium on the Internationalization of Higher Education. "My graduate students tell me that . . . the attractions of the UK are beginning to decline because of the cost of getting visas, the bureaucracy that is involved, and the petty harassment and humiliation they feel when they actually encounter the British immigration service." What's more, Dingwall argued, visa hassles aren't just a problem for a receiving nation that might benefit from the brainpower of foreign students, but also for the entire enterprise of international research collaboration. "This vision for a world without borders where knowledge flows freely is not matched by the free movement of people," he said. "Immigration law is a serious constraint on that vision; I am running down my collaborations with the U.S. because I just can't be bothered with the hassle of getting in and out of that country. I prefer to work with colleagues in Europe, where I can move across borders much more freely," he said.[27]

Again, these controversial entry-visa policies and bureaucratic impediments are typically not explicitly protectionist. And they certainly have a plausible security rationale in some instances. The trick, of course, is to find the right balance. Given the strong case for the benefits of academic mobility, it is problematic not only for would-be academic migrants, but also for receiving nations themselves, to impede students' and researchers' access unnecessarily. As Marburger's comments suggest, nations such as India and Britain are far from the only ones that have impeded the free movement of students across borders: despite its magnet status, the United States has certainly not always been a paragon of openness itself.

Beyond visa policies, at U.S. universities there has also been perennial ambivalence about the heavy representation of foreign students in certain graduate programs, mostly in science and engineering. On the one hand, being a magnet for overseas students shows that U.S. universities have passed a flattering market test. Their popularity provides tangible evidence of the sheer excellence of the research university model that has been perfected in the United States. On the other, it raises alarm bells: Why is there such a shortage of American students well prepared for, and interested in pursuing, fields that are key to scientific innovation and economic progress? Moreover, could it be that foreign students are crowding out Americans who might otherwise enter these PhD programs?

Despite these fears, many research universities continue to seek out the best students regardless of national origins. A few, however, have responded by placing explicit limits on the number of international students they will enroll. At the University of Tennessee, for example, the graduate school dean inaugurated a policy in the early 1980s that said foreign students could make up no more than 20 percent of enrollment in any graduate program. In addition, it permitted no more than seventy-five students from any one foreign country university-wide. The dean, C. W. Minkel, argued some years later that the state's taxpayers had a right to see their dollars used to train domestic students. But many department chairs complained that they were being forced to reject talented foreigners in favor of mediocre Americans. Eventually, the university dropped the quotas. At other universities, officials facing the same dilemmas say that the solution lies in making the case for the benefits of importing the world's best brains. "Foreign graduate students contribute to the State of Wisconsin," Virginia Hinshaw, then dean of the University of Wisconsin–Madison graduate school, told the *Chronicle of Higher Education*. "They are the colleagues of the future."[28]

In some cases, restrictionist impulses in one part of the economy can have follow-on effects elsewhere. The impulse to protect domestic jobs, for example, has the potential to affect foreign students and academics directly. One of the first acts of Barack Obama's presidency was the passage of a massive $787 billion economic stimulus package. The legislation contained a number of provisions intended to spur creation of American jobs and to require use of American-made goods. This led to immediate questions about whether new "Buy American" rules might prevent universities not only from using stimulus dollars to buy foreign-made research equipment but also from running research projects in which foreign grad students are involved.[29]

Some international students on the verge of graduation were immediately affected by the economic stimulus bill when Bank of America rescinded job offers to foreign citizens, who flock to American MBA programs and often seek employment in the United States after graduation. Although final rules had not yet been written immediately following the bill's passage, the so-called Made in America provision limits the ability of companies receiving government bailout funds to hire foreign employees; it affects those who might have sought coveted H-1B visas, which are issued in limited numbers each year to highly skilled foreign workers. One of the provision's sponsors was Vermont senator Bernard Sanders, an independent who said he thought the needs of laid-off U.S. workers should supersede those of foreign graduates of U.S. programs, however worthy their claims. U.S. workers "should have the first opportunity," he said. But others decried the restrictions on firms receiving federal stimulus funds. R. Glenn Hubbard, dean of Columbia University's business school, said American universities would be hurt when the new rules led foreign students to go elsewhere. "It gives an advantage to international institutions over American institutions," he told students. In the same vein, Bob Sakinawa of the American Immigration Lawyers Association asked, "Why cut off that avenue of talent?" The restriction, he said, "sends a protectionist-oriented message that's not necessarily conducive to fostering economic recovery."[30]

Even before passage of the stimulus bill, visa restrictions in the United States, combined with burgeoning opportunities at home, led many foreign students to abandon once-common plans to stay in the United States in favor of returning to their countries of origin. This new trend sparked fears of a "reverse brain drain"—the prospect that a nation once renowned for attracting the best talent from around the world, first to its universities and then to its research laboratories and start-up firms, might relinquish its role as a global innovation hub. Some, in fact, argue that the brain drain has already begun. Writing in the *Washington Post* under the headline "They're Taking Their Brains and Going Home," entrepreneur and scholar Vivek Wadhwa tells the story of Sandeep Nijsure, who traveled from Bombay to the United States to earn a master's in computer science from the University of North Texas. After graduation, he took a job at Microsoft—an apparent poster child for the talent migration to the United States that has become routine. But in Nijsure's case, the pattern reversed itself when the pull of family and cultural ties led him and his wife to move back to India, where he became a software developer for Amazon.com in Hyderabad. His quality of life is high, and his opportunity to chart the course of his own employment is not limited, as it would have been in the United States, by the need to obtain a scarce H-1B visa.[31]

Just 85,000 or so H-1B visas are issued each year.[32] These visas allow highly skilled foreigners, usually in science and engineering, to work temporarily in the United States. Only 120,000 permanent-resident visas are granted annually to skilled workers and their family members, meaning long waiting lists—more than a million people as of 2006. Opponents such as Wadhwa persuasively argue that these visa ceilings are far too low. Born of protectionist motivations—preserving American jobs—the visa restrictions have in fact hurt America's innovation economy by discouraging talented international students from settling in the United States. Wadhwa, executive in residence at Duke University, a senior research associate at Harvard Law School, and himself a serial entrepreneur, says that when he began teaching at Duke in 1985, almost all the foreign students in the Master of Engineering Management program said they intended to stay for at least a few years in the United States. By 2009, he writes, most "are buying one-way tickets home."[33]

Wadhwa notes that there are ample reasons for the United States to be worried about this new trend, given immigrants' extensive contributions to scientific innovation and research. Between 1995 and 2005, 25 percent of all American engineering and technology companies were founded by immigrants—including half of those in Silicon Valley. Nearly one-quarter of all international patent applications filed from the United States in 2006 named foreign nationals as inventors. Indeed, a 2004 study conducted by researchers at the University of Colorado and the World Bank found that a 10 percent rise in the number of foreign graduate students in the United States would increase overall patent applications by 3.3 percent and patents granted to universities by 6 percent.[34] The facts and figures go on and on. While immigrants made up just 12 percent of the U.S. workforce in 2000, they accounted for fully 47 percent of scientists and engineers with PhDs, according to an analysis of that year's census. Fully two-thirds of those who entered science and engineering fields between 1995 and 2006 were, yes, immigrants. "What will happen to America's competitive edge," asks Wadhwa, "when these people go home?"[35]

Further buttressing his case is an online survey Wadhwa conducted for the Kauffman Foundation in 2008, released in a 2009 foundation report entitled "Losing the World's Best and Brightest: America's New Immigrant Entrepreneurs, Part V."[36] International students were gloomy not only about their job prospects but also about their ability to get work visas, according to the survey, which was conducted on the social-networking site Facebook. It was based on the responses of 1,224 foreign students who were currently enrolled or had graduated by the end of 2008. While large numbers of international students in recent years have stayed in the United States to work or take postdoctoral positions, the informal survey found that half of Chinese students, 32 percent of Indians, and 26 percent of European students saw opportunities as brighter in their home countries. And although respondents still saw American universities as the best in the world, just 6 percent of Indians said they wanted to stay permanently in the United States, compared to 10 and 15 percent, respectively, of Chinese and European students.[37] These findings alarmed AnnaLee Saxenian, dean and professor in the School of Information at the University of California, Berkeley. "The U.S. has changed from a land of opportunity to a country where even highly skilled immigrants feel unwelcome," she said. "We have raised barriers for visas, limited access to public sector jobs and reduced the hiring of foreign students for fear of political backlash."[38] Robert Litan, the Kauffman Foundation's vice president for research and policy, told the *Chronicle of Higher Education* that policymakers are mistaken if they believe talented immigrants threaten American jobs. On the contrary, he said, "they, in fact, offer the promise of more jobs by building successful, high-growth companies, either in their own businesses or in those for which they work."[39]

What accounts for the high level of concern that periodically surfaces about letting foreign students into the United States (and other countries) and letting them stay on to work? More broadly, in an age of unprecedented academic mobility, a time when a veritable academic arms race is creating ever-stronger universities around the world, what accounts for the high level of concern in the West about what our academic competitors in the developing world are beginning to accomplish? It is certainly not hard to find evidence of increased alarm and hand-wringing about the threat to U.S. academic and technological dominance posed by the ascendance of the academic and innovation capacities of other countries. Perhaps best known is the 2005 report issued by the National Academies, "Rising Above the Gathering Storm," which warned ominously of the decline of U.S. science and technology. The report's authors, a group of business and academic leaders, highlighted the growing accomplishments of other nations to buttress their contention that the United States is falling behind.

In one of many articles that continued in the same vein, the following year Doug Fuller, a fellow in the Stanford Program on Regions of Innovation and Entrepreneurship, argued that China's ascendant academic system poses a serious competitive threat to the United States. He noted that China produces 214,000 more science and engineering bachelor's degrees than the United States, and that its global share of science and engineering doctorates has grown from zero in 1975 to 11 percent—not including PhDs earned overseas. During the same period, he wrote, U.S. doctorates fell from about 50 percent to 22 percent. Fuller disputed the findings of a Duke University report that downplayed worries about the science and engineering gap between the United States and developing economies, notably China. Fuller called for greater federal funding for basic research and more support for science education. "It would be a grave mistake," he wrote, "to drop our concerns about China's competitive challenge."[40]

Such concerns are more than just rhetorical. They have consequences, not only for Western attitudes toward ascendant universities overseas but also for academic collaboration. In 2007, for instance, the founding provost of Nottingham University's Chinese campus, Nottingham–Ningbo, sounded the alarm about China's desire to profit from Britain's science and technology strengths. In a report issued by the higher education think tank Agora, Ian Gow said China's partnerships with British institutions were being negotiated on a one-sided basis that provided too little benefit to British universities, which are being asked to send their top research scientists to work in China for stints of several years or more. "British institutions must stop viewing this aggressively ambitious country through rose-tinted spectacles," he said. "Make no mistake, China wants to be the leading power in higher education, and it will extract what it can from the UK."[41]

University presidents often make similar arguments in an effort to boost (or restore) government research funding. Testifying before a U.S. Senate hearing in 2008, Harvard president Drew Faust lamented the detrimental effects of trimmed-down government research budgets, from poor morale in laboratories to thinning the ranks of postdoctoral researchers to a worrisome tendency to neglect "the big research questions." Moreover, she cautioned, fierce competition from overseas is beginning to erode the U.S. talent pool. Countries such as China, India, and Singapore "have adopted biomedical research and the building of biotechnology clusters as national goals," she said. "Suddenly, those who train in America have significant options elsewhere."[42]

Politicians, too, are quick to voice apprehension about the downsides of global academic competition. Mark Warner, a former governor of Virginia and a Democratic Party star, told an audience of college presidents in 2006 that the growing academic competition with which U.S. universities must contend amounts to a national security matter. A globally competitive university system, he said, "is absolutely critical to America's security"—speaking in particular about the nation's economic security.[43] Indeed, President Obama sounded this theme when he was the Democratic nominee during the 2008 presidential campaign. Delivering a major campaign speech focused on education in Dayton, Ohio, Obama spoke in broad terms of the new era of globalization and its effects on schoolchildren. "In this economy, companies can plant their jobs wherever there's an Internet connection and someone willing to do the work, meaning that children here in Dayton are growing up competing with children not only in Detroit or Chicago or Los Angeles, but in Beijing and Delhi as well. What matters, then, isn't what you do or where you live, but what you know." Then he went on to speak in concerned tones about the shortcomings of U.S. higher education. "If we want to keep on building the cars of the future here in America, we can't afford to see the number of PhD's in engineering climbing in China, South Korea, and Japan even as it's dropped here in America."[44]

THE BENEFITS OF ACADEMIC TRADE

These calls to arms could be understood at one level as a healthy spur to global competition, an effort to increase university funding, to get the attention of policymakers, and to stir the rivalrous juices of provosts and the public alike. But the benign or at times even helpful function of such rhetoric can easily be overshadowed by its underlying alarmism. Every time those in the United States, or in other countries for that matter, are warned of the threat posed by other nations' academic advances, the implications are clear: the growing strengths of universities overseas—and by extension the entire enterprise of academic free trade—are allegedly damaging to the hand-wringing country's domestic universities and economy. In fact, just the opposite is true. The globalization of higher education, including the growth in the quality and quantity of universities in places like China, should be embraced, not feared. That's because the ever-more-open flow of people and knowledge is good for other nations and good for the United States.

George Mason University economist Tyler Cowen, who is known among other things for his popular blog, Marginal Revolution, offers a compelling case against the anxieties expressed by President Obama, rooting his argument in a broad defense of free trade across all economic sectors. Advocates of expanded international trade often focus on the benefits to consumers of, say, imported shoes from Italy or computer chips from Taiwan, he says. But the products of academic institutions are even more important. "New ideas are the real prize," according to Cowen. For that reason, he is quite unperturbed by the projection that by 2010 China will have more doctorate-holding scientists and engineers than the United States. Why the lack of concern? Because, he writes, "These professionals are not fundamentally a threat. To the contrary, they are creators, whose ideas are likely to improve the lives of ordinary Americans, not just the business elite." Noting that economists on the right and left of the political spectrum concur about the importance of new ideas, from biotechnology to cleaner energy, in creating higher living standards, Cowen says trade can enable the kind of access to higher education that will pave the way for innovation.[45]

Other analysts sound a similar note. In his 2008 book *The Venturesome Economy*, Columbia University business professor Amar Bhidé makes a compelling case against those who fear that the growth of high-level research and development in places such as India and China will hurt economic prosperity in the West. In fact, he argues, innovation overseas can actually enhance America's financial well-being. That is because ideas can't be contained within national boundaries, meaning that America's share of the world's research production matters far less than the proven ability of U.S. entrepreneurs, financiers, and consumers to take advantage of cutting-edge research wherever it comes from. "For the United States to hunker down or obsess about international technology races is folly," he concludes. "Today's conditions allow nations to gain from each other's advances, and our challenge lies in making the best of this good fortune."[46]

While Bhidé writes of technology and research generally rather than higher education per se, his arguments certainly apply to the knowledge created by universities. The same is true of the conclusions of a 2008 RAND study, sponsored by the U.S. Department of Defense, which found that new knowledge leads to worldwide gains and should not be viewed as a threat to domestic employment. "Advances overseas may be taken advantage of by U.S. entrepreneurs," said study coauthor James Hosek, a senior economist at RAND. "Really, what we're seeing is an acceleration of scientific discoveries."[47]

Moreover, while progress in international research need not be viewed as worrisome by the West, even the widespread premise that rising research powers in the developing world are overtaking most established nations is by no means universally accepted. The RAND report found that nearly two-thirds of highly cited articles in science and technology come from the United States. Seventy percent of Nobel Prize winners are employed by U.S. universities, which hold thirty of the forty top slots in the world. "Our review of the data suggests that the United States is not close to the brink of losing its [science and technology] leadership," the study concluded.[48] A British report published in 2009 by the Department for Business and Regulatory Reform took a similar tack, suggesting that China and India, home to surging numbers of high-skilled, low-cost workers, are less of a threat to Britain than is often claimed. "Although India and China have made substantial progress in improving their skills and innovation capabilities, protectionist fears about the competitive threat from these countries are often overdone," it contended. "In practice, over the next few decades they will (in general) continue to specialize in activities which complement rather than compete with those carried out in the UK." In the same vein, Yale University president Richard Levin reminds readers, in a *Newsweek* article entitled "The West Need Not Panic,"[49] that the United States accounts for 40 percent of global spending on higher education and 35 percent on research and development, spending 2.9 percent of its GDP in 2005 on postsecondary education, compared to the less than 1.3 percent spent by China, India, the European Union, and Japan. Little wonder that the United States is home to the lion's share of the world's top-rated universities.

Perhaps one of the most articulate defenders of the proposition that the spread of academic excellence around the world should be a cause for celebration rather than anxiety, Levin has made increasing internationalism one of the hallmarks of his presidency. A longtime professor of economics, Levin applies the logic of a confirmed free trader to his analysis of protectionist impulses in visa policy and the free movement of students and workers more generally. He is troubled by visa policies that require talented foreign students to return home after graduation rather than stay in the United States, unless they are "one of the lucky ones" to receive a prized H-1B visa. His solution—similar to one proposed by Carl Schramm and Robert Litan of the Kauffman Foundation—is to "staple a green card" (allowing permanent residency and work status) to every graduate's diploma. "I think reducing barriers to human mobility is crucial, so that if you make it easier for people to work anywhere in the world, that's going to be wealth-creating. And you'd also have nonpecuniary returns to people that are worth having," he said in an interview in his office at the center of the Yale campus.[50]

Indeed, beyond economic returns, the flow of students across borders "to a greater extent probably than ever before" creates a range of opportunities, Levin says, including preparing a new generation of graduates for citizenship in a global world and for the kind of "cross-cultural understanding" needed to foster "the future peace and prosperity of the planet," he said in a May 2008 speech in Athens, Greece.[51] On the research front, too, he stresses that international collaborations such as Yale's joint ventures in China bring huge potential gains—accelerating the scientific and technological advances that lead to improved health and economic prosperity.

It is true, of course, that other nations are working hard to recruit foreign students, gradually eroding U.S. market share, and that huge sums are being spent in the Middle East and China to upgrade existing universities or create new institutions. Such efforts may take a while to bear fruit. But as those nations continue their upward trajectory, Levin underscores that the spread of knowledge, the expansion of human capital globally, is "an opportunity, not a threat." Globalization, he writes "is a positive-sum game in education, as it is in economics." Echoing James Hosek, Tyler Cowen, and Amar Bhide, he says just as Asian universities and their Western partners may profit from collaboration, "so does everyone else, since knowledge is a public good that other scientists and engineers can use."[52]

Academic competition inevitably creates some costs and dislocation. Assessing the impact of the global expansion of higher education for the United States, Harvard University economist Richard Freeman notes that the growing number of college graduates from other nations does pose a threat to the U.S. comparative advantage in sectors of the economy that are heavily dependent on university graduates, particularly if those foreign graduate are much less expensive than American workers.[53]

However, the overall benefits will nevertheless be significant, he concludes: "My analysis suggests that the globalization of higher education should benefit the U.S. and the rest of the world by accelerating the rate of technological advance associated with science and engineering and by speeding the adoption of best practices around the world, which will lower the costs of production and prices of goods." Beyond purely economic benefits, Freeman suggests, worldwide academic competition is likely to strengthen America's role as an educational leader rather than weaken it. "My guess is that by educating some of the best students in the world, attracting some to stay and positioning the U.S. as an open hub of ideas and connections for university graduates worldwide," he maintains, "the country will be able to maintain excellence and leadership in the 'empire of the mind' and in the economic world more so than if it views the rapid increase in graduates overseas as a competitive threat."

If increased knowledge is not a zero-sum game, and greater competition is something Western institutions should welcome rather than fear, there is every reason to do what we can to expand the global academic marketplace. What will that require from policymakers, academics, and citizens? In practical terms, it means doing everything possible to sustain the movement toward meritocracy that has taken hold in many countries in recent years. Conversely, it means reexamining the barriers—from political corruption to caste preferences—that prevent the best students from finding the best professors, and vice versa. As students increasingly see themselves as citizens of the world, first at elite levels and eventually among a broader swath of the global population, all forms of academic protectionism should be removed. One opportunity to do this has receded from view with the collapse of the Doha round of world trade talks in 2006. The General Agreement on Trade in Services, or GATS, included provisions that would have required universities in nations entering the accord to open their own higher education markets in exchange for access to those in other member countries. The talks may yet be revived, but in the meantime a number of nations are entering similar bilateral higher education agreements—an imperfect, piecemeal solution to a global problem but at least a start. Meantime, numerous other steps should be taken: removing regulatory obstacles to forming foreign branch campuses and academic partnerships, scrapping unreasonable visa barriers that discourage talented students from crossing borders, and ending silly symbolic practices such as Germany's refusal to allow many foreign PhDs to use the title "Dr."

Beyond these concrete measures, however, a psychological barrier needs to be lowered as well: the tendency to view as a threat what is in fact the healthy rivalry that comes with the globalization of higher education. As with other kinds of free trade, it seems safe to predict that greater movement of people and ideas in the academic marketplace may create both winners and losers. But its net positive effect seems certain—which is why free trade in minds holds the key to sustaining the world's knowledge economy and ultimately to restoring global prosperity.

Afterword

In higher education, as in just about every twenty-first-century human endeavor, it seems hard to imagine that globalization will ever go away. National borders are simply less relevant than they once were. Student and faculty mobility has exploded. Cross-national research collaboration is more common than ever. Branch campuses abound. Research universities compete with rivals well beyond their own shores. Global college rankings proliferate. For-profit firms rush to cater to demand in new markets. The merit principle becomes increasingly dominant, both within and across nations. The best students shop for universities like consumers in a world-wide marketplace.

That said, numerous questions about the future of globalized higher education remain unanswered. The rising mobility of recent decades seems likely to continue—but at what rate and in which directions? Will the cross-border movement of students begin to shift from a mostly elite to a mass phenomenon? Will countries like India, which has erected among the world's highest barriers to foreign universities, continue on a protectionist path or take a new, market-oriented direction? What new forms might the increasingly popular global college rankings take? Will the explosive growth of vocationally oriented for-profit institutions continue?

Whatever direction global higher education takes going forward, one thing is clear: the growing number of internationally mobile students, intent on finding excellence in research and teaching, have already begun to create a world in which, to an unprecedented extent, talent can be identified and find the best possible academic home—a version of what, in real estate, is known as the "highest and best use." Policymakers seeking to reap the advantages of a thriving and open higher education system will make little headway toward creating good universities, let alone globally great ones, without understanding that meritocracy and the free exchange of ideas form the core of the university.

The World Bank's Jamil Salmi offers a cautionary tale that illustrates this lesson perfectly, by describing the divergent paths taken by the University of Malaya and the National University of Singapore after Malaysia became independent from Great Britain and Singapore was for several years a province of the Malaysian Kingdom. The two universities had similar cultural and colonial roots, thus offering what Salmi calls a "natural experiment" showing how different policies can produce quite different results.[1] Initially, the University of Malaya had two campuses, one in Kuala Lumpur and another in Singapore. The latter split off to become first the University of Singapore, then the National University of Singapore, or NUS, following a 1980 merger with Nanyang University. Today, NUS is a powerhouse both regionally and globally, and is pushing hard to become a global scholarly hub through partnerships with top universities around the world. It placed 19th in the 2006 *Times Higher* rankings. The University of Malaya, by contrast, "struggles as a second-tier research university," standing at 192nd in the *Times Higher* league tables.

How did this happen? To begin with, the Malaysian government gave preferential admissions treatment to the majority population of ethnic Malays, or Bumiputras. Between the early 1970s and the late 1980s, their numbers shot up from one-third to two-thirds of the student population. The downside of this affirmative-action policy, however, was that many talented ethnic Chinese and Indian students couldn't gain admission to the university; the percentage of Chinese students, for example, plummeted from 56 to 29 during the same period. Many sought education overseas, depriving the country of important human capital. Efforts to revisit this policy sparked student demonstrations and a sharp rebuke by the prime minister. The Malaysian Ministry of Higher Education didn't help matters by an overtly protectionist policy that places a limit of 5 percent on the number of foreign undergraduates who can enroll in the nation's public universities. Funding levels are also lackluster. And those financial constraints, combined with restrictive civil service rules, make it extremely hard to attract top-level faculty, in particular those from foreign countries.

By contrast, NUS seems to have done everything right. It has actively sought to recruit foreign students, who make up 20 percent of undergraduates and 43 percent of graduate students. In an effort to boost the university's intellectual capital, it also subsidizes their studies—a far cry from the predominant tuition-generating function that foreign students often serve in the United Kingdom and Australia. Its per-student spending is about 50 percent higher than the University of Malaya's, thanks to a combination of government spending, fund-raising, and investment revenue that have given NUS a budget almost twice as large as its nearby competitor's. One final distinguishing feature of NUS's rise to excellence is that it has cultivated a meritocratic culture, backed by resources and freed from bureaucratic hiring constraints, that has allowed it not only to hire away many of Malaysia's best researchers but also, as Salmi writes, "to bring in top researchers and professors from all over the world, pay a global market rate for them, and provide performance incentives to stimulate competition and to retain the best and the brightest." This story is not purely of historical interest. It should be read instead as a road map for countries striving for academic excellence.

Still, in many places that road is not easy to follow. As Philip Altbach noted in a 2007 speech, "Many of the world's universities are not meritocratic institutions. People are appointed because of who they know, because they're in certain categories of the population."[2] For nations and universities that want to become part of the global academic conversation, such corrupt policies are untenable. Will governments and universities seeking excellence in a global academic market take the right path? Altbach himself is pessimistic, at least when it comes to non-elite institutions. But a strong case can be made that the market pressures of academic globalization will make it harder than ever to cling to cronyism and mediocrity. Certainly, nobody will be able to say that the general contours of the route to success aren't clear. Nor is there much doubt about the benefits to be gained for nations that embrace the merit principle along with an open educational market.

The biggest factor driving continued growth in higher education worldwide, both within nations and across borders, is the mounting evidence of the economic benefits of postsecondary education for both individuals and societies. It may be a commonplace to say that the world has moved from a manufacturing to a service to a knowledge economy, but sometimes truisms are just that—true. Universities help individuals widen their intellectual horizons and improve their economic prospects. Universities also produce research that fosters innovation and entrepreneurship, and hence economic growth. As economists Claudia Goldin and Lawrence Katz write in their influential 2008 book *The Race between Education and Technology*, "Human capital, embodied in one's people, is the most fundamental part of the wealth of nations."[3]

To compete successfully in the community of nations, a modern economy clearly must embrace not only elementary and secondary schooling but also higher education. And improving universities will increasingly require taking part in a global conversation of ideas and a global exchange of scholars. The good news is that more and more nations are joining this movement. The bad news is that mercantilism—the outdated notion that a nation's economic prosperity rests on its ability to hold on to the maximum possible share of a finite amount of global capital—persists in higher education. Almost every day brings word of policy directives large and small that are apparently driven by restrictionist impulses. In October 2009, to take a small but telling example, administrators at Russia's prestigious St. Petersburg State University told professors that they must obtain advance approval to publish or present their scholarly work overseas.[4] Following alarmed reaction from faculty members, the university announced the following month that the policy would apply only to research with potential military applications. It maintained that concern about potential censorship of scholarship in the humanities and social sciences "stems from insufficient information about the real state of affairs."[5]

It is certainly hard to see how Russia's competitiveness could possibly be advanced by barring intellectual "exports." Nor, in other nations, does limiting the presence of foreign universities or foreign students do any favors for economic growth and innovation. *Just as constraining traditional forms of trade hurts consumers and stymies economic creativity, closing doors to the free flow of people and ideas thwarts knowledge generation, which is the lifeblood of successful economies.*

Broadly speaking, there is every reason to be optimistic about the continued globalization of higher education. If knowledge is not seen as a finite resource but as a public good open to all, educational institutions that generate knowledge should be welcomed everywhere. So should the talented students who roam the globe seeking the best opportunities they can find. The challenge will be to fend off periodic bouts of academic protectionism, whether directed at branch campuses, at foreign students, at the export of scholarship or human talent, or at ascendant institutions in distant lands that are wrongly perceived as a threat to domestic universities.

For a nation like the United States, long the front-runner in the race for global academic preeminence, today's changing international environment should not be a cause for panic. Neither a gradual erosion in the U.S. market share of students nor the emergence of ambitious new competitors in Asia, Europe, and the Middle East means that American universities are on some inevitable path to decline. Indeed, in many ways this new competition is flattering, testimony to the extraordinary post–War War II success of U.S. institutions. In almost every case, the American research university, combining top-quality research and teaching within one institution, has become the model every other nation wants to clone—just as U.S. universities themselves emulated the pioneering German universities of the nineteenth century.

The United States should respond to the globalization of higher education not with fear but with a sense of possibility. There is nothing wrong with nations competing, trying to improve their citizens' human capital and to reap the economic benefits that come with more and better education. Moreover, as many economists observe, research discoveries in other nations provide fodder for American innovators and may redound to the benefit of the U.S. economy. By continuing to recruit and welcome the best students in the world, by sending more students overseas, by fostering cross-national research collaboration, and by cooperating in efforts to better measure the effectiveness of universities, the United States not only will sustain its own academic excellence but also will continue to expand the sum total of global knowledge.

Today's period of university globalization is at first glance a far cry from the era inaugurated by the wandering scholars of medieval Europe, the earliest academic globe-trotters in the West. But there are unmistakable parallels. Knowledge changes the world. And with the right kind of encouragement, the far-reaching intellectual ferment now under way could have a transformational effect similar to that of the twelfth-century Renaissance of learning. From the United States and Britain to India, China, and the Middle East, policymakers should applaud—and encourage—the movement toward global universities. In changing economic times, the world's prosperity demands nothing less.

Notes

CHAPTER ONE. THE WORLDWIDE RACE FOR TALENT

1. Author interview with Claire Booyjzsen, Coventry, England, November 12, 2008.

2. University of Warwick International Representative Offices, http://www2 .warwick.ac.uk/international/world/office/.

3. Author interview with Nigel Thrift, Coventry, England, November 12, 2008.

4. Elizabeth Redden, "Higher Education on the Move," *Inside Higher Ed*, May 6, 2009.

5. Hugh Davis Graham and Nancy Graham, *The Rise of American Research Universities: Elites and Challengers in the Postwar Era* (Baltimore, MD: Johns Hopkins University Press, 1997), p. 9.

6. Redden, "Higher Education on the Move."

7. Susan Robertson, "International Student Mobility: Patterns and Trends," *GlobalHigherEd*, September 30, 2007.

8. Susan Robertson, "Trouble Ahead? US Council of Graduate Schools Survey Reports Overseas Student Applications Slow to 3%," *GlobalHigherEd*, April 15, 2008.

9. T. B. Hoffer, M. Hess, V. Welch Jr., and K. Williams. *Doctorate Recipients from United States Universities: Summary Report 2006* (Chicago: National Opinion Research Center, 2007), Table A-2, pp. 119–27. (The report gives the results of data collected in the Survey of Earned Doctorates, conducted for six federal agencies, NSF, NIH, USED, NEH, USDA, and NASA by NORC.)

10. Jeffrey Brainard, "Graduates of Chinese Universities Take the Lead in Earning American Ph.D.'s," *Chronicle of Higher Education*, July 14, 2008.

11. Philip G. Altbach, "Higher Education Crosses Borders," *Change*, March–April 2004, http://www.bc.edu/bc_org.

12. Kemal Gürüz, *Higher Education and International Student Mobility in the*

Global Knowledge Economy (Albany: State University of New York Press, 2008), p. 193.

13. Line Verbik and Veronica Lasanowski, "International Student Mobility: Patterns and Trends," Observatory on Borderless Higher Education, http://www .obhe.ac.uk/home.

14. Karin Fischer and Beth McMurtrie, "Conference Participants Discuss Key Issues in International Higher Education," *Chronicle of Higher Education*, May 28, 2008.

15. Author interview with Daniel Fallon, New York City, May 29, 2008.

16. Quoted in Charles Haskins, *The Renaissance of the Twelfth Century* (Cambridge, MA: Harvard University Press, 2005), 65.

17. Helene Wieruszowski, "The Cathedral Schools and the Study of Liberal Arts," in *The Medieval University* (New York: Van Nostrand, 1966), p. 16.

18. Wieruszowski, "Cathedral Schools," p. 36.

19. Gürüz, *Higher Education and International Student Mobility*, p. 120.

20. Wieruszowski, "Cathedral Schools," p. 36.

21. Pearl Kibre, "Scholarly Privileges: Their Roman Origins and Medieval Expression," *American Historical Review* 59 (1954): 543–67, http://www.jstor.org.

22. Gürüz, *Higher Education and International Student Mobility*, p. 121.

23. Kibre, "Scholarly Privileges," pp. 543–67.

24. Gürüz, *Higher Education and International Student Mobility*, p. 121.

25. Wieruszowski, "Cathedral Schools," p. 34.

26. Hilde Ridder-Symoens, *Mobility: A History of the University in Europe* (Cambridge: Cambridge University Press, 1992), p. 287.

27. *Stanford Encyclopedia of Philosophy*, s.v. "Desiderius Erasmus," http://plato .stanford.edu/entries/erasmus/; Gürüz, *Higher Education and International Student Mobility*, p. 122.

28. Ridder-Symoens, *Mobility*, p. 290.

29. Wieruszowski, "Cathedral Schools," pp. 96–97.

30. Daniel Fallon, "Wilhelm Von Humboldt and the Idea of the University," in *The German University: A Heroic Ideal in Conflict with the Modern World* (Boulder: Colorado Associated University Press, 1980), p. 19.

31. Gürüz, *Higher Education and International Student Mobility*, p. 129.

32. "Our Universities Show Increasing Foreign Attendance, but German Institutions Still Far in Lead," *New York Times*, November 10, 1912.

33. Gürüz, *Higher Education and International Student Mobility*, p. 132.

34. Ibid., p. 131.

35. Charles Thwing, *The American and German University* (New York: Macmillan, 1928), p. 66.

36. "Want American Students. French Universities Offer Inducements to Encourage Them," *New York Times*, June 3, 1917.

37. Daniel Fallon, "Recreating the Elite Research Universities in Germany: Policy Transfer Then and Now," in *Globalization's Muse: Universities and Higher Education Systems in a Changing World*, ed. John Aubrey Douglass, C. Judson King, and Irwin Feller (Berkeley: Berkeley Public Policy Press, 2009).

38. "Foreign Students Choose the U.S.," *New York Times*, June 16, 1957.

39. Güruz, *Higher Education and International Student Mobility*, p. 133.

40. Russell Kirk, "Growing Dangers in 'Campus Research,'" *New York Times*, September 17, 1961.

41. Ibid.

42. Güruz, *Higher Education and International Student Mobility*, p. 135.

43. Council for International Exchange of Scholars (CIES), "Fulbright Scholar Program," http://www.cies.org/about_fulb.htm (accessed July 8, 2008).

44. "Fulbright Scholars—Largest U.S. Group Sails for Year of Study in France," *New York Times*, October 18, 1953; CIES, "Fulbright Scholar Program."

45. John W. Finney, "US Is Broadening Scientific Grants," *New York Times*, July 18, 1960.

46. "News Notes: Classroom and Campus," *New York Times*, July 26, 1964.

47. Anthony dePalma, "Graduate Schools Fill with Foreigners," *New York Times*, November 29, 1990.

48. "The Future Is Another Country," *The Economist*, January 3, 2009.

49. Richard Levin, "The West Need Not Panic," *Newsweek*, August 9, 2008.

50. Brendan O Malley, "US Share of Foreign Students Drops," *University World News*, October 21, 2007.

51. Susan Robertson, "Battling for Market Share 1: The 'Major Players' and International Student Mobility," *GlobalHigherEd*, October 1, 2007.

52. Aisha Labi, "British Universities Warned of Need to Rethink International Strategy," *Chronicle of Higher Education*, October 23, 2008.

53. Verbik and Lasanowski, "International Student Mobility."

54. Güruz, *Higher Education and International Student Mobility*, pp. 192–93.

55. Margaret Spellings, U.S. Secretary of Education (Secretary's remarks, Higher Education Summit for Global Development, Washington, DC, April 30, 2008).

56. David Cohen, "Returning to Singapore," *Inside Higher Ed*, February 14, 2008.

57. "The Future Is Another Country."

58. Alison Campsie, "20% of Students Are from Overseas," *Herald Scotland*, March 19, 2008.

59. Andrew Denholm, "Warning to Universities over Rise in Overseas Students," *Herald Scotland,* April 7, 2008.

60. Fischer and McMurtrie, "Conference Participants Discuss Key Issues."

61. Rajika Bhandari and Peggy Blumenthal, "Global Student Mobility: Moving Towards Brain Exchange," in *Higher Education on the Move: New Developments in Global Mobility* (New York: Institute of International Education/AIFS Foundation, 2008).

62. Tamar Lewin, "Matching Newcomer to College, While Both Pay," *New York Times*, May 11, 2008.

63. Martha Ann Overland, "Ad Campaign by New Zealand's Colleges Seems to Promise Carnal Knowledge," *Chronicle of Higher Education*, April 17, 2008.

64. UNESCO, *Global Education Digest 2009: Comparing Education Statistics Across the World* (Montreal: UNESCO Institute for Statistics, 2009), p. 44, http://www.uis.unesco.org/template/pdf/ged/2009/GED_2009_EN.pdf.

65. Author interview with Ellen Hazelkorn, Paris, September 10, 2008.

66. For official biography and related articles, see "President's Office," King Abdullah University of Science and Technology, http://www.kaust.edu.sa/about/admin/president/presidentoffice.html; "Choon Fong Shih Named the Founding President of KAUST of Saudi Arabia," iMechanica: Web of Mechanics and Mechanicians, http://imechanica.org/node/2561; and "Shih Choon Fong Biography," Cisco.com, http://www.cisco.com/web/learning/le21/le34/nobel/2006/popups/fong.html.

67. Richard Byrne, Goldie Blumenstyk, and Aisha Labi, "Yale's Provost Will Run Oxford," *Chronicle of Higher Education*, June 13, 2008.

68. University of Cambridge, Vice-Chancellor's Office, "Professor Alison Richard," http://www.admin.cam.ac.uk/offices/v-c/richard.html.

69. David McNeill, "South Korea Seeks a New Role as a Higher-Education Hub," *Chronicle of Higher Education*, March 21, 2008.

70. David Cohen, "A University in Milan Shops for Professors Elsewhere," *Inside Higher Ed*, June 9, 2008.

71. Bhandari and Blumenthal, "Global Student Mobility."

72. Bhandari and Blumenthal, "Global Student Mobility."

73. Jane Knight, "New Developments and Unintended Consequences: Whither Though Goest, Internationalization?" in *Higher Education on the Move: New Developments in Global Mobility* (New York: Institute of International Education/AIFS Foundation, 2008).

74. Showkat Ali et al., "Elite Scientists and the Global Brain Drain" (paper presented at the Second International Conference on World-Class Universities, Shanghai Jiao Tong University, October 31–November 3, 2007), http://www

.international.ac.uk/resources/Elite%20Scientists%20and%20the%20Global%20Brain%20Drain.pdf.

75. Organisation for Economic Co-operation and Development (OECD), Directorate for Science, Technology and Industry, *The Global Competition for Talent: Mobility of the Highly Skilled*, pp. 70–71, www.oecd.org/sti/stpolicy/talent.

76. Ibid., pp. 101–2.

77. Scott Jaschik, "The Science Lab Is Flat," *Inside Higher Ed*, July 16, 2007.

78. James D. Adams, Grant D. Black, J. Roger Clemmons, and Paula E. Stephan, "Scientific Teams and Institutional Collaborations: Evidence from U.S. Universities, 1981–1999" (Working Paper 10640, National Bureau of Economic Research, July 2004).

79. OECD, *Global Competition for Talent*, p. 103.

80. Stanford University, "Stanford Facts: The Undergraduate Program and Admission," http://www.stanford.edu/about/facts/undergraduate.html.

81. Author interview with Roberta Katz, Stanford, CA, June 25, 2008.

82. Author interview with Richard Levin, New Haven, CT, June 16, 2008.

83. Hopkins-Nanjing Center, "About the Center," http://nanjing.jhu.edu/about/index.htm.

84. MIT Open Courseware, "Courses by Department," http://ocw.mit.edu/OcwWeb/web/courses/courses/index.htm.

85. Simon Marginson, e-mail message to author, June 26, 2009.

86. Don Olcott, e-mail message to author, June 17, 2009.

87. Masamicho Sasaki, Tatsuzo Suzuki, and Masato Yoneda, "English as an International Language in Non-Native Settings in an Era of Globalization," *International Studies in Sociology and Social Anthropology* 109 (2009): 379–404.

88. Author interview with Peggy Blumenthal, New York City, July 10, 2008. Subsequent quotes from Blumenthal come from this interview and a telephone interview with Blumenthal on June 16, 2009.

89. Author interview with Allan Goodman, New York City, July 10, 2008.

90. Altbach, "Higher Education Crosses Borders."

91. Philip G. Altbach, "The Giants Awake: Higher Education Systems in China and India," *Economic and Political Weekly*, June 6, 2009, p. 39.

92. Author telephone interview with Philip Altbach, June 11, 2009.

93. Olcott, e-mail message to author, June 17, 2009.

94. Line and Lasanowski, "International Student Mobility."

95. Mary Beth Marklein, "USA Sees First Increase in Foreign Students since 9/11," *USA Today*, November 11, 2007.

96. Shailaja Neelakantan, "Weak Economy Could Curtail Flow of Indian Students into the U.S.," *Chronicle of Higher Education*, January 9, 2009.

97. Martin Fackler, "Global Financial Crisis Upends the Plans of Many South Koreans to Study Abroad," *New York Times*, January 9, 2009.

98. Mara Hvistendahl, "A Poor Job Market and a Steady Currency Feed 'Overseas Study Fever' in China," *Chronicle of Higher Education*, February 27, 2009.

99. Ibid.

100. "The Future Is Another Country."

101. Ibid.

CHAPTER TWO. BRANCHING OUT

1. Author interview with Nigel Thrift, Coventry, England, November 12, 2008.

2. Author interview with John Sexton, New York City, July 9, 2008. Subsequent quotations are taken from this interview, a group discussion in New York City on October 16, 2008, and an interview with Sexton in Abu Dhabi on November 16, 2008.

3. New York University, Office of Public Affairs, "NYU to Open Campus in Abu Dhabi" (press release, October 12, 2007), http://www.nyu.edu/public.affairs/releases/detail/1787.

4. Tamar Lewin, "U.S. Universities Rush to Set Up Outposts Abroad," *New York Times*, February 10, 2008.

5. Author interview with Mariët Westermann, Abu Dhabi, November 17, 2008.

6. NYU Abu Dhabi, "Faculty Positions, Political Science, NYU Abu Dhabi," http://nyuad.nyu.edu/pdfs/nyuad_poliScience_10-23-08.pdf.

7. Author interview with Ayesha Alateeqi, Abu Dhabi, November 16, 2008.

8. Author interview with Alia Rashid Al-Shamsi, Abu Dhabi, November 16, 2008.

9. NYU Abu Dhabi, announcement about Sheikh Mohamed Scholars Program, http://nyuad.nyu.edu/sheikh.mohamed.scholars/.

10. Author interview with Khulood "Eternity" Al-Atiyat, Abu Dhabi, November 16, 2008.

11. "Global U.," *Inside Higher Ed*, February 15, 2008.

12. Zvika Krieger, "The Emir of NYU," *New York*, April 13, 2008.

13. Judith Miller, "Abu Dhabi: East Leans West," *City Journal* 18 (Winter 2008), http://www.city-journal.org.

14. Itamar Rabinovich, "Narrowing the Gulf," *Haaretz.com*, January 6, 2008.

15. Author telephone interview with Robert Baxter, November 3, 2008.

16. Author interview with James Reardon-Anderson, Doha, Qatar, November 18, 2008.

17. Author interview with Sheikha al-Misnad, Doha, Qatar, November 18, 2008.

18. Katherine Mangan, "Cornell Graduates Its Inaugural Class at Its Medical College in Qatar," *Chronicle of Higher Education*, May 7, 2008.

19. Author interview with Richard Roth, Doha, Qatar, November 19, 2008.

20. GuideStar, Form 990, "Return of Organization Exempt From Income Tax," 2007, http://www.guidestar.org/FinDocuments//2008/530/196/2008-530196603-05117427-9.pdf.

21. Author interview with John Bryant, Doha, Qatar, November 19, 2008.

22. Brady Creel, communications manager, Texas A&M University at Qatar, e-mail message to author, March 3, 2009.

23. Author interview with Mark Weichold, Doha, Qatar, November 18, 2008.

24. Author interview with Fathy Saoud, Doha, Qatar, November 18, 2008.

25. The Doha Debates, "This House Believes That Gulf Arabs Value Profit over People," November 17, 2008, http://www.thedohadebates.com/debates/past.asp.

26. John Bryant, e-mail message to author as forwarded by Norma Haddad, director, Office of Marketing and Communications, Texas A&M University at Qatar, April 6, 2009.

27. Grant McBurnie and Christopher Ziguras, "The International Branch Campus," Institute of International Education, http://www.iienetwork.org/page/84656/.

28. Ibid.

29. "International Campuses on the Rise," *Inside Higher Ed*, September 3, 2009.

30. "Jewel in the Crown," Observatory on Borderless Higher Education Breaking News, June 17, 2005, quoted in McBurnie and Ziguras, "The International Branch Campus."

31. Andrew Denholm, "Scottish University to Open Campus in Singapore," *Herald Scotland,* February 20, 2008.

32. Geoff Maslen, "South Africa: Monash Slowly Recovers Investment," *University World News*, May 11, 2008.

33. Monash University, "Monash Campuses," http://www.monash.edu/campuses/.

34. Huong Le and Vinh Bao, "Foreign Interests Make Inroads into Higher Education," *Thanh Nien News.com*, September 19, 2008.

35. "Asia: It's Nottingham, but Not as We Know It," *The Economist*, November 10, 2005.

36. Elizabeth Redden, "The Phantom Campus in China," *Inside Higher Ed*, February 12, 2008.

37. Scott Jaschik, "Rose-Colored Glasses on China?" *Inside Higher Ed*, December 7, 2007.

38. Observatory on Borderless Higher Education, "Sino-Foreign Joint Education Ventures: A National, Regional and Institutional Analysis," referenced in Redden, "Phantom Campus in China."

39. Geoff Maslen, Chinese Students to Dominate World Market," *University World News*, November 4, 2007.

40. According to the Open Doors 2009 "Fast Facts" report from the Institute of International Education, India is the leading source of overseas students in the United States, while China is second; http://opendoors.iienetwork.org/file_depot/0-10000000/0-10000/3390/folder/78747/Fast+Facts+2009.pdf.

41. Shailaja Neelakantan, "In India, Limits on Foreign Universities Lead to Creative Partnerships," *Chronicle of Higher Education*, February 8, 2008.

42. Author interviews with Steven Sheetz and Anamitra Ghatak, Mumbai, India, January 28, 2008.

43. Author interview with Richard Levin, New Haven, CT, June 16, 2008.

44. Author interview with Edward Harcourt, Coventry, England, November 12, 2008.

45. Redden, "Phantom Campus in China."

46. David Cohen, "Returning to Singapore," *Inside Higher Ed*, February 14, 2008.

47. David McNeill, "South Korea Seeks a New Role as a Higher-Education Hub," *Chronicle of Higher Education*, March 21, 2008.

48. Author telephone interview with Philip Altbach, June 11, 2009.

49. Olcott, e-mail message to author, June 17, 2009.

50. Author telephone interview with Kris Olds, June 17, 2009.

51. George Mason University, "Ras Al Khaimah Campus in the United Arab Emirates," http://rak.gmu.edu/.

52. Author interview with Alan Merten, Fairfax, VA, March 17, 2008; author telephone interview with Merten, July 2009.

53. David Cohen, "Border-Crossing Universities," *Inside Higher Ed*, October 1, 2008.

CHAPTER THREE. WANTED: WORLD-CLASS UNIVERSITIES

1. Quoted in Jamil Salmi, "The Challenge of Creating World Class Universities" (paper presented at the Second International Conference on World-Class Universities, Shanghai Jiao Tong University, October 31–November 3, 2007).

2. Ibid.

3. "International Rankings and Chinese Higher Education Reform," *World Education News & Reviews*, October 2006, http://www.wes.org/eWENR/06oct/practical.htm.

4. Ibid.

5. "Over 10 Billion Yuan to Be Invested in '211 Project,'" *People's Daily Online*, March 26, 2008.

6. Kathryn Mohrman, "Educational Exchanges: What World-Class Universities Should *Not* Adopt from U.S. Higher Education" (paper presented at the Second International Conference on World-Class Universities, Shanghai Jiao Tong University, October 31–November 3, 2007).

7. "International Rankings and Chinese Higher Education Reform."

8. "China's Ivy League," *Inside Higher Ed*, October 28, 2009.

9. Mara Hvistendahl, "China Entices Its Scholars to Come Home," *Chronicle of Higher Education*, December 19, 2008.

10. Ibid.

11. Ibid.

12. "China's Reverse Brain Drain," *Newsweek*, September 9, 2008.

13. Doug Lederman, "Documenting China's Higher Ed Explosion," *Inside Higher Ed*, April 1, 2008.

14. Yao Li et al., "The Higher Educational Transformation of China and Its Global Implications" (Working Paper 13849, National Bureau of Economic Research, March 2008).

15. Ibid.

16. Lederman, "Documenting China's Higher Ed Explosion."

17. Institute of International Education, Atlas of Student Mobility, "Global Destinations for International Students at the Post-Secondary (Tertiary) Level, 2008," http://atlas.iienetwork.org/?p=48027.

18. Mara Hvistendahl, "China Moves Up to Fifth as Importer of Students," *Chronicle of Higher Education*, September 19, 2008.

19. Hao Xin and Dennis Normile, "Chinese Universities: Gunning for the Ivy League," *Science Magazine*, January 11, 2008, http://www.sciencemag.org.

20. Ibid.

21. Howard W. French, "China Spending Billions to Better Universities," *New York Times*, October 27, 2005.

22. Paul Mooney, "Top Chinese Universities Now Seek Donations from Alumni," *Chronicle of Higher Education*, June 11, 2008.

23. Philip G. Altbach and N. Jayaram, "India: Effort to Join 21st Century Higher Education," *University World News*, January 11, 2009.

24. Author interview with Narayana Murthy, Bangalore, India, January 29, 2008.

25. Author interview with M. S. Ananth, Madras, India, January 31, 2008.

26. Jason Overdorf, "When More Is Worse," *Newsweek*, August 9, 2008.

27. Anubhuti Vishnoi, "Citing Quality, IITs Get HRD to Drop Proposal for Quota in Faculty Hiring," *Indian Express.com*, November 15, 2009.

28. Ibid.

29. Shailaja Neelakantan, "India Plans Big Budget Increase to Finance Higher-Education Expansion," *Chronicle of Higher Education*, February 20, 2009.

30. Altbach and Jayaram, "India: Effort to Join 21st Century Higher Education."

31. Author interview with Montek Singh Ahuwahlia, New Delhi, February 4, 2009.

32. Shailaja Neelakantan, "Rapid Expansion Strains Elite Indian Institutes," *Chronicle of Higher Education*, January 30, 2009.

33. Ibid.

34. Altbach and Jayaram, "India: Effort to Join 21st Century Higher Education."

35. Ibid.

36. While South Korea's economy has generally been strong, the global financial crisis is leading to mounting prospects for recession there. See "S. Korea Faces Growing Risk of Recession," *Korea Times*, February 5, 2009.

37. David McNeill, "South Korea Seeks a New Role as a Higher-Education Hub," *Chronicle of Higher Education*, March 21, 2008. The paragraphs that follow draw heavily on this article.

38. David McNeill, "Science Institute's New President Sets a Blistering Pace for Reform," *Chronicle of Higher Education*, March 21, 2008.

39. David McNeill, "South Korea Creates Grant Program to Lure Top Foreign Scholars to Its Universities," *Chronicle of Higher Education*, October 10, 2008.

40. Institute of International Education Network, "Singapore: The Global Schoolhouse," http://www.iienetwork.org/page/116259.

41. Michael Richardson, "Singapore Woos Top Schools with Vision of Regional Hub," *New York Times*, February 15, 1999.

42. Cris Prystay, "In Bid to Globalize, US Colleges Offer Degrees in Asia," Global Policy Forum, July 12, 2005, http://www.globalpolicy.org/globaliz/cultural/2005/0712degrees.htm.

43. Singapore-MIT Alliance for Research and Technology (SMART), http://web.mit.edu/smart/.

44. National Research Foundation, Prime Minister's Office, Republic of Singapore, "Campus for Research Excellence and Technological Enterprise (CREATE)," http://www.nrf.gov.sg/nrf/otherProgrammes.aspx?id=188.

45. Bioinformatics Institute, "Singapore International Pre-Graduate Award (SIPGA)," http://www.bii.a-star.edu.sg/research/opportunities/sipga.php.

46. "Singapore Aims to Attract over 1.5 Lakh International Students by 2015," *The Hindu*, September 21, 2008, http://www.hindu.com/thehindu/holnus/003200809211031.htm.

47. Martha Ann Overland, "In Asia, American-Style Fund Raising Takes Off," *Chronicle of Higher Education*, December 5, 2008.

48. Ibid.

49. Simon Montlake, "Singapore Officials Envision 'Boston of the East,'" *Christian Science Monitor*, October 2, 2007.

50. Ibid.

51. Human Rights Watch, "Singapore" (country summary, January 2008), http://www.hrw.org/legacy/wr2k8/pdfs/singapore.pdf.

52. Author interview with Edward Harcourt, Coventry, England, November 12, 2008.

53. "Saudi Arabia Unveils Co-ed 'House of Wisdom'/Postcards from Saudi Arabia: The KAUST Inauguration," *GlobalHigherEd*, October 5, 2009.

54. Zvika Krieger, "Saudi Arabia Puts Its Billions Behind Western-Style Higher Education," *Chronicle of Higher Education*, September 14, 2007.

55. Henny Sender, "Suitors Queue to Run $10bn Saudi Fund," *Financial Times*, May 18, 2008.

56. Krieger, "Saudi Arabia Puts Its Billions."

57. Ibid.

58. "Saudi Arabia 'May Allow' Cinemas after Three-Decade Ban," *Telegraph.co.uk*, December 21, 2008.

59. Author telephone interview with Walter Murray, June 26, 2008.

60. Stanford Artificial Intelligence Laboratory, "Jean-Claude Latombe," http://robotics.stanford.edu/~latombe/; author telephone interview with Jean-Claude Latombe, July 3, 2008.

61. Tamar Lewin, "U.S. Universities Join Saudis in Partnerships," *New York Times*, March 6, 2008.

62. Ibid.

63. William Drummond, "Concerns Had Merit," *Contra Costa Times*, March 8, 2008.

64. Ibid.

65. Steve Chawkins, "College's Saudi Plan Stirs Anger," *Los Angeles Times*, February 26, 2008.

66. "Saudi King Removes Cleric Who Criticized New University," *Inside Higher Ed*, October 5, 2009.

67. Fallon, "Recreating the Elite Research Universities in Germany."

68. Daniel Fallon, "Germany's 'Excellence Initiative,'" *International Higher Education* 52 (Summer 2008): 16.

69. Aisha Labi, "Germany Awards 'Elite' Status, and $26-Million, to 3 Universities," *Chronicle of Higher Education*, October 27, 2006.

70. Fallon, "Germany's 'Excellence Initiative.'"

71. Labi, "Germany Awards 'Elite' Status."

72. Fallon, "Germany's 'Excellence Initiative.'"

73. Aisha Labi, "Germany's Share of Foreign-Student Market Begins to Stagnate," *Chronicle of Higher Education*, May 1, 2008.

74. Ibid.

75. Fischer and McMurtrie, "Conference Participants Discuss Key Issues."

76. Jane Marshall, "France: First Super-Campuses Chosen," *University World News*, June 15, 2008.

77. Ibid.

78. Aisha Labi, "French President Attacks 'Infantilizing System' of 'Weak Universities,'" *Chronicle of Higher Education*, January 28, 2009.

79. Data on student demographics from *Sciences Po Paris* brochure (http://www .sciences-po.fr) and author interview (Paris, September 10, 2008) with Francis Vérillaud, vice president of Sciences Po Paris since 2002 and the organization's director of International Affairs and Exchanges since 1995.

80. Aisha Labi, "Lessons from—Quelle Horreur!—les Américains," *Chronicle of Higher Education*, September 2, 2005; additional data on Sciences Po from *Sciences Po Paris* brochures, Web site, and author interview with Richard Descoings, president of Sciences Po, Paris, September 10, 2008.

81. Author interview with Richard Descoings.

82. Author interview with Pascal Delisle, Washington, DC, August 27, 2008.

83. Author interview with Francis Vérillaud, Paris, September 10, 2008.

84. Second International Conference on World-Class Universities, Shanghai Jiao Tong University, October 31–November 3, 2007.

85. Author telephone interview with Tyler Cowen, June 17, 2009.

86. Author telephone interview with Jamie Merisotis, June 15, 2009.

87. Author telephone interview with Philip Altbach, June 11, 2009.

88. Jamil Salmi, *The Challenge of Establishing World-Class Universities* (Washington, DC: World Bank Publications, 2009).

CHAPTER FOUR. COLLEGE RANKINGS GO GLOBAL

1. Tia T. Gordon, "Global Ranking Systems May Drive New Decision Making at U.S. Higher Education Institutions," Institute for Higher Education

Policy, May 21, 2009, http://www.ihep.org/press-room/news_release-detail.cfm? id=166.

2. William Carey Jones, *Illustrated History of the University of California* (San Francisco: F. H. Dukesmith, 1895), p. 217.

3. The historical information in the two paragraphs that follow is drawn from Luke Myers and Jonathan Robe, *College Rankings: History, Criticism and Reform* (Washington, DC: Center for College Affordability and Productivity, March 2009), pp. 7–13, http://www.centerforcollegeaffordability.org/uploads/College_ Rankings_History.pdf.

4. Michael Planty et al., *The Condition of Education 2009* (Washington, DC: U.S. Department of Education, National Center for Education Statistics, Institute of Education Sciences, June 2009), http://nces.ed.gov/pubs2009/2009081.pdf.

5. Myers and Robe, *College Rankings*, p. 15.

6. Edward B. Fiske, e-mail message to author, March 5, 2009.

7. Alvin B. Sanoff, "The *U.S. News* College Rankings: A View from the Inside," in *College and University Ranking Systems: Global Perspectives and American Challenges* (Washington, DC: Institute for Higher Education Policy, April 2007). Much of the discussion here of the history of the rankings is drawn from Sanoff's account.

8. National Opinion Research Center (NORC) report quoted in Sanoff, "*U.S. News* College Rankings."

9. Eric Hoover, "U. of Chicago's 'Uncommon' Admissions Dean to Step Down," *Chronicle of Higher Education*, March 4, 2009.

10. John Walshe, "OECD: Worldwide 'Obsession' with League Tables," *University World News*, November 11, 2007.

11. Gordon, "Global Ranking Systems."

12. Jamil Salmi, "Recent Developments in Rankings: Implications for Developing Countries?" (presentation at Third Meeting of the International Ranking Expert Group, Shanghai Jiao Tong University, October 28–31, 2007).

13. Ellen Hazelkorn, "Learning to Live with League Tables and Rankings: The Experience of Institutional Leaders" (presentation at Third Meeting of the International Ranking Expert Group, Shanghai Jiao Tong University, October 28–31, 2007).

14. Ibid.

15. Quoted in Hazelkorn, "Learning to Live with League Tables."

16. Angela Yung-Chi Hou, "A Study of College Rankings in Taiwan" (presentation at Third Meeting of the International Ranking Expert Group, Shanghai Jiao Tong University, October 28–31, 2007).

17. P. Agachi et al., "What Is New in Ranking the Universities in Romania?

Ranking the Universities from the Scientific Research Contribution Perspective" (presentation at Third Meeting of the International Ranking Expert Group, Shanghai Jiao Tong University, October 28–31, 2007).

18. Sholpan Kalanova, "The Methodology of Higher Education Institutions Ranking in Kazakhstan" (presentation at Third Meeting of the International Ranking Expert Group, Shanghai Jiao Tong University, October 28–31, 2007).

19. Alex Usher and Massimo Savino, "A Global Survey of Rankings and League Tables," *College and University Ranking Systems: Global Perspectives and American Challenges* (Washington, DC: Institute for Higher Education Policy, April 2007).

20. Griffith University, "University Ranks," "World Rankings of Universities," http://www.griffith.edu.au/cgi-bin/frameit?http://www.griffith.edu.au/vc/ate/content_inst_ranks.html.

21. Mara Hvistendahl, "The Man Behind the World's Most-Watched College Rankings," *Chronicle of Higher Education*, October 17, 2008.

22. Nian Cai Liu, "Academic Ranking of World Universities Methodologies and Problems" (presentation at Shanghai Jiao Tong University, February 8, 2007). Details of ranking methodology and rationale drawn from this presentation; http://www.authorstream.com/presentation/Heather-19518-Nian-Cai-Liu-presentation-Outline-Dream-Chinese-WCU-Goals-Top-Universities-Questions-Academic-Ranking-World-Featu-as-Entertainment-ppt-powerpoint/.

23. Hvistendahl, "The Man Behind the World's Most-Watched College Rankings."

24. John O'Leary, "THE-QS World University Rankings Preview, October 7, 2008, http://www.topuniversities.com.dev.quaqs.com/worlduniversityrankings/university_rankings_news/article/2008_the_qs_world_university_rankings_preview/.

25. "Methodology: A Simple Overview," Top Universities, www.topuniversities.com/worlduniversityrankings/methodology/simple_overview.

26. "University Rankings FAQs," Top Universities, http://www.topuniversities.com.dev.quaqs.com/worlduniversityrankings/faqs/.

27. "World University Rankings: Methodology," Top Universities, http://www.topuniversities.com/university-rankings/world-university-rankings/methodology/simple-overview.

28. Author interview with Ann Mroz, London, November 13, 2008.

29. Simon Marginson, "Global University Rankings" (presentation version, Thirty-second Annual Conference of the Association for the Study of Higher Education, Louisville, KY, November 10, 2007); http://www.cshe.unimelb.edu.au/people/staff_pages/Marginson/ASHE%202007%20PRESENT%20global%20university%20rankings.pdf.

30. "Methodology: Weightings and Normalization," Top Universities, http://www.topuniversities.com/worlduniversityrankings/methodology/normalization/.

31. Marginson, "Global University Rankings."

32. John Gerritsen, "Global: US Dominance in Rankings Erodes," *University World News*, October 11, 2009.

33. Phil Baty, "New Data Partner for World University Rankings," *Times Higher Education*, October 30, 2009.

34. David Jobbins, "Break-Up Means New Global Rankings," *University World News*, November 8, 2009.

35. Ellen Hazelkorn, "OECD: Consumer Concept Becomes a Policy Instrument," *University World News*, November 11, 2007.

36. Walshe, "Worldwide 'Obsession' with League Tables."

37. Aisha Labi, "Obsession with Rankings Goes Global," *Chronicle of Higher Education*, October 17, 2008.

38. Author interview with Montek Singh Ahluwalia, New Delhi, February 4, 2008.

39. Jane Porter, "How to Stand Out in the Global Crowd," *BusinessWeek*, November 24, 2008.

40. Myers and Robe, *College Rankings*.

41. "Top-Tier Global Rankings," China Europe International Business School (CEIBS), http://www.ceibs.edu/today/rankings/.

42. Robert J. Samuelson, "In Praise of Rankings," *Newsweek*, August 1, 2004.

43. Marguerite Clarke, "The Impact of Higher Education Rankings on Student Access, Choice, and Opportunity" (background paper prepared for the Institute for Higher Education Policy and the Lumina Foundation for Education, September 2006).

44. Marginson, "Global University Rankings."

45. "A Shocking Global Slide," Little Speck, October 31, 2005, http://www.littlespeck.com/region/CForeign-My-051031.htm.

46. Francis Loh, "Crisis in Malaysia's Public Universities? Balancing the Pursuit of Academic Excellence and the Massification of Tertiary Education," *Aliran Monthly* 25 (2005), http://www.aliran.com.

47. Salmi, *The Challenge of Establishing World-Class Universities*, p. 1.

48. John Gill, "Malaysian Rankings Flop 'Shames' the Nation," *Times Higher Education*, December 4, 2008.

49. Graeme Paton, "British Universities Slip in Global League," *Telegraph.co.uk*, October 8, 2008.

50. Wendy Piatt, "Without Investment Our Top Universities Will Fall Behind Global Competition," *Telegraph.co.uk*, October 10, 2008.

51. Ross Williams and Nina Van Dyke, "Measuring University Performance at the Discipline/Departmental Level" (paper presented at the Symposium on International Trends in University Rankings and Classifications, Griffith University, February 12, 2007).

52. Tony Sheil, e-mail message to author, October 20, 2009.

53. "Breaking Ranks," *OECD Observer* 269 (October 2008), http://www.oecdobserver.org.

54. André Siganos, "Rankings, Governance, and Attractiveness: The New French Context" (paper presented at the Second International Conference on World-Class Universities, Shanghai Jiao Tong University, October 31–November 3, 2007).

55. Anubhuti Vishnoi, "No Indian Universities in Global Toplist so UGC Has a Solution: Let's Prepare Our Own List," *Indian Express.com*, March 10, 2009.

56. Jane Marshall, "France: French Do Well in French World Rankings," *University World News*, October 26, 2008.

57. "Methodology," Ranking Web of World Universities, http://www.webometrics.info/methodology.html.

58. Ranking Web of World Universities, http://www.webometrics.info/.

59. Rankings, *Zeit Online*, http://ranking.zeit.de/che9/CHE_en?module=Show&tmpl=p511_methodik.

60. Ibid.

61. Alex Usher and Massimo Savino, "A Global Survey of Rankings and League Tables," in *College and University Ranking Systems: Global Perspectives and American Challenges* (Washington, DC: Institute for Higher Education Policy, April 2007), p. 32.

62. Organisation for Economic Co-operation and Development (OECD), Directorate for Education, "OECD Feasibility Study for the International Assessment of Higher Education Learning Outcomes (AHELO)," http://www.oecd.org/document/22/0,3343,en_2649_35961291_40624662_1_1_1_1,00.html.

63. OECD, Directorate for Education, "AHELO: The Four Strands," http://www.oecd.org/document/41/0,3343,en_2649_35961291_42295209_1_1_1_1,00.html.

64. OECD, Directorate for Education, "PISA for Higher Education," http://www.paddyhealy.com/PISA_HigherEduc_OECD.pdf.

65. OECD, "OECD Feasibility Study."

66. Doug Lederman, "A Worldwide Test for Higher Education?" *Inside Higher Ed*, September 19, 2007.

67. "Measuring Mortarboards," *The Economist*, November 15, 2007.

68. Author telephone interview with Jamie Merisotis, June 15, 2009.

69. Aisha Labi, "Europe Starts Work on Its Own University-Ranking System," *Chronicle of Higher Education,* June 3, 2009.

70. "Ranking—in a Different (CHE) Way?" *GlobalHigherEd*, January 18, 2009.

71. Geri H. Malandra, "Creating a Higher Education Accountability System: The Texas Experience" (speech delivered at the OECD conference Outcomes of Higher Education: Quality, Relevance, and Impact, Paris, September 8–10, 2008), http://www.oecd.org/dataoecd/3/31/41218025.pdf.

72. Voluntary System of Accountability Program, http://www.voluntarysystem .org/index.cfm?page=about_vsa.

73. Kevin Carey, "Rankings Go Global," *Inside Higher Ed*, May 6, 2008.

CHAPTER FIVE. FOR-PROFITS ON THE MOVE

1. Author telephone interview with Douglas Becker, May 7, 2009.

2. Ron Perkinson, "Seizing the Opportunity for Innovation and International Responsibility!" (paper based on notes from plenary speech at the "Global 2" Education Conference, Edinburgh, December 2006).

3. Ibid.

4. Monica Campbell, "A Texas Company Sees Online Learning as Growth Industry in Latin America," *Chronicle of Higher Education*, September 12, 2008.

5. Doug Lederman, "Apollo Goes Global," *Inside Higher Ed*, October 23, 2007.

6. Goldie Blumenstyk, "Apollo Global in Talks to Buy British Higher-Education Company," *Chronicle of Higher Education*, April 29, 2009.

7. Jack Stripling, "From Princeton to DeVry," *Inside Higher Ed*, January 7, 2009.

8. "DeVry Inc. to Acquire Majority Stake in Fanor," March 10, 2009, http:// phx.corporate-ir.net/phoenix.zhtml?c=93880&p=irol-archiveNewsArticle&ID= 1264864&highlight=.

9. Perkinson, "Seizing the Opportunity," p. 17.

10. Doug Lederman, "The Private Sector Role in Global Higher Education," *Inside Higher Ed*, May 15, 2008.

11. Debra Epstein, vice president of corporate communications, Laureate Education, e-mail message to author, October 9, 2009.

12. Lederman, "The Private Sector Role in Global Higher Education."

13. Epstein, e-mail message to author.

14. Douglas Becker, "Higher Education and the Global Marketplace: Entrepreneurial Activity in a Dynamic Environment" (Twenty-seventh Annual Earl V. Pullias Lecture, USC Center for Higher Education Policy Analysis, Fall 2004),

http://www.usc.edu/dept/chepa/pullias/2005/pullias_booklet_2005.pdf; http://
www.researchchannel.org/prog/displayevent.aspx?rID=3357 (video link).

15. Perkinson, "Seizing the Opportunity," p. 10.

16. Ibid.

17. Kris Olds, "Cisco, KAUST, and Microsoft: Hybrid Offerings for Global Higher Ed," *GlobalHigherEd*, May 6, 2008.

18. Author telephone interview with Daniel Levy, May 14, 2009.

19. Author telephone interview with Brooke Coburn, May 18, 2009.

20. Perkinson, "Seizing the Opportunity," p. 21.

21. Ibid., pp. 21–22.

22. Peter Stokes, executive vice president and chief research officer, Eduventures, e-mail message to author, October 5, 2009.

23. Campbell, "A Texas Company Sees Online Learning as Growth Industry."

24. Perkinson, "Seizing the Opportunity," p. 15.

25. Campbell, "A Texas Company Sees Online Learning as Growth Industry."

26. John Daniel, Aha Kanwar, and Stamenka Uvalic-Trumbic, "A Tectonic Shift in Global Higher Education," *Change*, July–August 2006.

27. Perkinson, "Seizing the Opportunity," p. 15.

28. Author telephone interview with Mark Harrad, April 24, 2009.

29. Author telephone interview with Gerald Rosberg, June 9, 2009.

30. Author interview with Joseph Duffey, Washington, DC, May 28, 2009.

31. Jeff Langenbach, e-mail message to author, May 28, 2009.

32. Epstein, e-mail message to author.

33. Author telephone interview with Gerald Heeger, May 19, 2009.

34. Campbell, "A Texas Company Sees Online Learning as Growth Industry."

35. Author telephone interview with Levy.

36. Daniel C. Levy, "Access through Private Higher Education: Global Patterns and Indian Illustrations" (PROPHE Working Paper 11, April 2008).

37. Author telephone interview with Jason Lane, June 6, 2009.

38. Jessica Shepherd, "Privatisation of Higher Education Threatens Universities," *The Guardian*, September 4, 2008.

39. Ibid.

40. Daniel, Kanwar, and Uvalic-Trumbic, "A Tectonic Shift in Global Higher Education."

41. John Fielden and Norman LaRocque, "The Evolving Regulatory Context for Private Education in Emerging Economies" (discussion paper presented at International Finance Corporation International Forum on Private Education, Washington, DC, May 16, 2008).

42. Karin Fischer and Beth McMurtrie, "Forum Focuses on Private Role in

Expanding Global Access to Higher Education," *Chronicle of Higher Education*, May 16, 2008.

43. International Finance Corporation, World Bank Group, "Regulating Private Education," http://www.ifc.org/ifcext/che.nsf/Content/Education_Regulating_Private_Education (link leads to interview with Douglas Becker).

44. Fischer and McMurtrie, "Forum Focuses on Private Role."

45. International Finance Corporation, World Bank Group, "Regulating Private Education," http://www.ifc.org/ifcext/che.nsf/Content/Education_Regulating_Private_Education (link leads to interview with Daniel Levy).

CHAPTER SIX. FREE TRADE IN MINDS

1. Jessica Shepherd, "Why I Chose the University of Wherever," *The Guardian*, February 5, 2008.

2. David Rothkopf, *Superclass: The Global Power Elite and the World They Are Making* (New York: Farrar, Straus and Giroux, 2008), p. 126.

3. Ibid., pp. 290–91.

4. Author interview with Peggy Blumenthal, New York City, June 16, 2009.

5. "Confucianism and the Chinese Scholastic System" and "The Chinese Imperial Examination System," Confucian and Chinese Education, http://www.csupomona.edu/~plin/ls201/confucian3.html.

6. Olivia Chavassieu, "Learning a Discipline on a Grande Scale," *Sydney Morning Herald*, May 12, 2008.

7. Author interview with Vivek Upadhyay, Mumbai, India, January 28, 2008.

8. Manuela Zoninsein, "China's SAT," *Slate*, June 4, 2008. The information in this section about Chinese university admissions draws heavily on this article.

9. Nicholas Lemann, *The Big Test: The Secret History of the American Meritocracy* (New York: Farrar, Straus and Giroux, 1999).

10. Tracy Jan, "Colleges Scour China for Top Students," *Boston Globe*, November 9, 2008.

11. Ibid.

12. Hilde Ridder-Symoens, *Mobility: A History of the University in Europe* (Cambridge: Cambridge University Press, 1992), p. 287.

13. "India, in a Slap at U.S., Decides to Restrict American Scholars," *New York Times*, September 3, 1973.

14. Shailaja Neelakantan, "In India: No Foreign Colleges Need Apply," *Chronicle of Higher Education*, February 8, 2008.

15. Ibid.

16. Shailaja Neelakantan, "India's Higher-Education Minister Calls for Foreign Entries into University System," *Chronicle of Higher Education*, October 18, 2009.

17. Shailaja Neelakantan, "Elite Engineering School in India Bans Foreign Internships," *Chronicle of Higher Education*, June 4, 2008.

18. Vivek Upadhyay, e-mail message to author, June 5, 2008.

19. Akshaya Mukul, "Govt Lays Down Stricter Norms for Setting Up Offshore Campus," *Times of India*, January 10, 2009.

20. Shailaja Neelakantan, "India Stymies Local Private Universities from Expansion Abroad," *Chronicle of Higher Education*, January 10, 2009.

21. Shailaja Neelakantan, "Facing a Doctor Shortage, India Will Recognize Foreign Medical Degrees," *Chronicle of Higher Education*, March 28, 2008.

22. "New Immigration Rules to Restrict International Medical Graduates' Access to UK Post-graduate Medical Training," *Medical News Today*, February 7, 2008.

23. Craig Whitlock and Shannon Smiley, "Non-European PhDs in Germany Find Use of 'Doktor' Verboten," *Washington Post*, March 14, 2008.

24. Ned Stafford, "Germany Set to Resolve Foreign Doctorates Spat," *Chemistry World*, March 13, 2008.

25. Associated Press, "Changes Restrict Foreign Students' Research Involvement," August 2, 2005, available at http://opendoors.iienetwork.org/?p=65973; Scott Jaschik, "Badges and Segregation," *Inside Higher Ed*, July 18, 2005; "Defense Dept. Won't Segregate Foreign Staffers," *Boston Globe*, August 16, 2006.

26. "Scientists Fear Visa Trouble Will Drive Foreign Students Away," *New York Times*, March 3, 2009.

27. John Gill, "Immigration Hassles Impair International Partnerships," *Times Higher Education*, September 25, 2008.

28. Robin Wilson, "A University Uses Quotas to Limit and Diversify Its Foreign Enrollments," *Chronicle of Higher Education*, May 14, 1999.

29. Paul Basken, "'Buy American' Provisions in Stimulus Law Could Limit University Actions," *Chronicle of Higher Education*, February 20, 2009.

30. Jonathan D. Glater, "A Hiring Bind for Foreigners and Banks," *New York Times*, March 9, 2009.

31. Vivek Wadhwa, "They're Taking Their Brains and Going Home," *Washington Post*, March 8, 2009.

32. Vivek Wadhwa, "The Visa Shortage: Big Problem, Easy Fix," *BusinessWeek*, October 17, 2007.

33. Wadhwa, "They're Taking Their Brains and Going Home."

34. "Keith Maskus, "U.S. Innovation Hurt by Restrictions on Foreign Grad

Students, CU Study Shows," University of Colorado at Boulder, December 7, 2004, http://www.colorado.edu/news/releases/2004/384.html.

35. Wadhwa, "They're Taking Their Brains and Going Home."

36. Vivek Wadhwa et al., "Losing the World's Best and Brightest: America's New Immigrant Entrepreneurs, Part V," March 2009, Kauffman Foundation, http://www.kauffman.org/uploadedFiles/ResearchAndPolicy/Losing_the_World's_Best_and_Brightest.pdf.

37. Katherine Mangan, "Foreign Students Are Less Inclined to Seek Jobs in the U.S., Survey Finds," *Chronicle of Higher Education*, March 19, 2009.

38. AnnaLee Saxenian, "Unwelcome in the Land of Opportunity," *Financial Times*, March 30, 2009.

39. Mangan, "Foreign Students Are Less Inclined to Seek Jobs in the U.S."

40. Doug Fuller, "The Fact Remains, U.S. Tech Leadership Must Be Reinforced," *San Jose Mercury News*, April 7, 2006.

41. Anthea Lipset, "Academics Urge Cautions Over Chinese Collaboration," *The Guardian*, December 6, 2007.

42. Quoted in Thomas L. Friedman, "Who Will Tell the People?" *New York Times*, May 4, 2008.

43. Paul Fain and Jeffrey Selingo, "Virginia Governor Says Global Competition in Higher Education Is a Matter of National Security," *Chronicle of Higher Education*, February 2, 2006.

44. Lynn Sweet, "Obama Education Speech in Onio" (transcript), *Chicago Sun-Times*, September 9, 2008.

45. Tyler Cowen, "This Global Show Must Go On," *New York Times*, June 8, 2008.

46. Amar Bhidé, *The Venturesome Economy: How Innovation Sustains Prosperity in a More Connected World* (Princeton, NJ: Princeton University Press, 2008), p. 438.

47. Richard Monastersky, "Despite Recent Obits, U.S. Science and Engineering Remain Robust," *Chronicle of Higher Education*, June 12, 2008.

48. Ibid.

49. Levin, "The West Need Not Panic."

50. Author interview with Richard Levin, New Haven, CT, June 16, 2008.

51. Richard Levin, "The Internationalization of the University" (speech, Athens, Greece, May 6, 2008), http://athens.usembassy.gov/levinspeech_zappeion.html.

52. Levin, "The West Need Not Panic."

53. Richard Freeman, "What Does Global Expansion of Higher Education Mean for the US?" (paper prepared for "U.S. Universities in a Global Market," National Bureau of Economic Research conference, October 3–4, 2009).

AFTERWORD

1. Salmi, *The Challenge of Establishing World-Class Universities.* The account that follows comes from Salmi.

2. Philip G. Altbach, "Empires of Knowledge: The Challenges of World-Class Research Universities in Developing Countries" (author notes from speech delivered at Second International Conference on World-Class Universities, Shanghai Jiao Tong University, November 1, 2007).

3. Claudia Goldin and Lawrence F. Katz, *The Race between Education and Technology* (Cambridge, MA: Harvard University Press, 2008), p. 41.

4. "Professors at Russian University Must Get Approval to Publish or Present Overseas," *Chronicle of Higher Education*, October 28, 2009.

5. Ellen Barry, "Major University in Russia Eases Fears on Rules," *New York Times*, November 1, 2009.

Index

Abayas, 3, 48, 52

Abdullah, King of Saudi Arabia, 84–88, 97

Abington Township School District v. Schempp, 49

Abu Dhabi, 3, 34; academic freedom and, 52; censorship and, 51; financial incentives and, 47; gender issues and, 51–52; Israelis and, 53; Knowledge Village and, 55; New York University partnership and, 43–53, 85; Sexton and, 43–53; Sorbonne and, 61; Yale and, 64

Academic Ranking of World Universities, 111–12

ACT scores, 105, 129

admissions standards: Education City and, 55–56; quotas and, 56, 163, 172–79, 183. *See also* elitism

affirmative action, 16, 77, 93, 195

Agora, 187

Ahluwalia, Montek Singh, 78, 119–20

Al-Ain, 50

Alateeqi, Ayesha, 50

Al-Atiyat, Khulood "Eternity," 51

alcohol, 86

Al Jazeera Children's Channel, 54

Al-Misnad, Sheikha, 55, 59

Al-Shamsi, Alia Rashid, 50

Altbach, Philip: branch campuses and, 65–66, 70, 75, 79, 98–99; future policy and, 196; rankings and, 110; talent and, 35–38

American Association of State Colleges and Universities, 137–38

American Council on Education, 132–33

American University, 157

America's Best Colleges (*U.S. News & World Report*), 104

Amherst College, 101

Ananth, M. S., 1, 76

Anti-Defamation League, 53

Apollo Group, 11, 144–45, 149–51, 157, 159–60, 164–65

APTECH, 147–48, 155

Aramco, 85

Archana, K., 39

architecture: NYU Abu Dhabi campus and, 45; University of Nottingham's Ningbo campus and, 61

Argentina, 109, 144, 158–59

Arts and Humanities Indices (ACHI), 113

Ashahi Shimbun journal, 138

Asiaweek, 111

Assessment of Higher Education Learning Outcomes (AHELO), 128–39

Assessment of Quality in Graduate Education (Cartter), 102

Association of Public and Land-grant Universities, 108, 138

Australia, 4, 23–24, 28, 196; branch campuses and, 60–61; for-profit institutions and, 146–47, 151, 165; global financial crisis and, 40; *The Good Universities*

Australia (*cont.*)
  Guide and, 110; online learning and,
  153–55; rankings and, 123–24; regional
  globalism and, 38; Singapore and,
  83–84; world-class status and, 70
Austria, 128, 179
authentica Habita rules, 18

Baby Boomers, 104
backward castes, 77, 172
Baldwin, Ian Thomas, 180
Barbarossa, Frederick, 18
Barron's guide, 108
Bates, Luke, 154
Baxter, Robert, 55
Becker, Douglas, 141–42, 146, 148,
  157–58, 162, 164
Bédier, Joseph, 17
Belgium, 18, 179
Bell, Daniel, 27
Benavidas, Jimmy, 153
Bertelsmann Stiftung, 110
Best, Randy, 144
Bhandari, Rajika, 27
Bhidé, Amar, 189–90, 192
Bible readings, 49
Big Test, The (Lemann), 173
Bing Overseas Studies programs, 31
bin Khalifa Al-Thani, Sheikh Hamad
  (Emir of Qatar), 54
bin Sultan Al Nahyan, Sheikh Zayed, 45
bint Nasser al Missned, Sheikha Mozah, 54
bin Zayed, Sheikh Mohamed, 48
Blackboard, Inc., 149–50
Blair, Tony, 23
Bloom, Alfred, 46
Blue Cross/Blue Shield, 141
Blumenthal, Peggy, 27, 36–40, 170
Bobst Library (NYU), 43
Bocconi University, 9, 27
Bollywood, 96
Bologna Process, 38

Booyjzsen, Claire, 14–15, 168
Boston College, 35, 37, 65–66, 75, 110, 907
Boston Consulting, 172
Boston University, 96
BPP Professional Education, 145
brain circulation, 8, 27–28
brain drain, 8, 18, 25–28, 72, 176, 184
brain exchange, 27
brain gain, 8, 28
brain train, 28
branch campuses, 9; academic freedom
  and, 52; Australia and, 60–61; branding and, 6, 64; censorship and, 51; China
  and, 4, 41, 61–62; classic firm theory
  and, 42–43; closing of, 67–68; difference from study-abroad centers, 42;
  Education City and, 53–60; financial
  risks and, 64–65; for-profit institutions
  and, 62, 68–69; free speech and, 64–65;
  funding and, 66–67; gauging student
  demand and, 65; global economic crisis
  and, 66; growing demand for Western
  higher education and, 42–43; growing
  popularity of, 42–43; human rights and,
  64–65; ICE assets and, 45; as idea capitals, 44–45; immigration restrictions
  and, 53; Incheon Free Economic Zone
  and, 68; India and, 62–63; Japan and,
  65; logistical problems of, 65; non-U.S.,
  60–69; number of, 61; numerous forms
  of, 60–61; one-two-one program and, 68;
  Persian Gulf and, 6; politics and, 51–52;
  portal campuses and, 4; regional students and, 42; research and, 61; risk
  aversion and, 43–44; sender countries
  and, 15; Sexton and, 43–45; subordination principle and, 43; tuition and,
  63–64; twinning arrangements and, 62;
  U.S., 43–60
Brandenburg, Uwe, 135–36
branding, 32, 40; branch campuses and, 6,
  64; dilution of, 6, 55–56, 64; Education
  City and, 55–56; France and, 93–95;

free trade and, 167; mentality of, 168; Open Courseware and, 34–35; Singapore and, 84. *See also* quality issues
Brazil, 23, 145–46
British Broadcasting Corporation (BBC), 58
British Council, 23
Brown University, 1, 174
Bryant, John, 57, 59
Bulgaria, 16, 91
Bush, George W., 182
Bush, Simon, 168
BusinessWeek, 121
Buy American rules, 183–84

California Institute of Technology, 65, 76, 114, 118, 180
California Polytechnic State University, 88
Cambodia, 69
Campus for Research Excellence and Technological Enterprise (CREATE), 82
Canada, 2, 26–27, 96, 109–10, 133, 138
Canter and Associates, 141
Canto-Sperber, Monique, 100, 110, 125–26
Carey, Kevin, 139
Carlyle Group, 145, 149–50, 163
Carnegie Classifications, 104–6
Carnegie Foundation for the Advancement of Teaching, 104, 180
Carnegie Mellon University, 53–54, 62, 65
Cartter, Allan, 102
Castiblanco, Marta, 152
Catholic Church, 18, 35–36
cell phones, 48
Center for Advanced Study in the Behavioral Sciences, 27
Center for Higher Education Development (CHE), 109, 127–28, 136
Centre for Policy Research, 177
Challenge of Establishing World-Class Universities, The (Salmi), 98

Chamberlain College of Nursing, 145
Charles IV, King of France, 19
cheating, 79
Chen Fangrou, 73
Chen Shiyi, 72
Chen Zhil, 74
Cheung Kong Scholars Program, 72
Chile, 36, 146, 162
China, 16, 51, 186; academic freedom and, 74–75; affirmative action and, 195; American PhDs and, 16; brain drain and, 8; branch campuses and, 4, 44, 61–62; bureaucratic barriers of, 6; Cheung Kong Scholars Program and, 72; C9 conference and, 72; competition and, 23–27, 32; Cultural Revolution and, 71; Deng Xiaoping and, 71; economic growth of, 72; engineering and, 187; English and, 36; entrance exams and, 74, 172–74; for-profit institutions and, 143, 151; free speech and, 64–65; free trade and, 167; future issues and, 37–38; *gaokao* test and, 172–74; German universities and, 90–91; global financial crisis and, 39–40; human rights and, 64–65; increased enrollment in, 71–74; international students in, 73–74; Ivy League of, 72; Jiang Zemin and, 71–72; Johns Hopkins University partnership and, 33–34; liberal arts and, 174; Mao and, 71; meritocracy and, 170–75; Ministry of Education and, 72; one-two-one program and, 68; online learning and, 155, 158; overseas-study fever of, 40; perceived threat of, 7; postsecondary system of, 73; Project 211 and, 71, 74; Project 985 and, 71–72; protectionism and, 6, 190–91; quality issues and, 10, 71–75; rankings and, 119; recruitment and, 72–73; regional globalism and, 38, 42; regulatory obstacles in, 65; research and, 73, 188; reverse brain drain and, 72–73; "sea turtle" returnees and, 72–73;

China (*cont.*)
  security issues and, 180–81; as sender
  country, 15; world-class universities
  and, 70–75, 83–84, 91, 94–95, 97; Yale
  partnerships and, 34
China Europe International Business
  School (CEIBS), 121
Chinese Ministry of Education, 65
Chronicle of Higher Education, The, 39,
  72, 80–81, 114, 144, 152, 176, 183,
  186
Cisco Systems, 148
Clemson University, 62, 106
C9 conference, 72
coaching centers, 2
Coburn, Brooke, 149–51, 163
Coca-Cola, 176
Cohen, Jake, 2–3
Cold War, 22
Collegiate Learning Assessment (CLA),
  129–30, 132, 137–38
Columbia University, 92–93, 114, 118,
  144, 152–53, 159, 176, 184
communications, 32, 53, 55, 77, 145, 155
Communists, 61, 163, 177
competition: Australia and, 23–24; benefits of academic trade and, 188–93;
  Blair program and, 23; brain drain and,
  8, 18, 25–28, 72, 176, 184; branding
  and, 32; British Council and, 23; China
  and, 23–27, 32; for faculty, 22–36; for-
  profit institutions and, 160; free trade
  in minds and, 5–13 (*see also* markets);
  future issues for, 36–41, 194–98; graduate students and, 24–25; India and, 23;
  industrial, 76–77; "international" term
  and, 32; language issues and, 35–36;
  Malaysia and, 23; metaphorical view of,
  29–36; Operation Campus and, 91–92;
  partnerships and, 33–34; PhD goals and,
  25; protectionism and, 6, 12, 175–93,
  197–198; race for talent and, 14–41;

rankings and, 10–11, 106 (*see also*
  rankings); researchers and, 28–29; Yale
  policy and, 32–35
computer science, 6, 16
Consumer Reports, 137
Contra Costa Times, 87–88
Cornell University, 20, 56, 65, 101,
  157–58, 176, 180
correspondence courses, 154. *See also*
  online learning
Costa Rica, 146
Council for Aid to Education, 129
Cowen, Tyler, 96–97, 189, 192
cram schools, 2
Cultural Revolution, 71

Daily Telegraph, 123
Daniel, John, 154, 161, 163
Davies, Graeme, 164
Davis, Larry, 171
Davos Man, 169
Delisle, Pascal, 94
Deng Xiaoping, 71
Denmark, 147
Descoings, Richard, 93–94
DeVry University, 144–46
Dingwell, Robert, 182
dishdasha, 48
distance learning, 147, 151–55. *See also*
  online learning
Doha. *See* Qatar
Dow Jones, 96
Drummond, William, 87–88
Dubai, 47, 50, 55, 61, 120
Dublin Institute of Technology, 25, 110,
  118
Duderstadt, James, 3
Duffey, Joseph, 157, 160–63
Dugan, Renee, 46
Duke University, 65, 185, 187
Dutch Renaissance, 18

École Normale Supérieure, 100, 110, 125–26
economic issues, 3, 97; *authentica Habita*
and, 18; compensation boosts and,
56–57; Education City and, 54–55;
fellowships and, 14, 24–25, 27, 83, 85;
Fulbright Program and, 21; full-pay
status and, 14; General Agreement on
Trade in Services (GATS) and, 193;
global financial crisis and, 39–40, 66;
Incheon Free Economic Zone and, 68,
80; knowledge-based economies and,
5–8, 33, 62, 70–75, 78–82 (*see also*
knowledge-based economies); online
learning and, 153–54; Open Courseware program and, 34–35; Project 211
and, 71, 74; Project 985 and, 71–72;
protectionism and, 6–7, 12, 175–93,
197–98; tuition and, 9, 14, 23–24,
38–39, 47, 60, 63, 74, 85, 93, 144,
147, 155, 158, 165, 177, 196
Economist, The, 40, 61, 121
Edrak, 68
Educate, Inc., 142
Educational Policy Institute, 133
Education City, 9, 68, 178; admissions
standards and, 55–56; branding and,
55–56; compensation boosts and, 56–57;
diplomas from, 55; governmental motivations for, 54–55; housing for, 54; human capital strategy and, 55; language
and, 56; luxury of, 54; monthly debates
and, 58; prayer and, 54; quality issues
and, 55–58; quotas and, 56; RAND
and, 54; recruitment and, 56–57; segregation and, 59; sexual harassment and,
59; sustainability and, 59–60; tuition
and, 60; Western franchises in, 54;
women and, 59
Education Sector, 139
Eduventures, 151
elitism, 2; brand dilution and, 6 (*see also*
branding); for-profit institutions and,

148–49; language and, 35–36; market
issues and, 168–69; meritocracy and, 5,
12, 19, 79, 103, 169–75, 192, 195–96;
new free trade and, 5–13; Nobel Prize
and, 4; protectionism and, 175–88;
rankings and, 100 (*see also* rankings);
Russell Group and, 123; superclass and,
168–69; talent and, 1, 5, 7, 12–46, 55,
75, 82–84, 170–71, 177, 183–88, 191–
98; world-class universities and, 79–99
Engel v. Vitale, 49
engineering, 1, 3, 7, 144, 146, 192; branch
campuses and, 55–59; China and, 187;
India and, 75–76; KAUST and, 86; protectionism and, 181–88; rankings and,
102, 104, 112–13, 124, 140; talent
race and, 16, 21–22, 25–26, 30, 36;
world-class universities and, 72, 75–78,
81, 85–88
English language: Education City and, 55–
56; France and, 93–94; as language of
international exchange, 93–94; Sciences
Po and, 93; South Korea and, 80–81;
talent race and, 24–25, 36; world-class
universities and, 93–94, 97
enrollment management, 108
entrance exams, 12, 120; China and, 74,
172–74; *gaokao* test and, 172–74; Indian
Institutes of Technology (IITs) and, 2,
76, 171; meritocracy and, 172–74
Erasmus, Desiderius, 18
Erasmus Mundus program, 36, 66
Estacia University Group, 146
ETH, 172
European Center for Strategic Management of Universities, 125
European Commission, 36
European Union (EU), 14; Bologna Process and, 38; declining research in, 73;
Erasmus program and, 18, 36; free trade
in minds and, 179–80, 191; PhD goals
of, 25; rankings and, 111, 126–27,

European Union (EU) (*cont.*)
134–35; world-class universities and,
88–95
Excellence Initiative (German program),
89–90

faculty, 194; censorship in Abu Dhabi and,
51; Cheung Kong Scholars Program
and, 72; class size and, 77; competition
for, 22–36; Education City and, 55–57;
favoritism and, 79; financial incentives
and, 47, 56–57, 72; future policy for,
195–98; increased mobility of, 26, 28–
31, 35; Indian Institutes of Technology
(IITs) and, 76–77; KAUST and, 86–88;
moonlighting and, 141; NYU and, 46–
47; online learning and, 53, 152–53; private research and, 21–22, 26; rankings
and, 105; returnees to China and, 72–
73; reverse commutes and, 27; spouses
and, 47
Fallon, Daniel, 17, 89–90
Fanor, 145–46
Faust, Drew, 188
fellowships, 14, 24–25, 27, 83, 85
Fertile Crescent, 46
Fields Medal, 113
Financial Services Institute of Australasia,
154
Financial Times, 109, 121
FIRE (finance, insurance, and real estate),
44–45
firm theory, 42–43
First Amendment, 47, 48–50
Fiske, Edward T., 103, 106
Fitzsimmons, William, 174–75
Forbes, 121
for-profit institutions, 4–5, 11–12; Asia
and, 143; blended delivery and, 151;
branch campuses and, 62, 68–69;
competition and, 160; foreign subsid-
iaries and, 43; growth in, 143; higher

education and, 143; learning methods
and, 151–59; new market potential of,
142–51; non-elite learners and, 142–43;
online learning and, 151–59; postsecondary education and, 143–44; quality
issues and, 155–66; rankings and, 147;
soaring enrollment in, 143; technology
and, 151–59; test preparation business
and, 144–45
Fortune, 126
Foxman, Abraham, 53
France, 3, 10; academic influx to, 20;
branch campuses and, 4; branding
and, 93–95; English and, 93–94; first
Western universities and, 17; foreign
student demographics of, 16; free trade
and, 167; Great Dispersion and, 18;
meritocracy and, 170–71; National
Assembly and, 91; Operation Campus
and, 91–92; quality issues and, 91–95;
rankings and, 100, 110, 119, 125–27;
record enrollment in, 20; regional
globalism and, 38; research and, 92–95;
Sarkozy and, 91–92, 125–26; Sciences
Po and, 92–95; world-class universities
and, 70, 91–95, 98
Freeman, Richard, 192
free speech, 6, 51, 52, 64–65, 75
free trade: branding and, 167; meritocracy
and, 171–72 (*see also* meritocracy); new
form of, 5–13; protectionism and, 175–
88; quality issues and, 171, 176–80, 185,
189, 191; talent and, 5–13, 170–71,
177, 183–88, 191–93
Friedman, Thomas, 3
Fudan University, 34
Fulbright Program, 21
Fuller, Doug, 187
full-pay status, 14

gaokao, 172–74
gays, 6, 51

Gazzola, Ana Lucia, 159

General Agreement on Trade in Services (GATS), 193

General Electric Corporate Research Lab, 26

General Motors, 176

George Mason University, 67–68, 96, 189

Georgetown University, 9, 53, 55–60

Georgia Tech, 62, 72

German University, The (Fallon), 89

Germany, 10, 17–18; academic influx to, 19–20; Bertelsmann Stiftung and, 110; branch campuses and, 4; Center for Higher Education Development (CHE) and, 109, 127–28, 136; Chinese students and, 90–91; English language and, 36; Excellence Initiative and, 89–90; Federal Ministry of Education and Research and, 90–91; foreign enrollment in, 16, 89–91; free trade and, 167; futures concepts and, 90; Indian Institutes of Technology (IITs) partnership and, 76; protectionism and, 179–80; quality issues and, 89–91; rankings and, 109, 119; regional globalism and, 38; research universities and, 19–20; world-class universities and, 70, 89–91, 98

Ghana, 51

Ghatak, Anamitra, 63

"Global Competition for Talent, The: Mobility of the Highly Skilled" (OECD report), 28

global financial crisis, 39–40, 66

GlobalHigherEd (blog), 66

globalization: benefits of academic trade and, 188–93; brain drain and, 8, 18, 25–28, 72, 176, 184; competition and, 3–9, 28, 40, 65, 70, 81–82 (*see also* competition); English and, 36; foreign coauthored papers and, 29; for-profit institutions and, 141–51 (*see also* for-profit institutions); future issues for, 36–41, 194–98; "international" term and, 32; international trade and, 29,

167–73; language issues and, 35–36; mercantilism and, 197; meritocracy and, 169–71; mobility and, 3–9, 12, 15–20, 26–41 (*see also* mobility); multiculturalism and, 14, 54; national boundaries and, 70; new free trade and, 5–13; online learning and, 151–59; Open Courseware and, 34–35; perceived threat of, 7; political instability and, 38–39; porous boundaries of, 2–3; protectionism and, 6, 12, 175–93, 197–98; quality issues and, 6, 171, 176–80 (*see also* quality issues); rankings and, 109–27 (*see also* rankings); superclass and, 168–69; visas and, 6–7, 17, 27, 31, 38, 63, 121, 180–86, 191–93; world-class universities and, 70–99; Yale policy and, 32–35; zero-sum games and, 7

global network universities, 44

Goldin, Claudia, 197

Goodman, Allan, 36

Good Universities Guide, The, 110

Google, 1

Gourman Report, The, 103

Gow, Ian, 187

Graduate Research School, 25

Grancolombiano Polytechnic, 144, 152–53

Great Dispersion, 18

Greece, 111

Griffith University, 124

GUILDHE, 161

Hamilton, Andrew, 26

Hanoi, 61

Harcourt, Edward, 64–65, 84

Harrad, Mark, 155–56

Hartle, Terry, 133

Harvard Law School, 43, 185

Harvard University, 26; Fitzsimmons and, 174–75; meritocracy and, 172–73; prestige of, 97–98; ranking of, 114, 118; superclass and, 168–69

Hazelkorn, Ellen, 25, 110, 114, 118–19
Heeger, Gerald, 158–59
Henry III, King of England, 18
Heriot-Watt University, 61
Higher Colleges of Technology (HCT), 50
higher education: brain drain and, 8, 18, 25–28, 72, 176, 184; business professors and, 73; competition and, 3–9, 28, 40, 65, 70, 81–82, 90–91, 101–3 (*see also* competition); economic benefits of, 33 (*see also* knowledge-based economies); for-profit institutions and, 141–66; as free trade, 5–13, 167–93; future policy for, 194–98; growth rate of, 35; importance of global, 1–13; missteps of, 5–6; online learning and, 151–59; porous boundaries of, 2–3; quality issues and, 6, 171, 176–80 (*see also* quality issues); rankings and, 117–19, 123, 125, 135 (*see also* rankings); recruitment and, 4, 23, 42, 86, 120, 161, 164; zero-sum games and, 7
Higher Education Policy Research Unit, 25
Hinshaw, Virginia, 183
Hippler, Horst, 90
Ho Chi Minh, 163
Ho Chi Minh City, 61
Hollywood, 96
Holmes, Richard, 127
Holyoke Community College, 133
Hong Kong, 2, 15, 27, 72, 109, 146, 151, 172
Hood, John, 26
Hosek, James, 7, 190, 192
Hou, Angela Yung-chi, 110
House of Wisdom, 84
Hubbard, R. Glenn, 184
human capital, 8, 10, 197–98; branch campuses and, 55; for-profit institutions and, 149, 158–59, 166; free trade in minds and, 191–192, 195; rankings and, 136; world-class universities and, 71, 75, 79

human rights, 64–65, 195, 172
Humboldt University, 19
Hungary, 17
Hunt, Sally, 161
Huntington, Samuel, 169
Hynes, Alice, 161

ICE (intellectual, cultural, educational) assets, 54
idea capitals, 44–45
IDP Education, 16
I-graduate, 168
Illustrated History of the University of California, 101
Imperial College, London, 2, 85, 118
Incheon Free Economic Zone, 68, 80
India, 1, 16, 37, 186; affirmative action and, 195; Andra Pradesh and, 62; backward castes and, 77, 172; branch campuses and, 61–63; bureaucratic barriers of, 6; Carnegie Classifications and, 104; class size and, 77; competition and, 23; culture of mediocrity in, 79; dearth of scholarship in, 76; doctor shortage in, 178–79; elitism and, 2; engineering and, 75–76; for-profit institutions and, 146–48; free speech and, 75; future issues and, 37–38; global financial crisis and, 39–40; need for reform in, 75–79; Planning Commission and, 78; protectionism and, 176–78, 191, 194; quality issues and, 62–63, 75–79; rankings and, 127; regional globalism and, 38; regulatory obstacles in, 62; research and, 188; security issues and, 180–81; as sender country, 15; twinning arrangements and, 62; world-class universities and, 70–71, 75–79, 84, 90, 94–95, 97–98
India Education Index, 126
Indian Institute of Science, 120
Indian Institutes of Technology (IITs), 1, 10, 62, 75; elitism and, 2; entrance

exams of, 2, 76, 171; faculty building in, 76–77; meritocracy and, 171–72; Nehru and, 76; plans for additional, 77–78; protectionism and, 6; rankings and, 119–20; Western partnerships and, 76

Indian Institutes of Management (IIMs), 62, 75, 77, 120, 172

Indiresan, P. V., 78

Indonesia, 69, 122

information technology (IT), 147–48

Infosys, 1, 75

innovation: alumni funding and, 83; British Office of Science and Innovation and, 29, Chinese research and, 7; entrepreneurship and, 107; for-profit institutions and, 163–64; France's lack in, 92; free trade in minds and, 175, 181, 183–90; government-funded universities and, 101; quality issues and, 10 (see also quality issues); ranking and, 126, 136; regulatory impediments to, 163–64; sclerotic bureaucracy of India and, 79; Singapore and, 83; world-class universities and, 79, 83, 92, 95

INSEAD, 2–3, 120–21, 151

Inside Higher Ed, 133

Insider's Guide to the Colleges, The (Yale Daily News), 103

Institute for Computational Earth Sciences and Engineering, 85

Institute for Higher Education Policy, 133

Institute for International Education (IIE), 15, 23, 27, 36, 39–40, 170

Intercontinental Hotel, 48

International Adult Literacy Survey, 133

Ireland, 17

Islam, 86

Israel, 6, 53, 87– 88

Italy, 9–10, 128; Bologna Process and, 38; branch campuses and, 61; first Western universities and, 17; quality issues and, 96; rankings and, 109; talent race and, 18, 27

James, Nidia Mercedes, 153

Japan, 4, 16, 23–24, 138, 191

Jayaram, N., 75, 79

Jiang Zemin, 71–72

Johns Hopkins University, 20, 33–34, 62, 72, 83

Jordan, 24, 46

journalism, 9, 53, 55–56, 58

Jubail University College, 88

Kang Youn-mo, 39

Kanwar, Asha, 154, 159, 161, 163

Kaplan, Inc., 11, 62, 144–45, 149, 153, 155–56, 159–60, 164–65

Katz, Lawrence, 197

Katz, Roberta, 30–32

Kazakhstan, 10, 98, 111, 136

Kean University, 65

Kiang, C. S., 72

King, Roger, 160–61

King Abdullah University of Science and Technology (KAUST), 1–2, 10, 97–98; Abdullah endowment and, 84–85; controversy over, 87–88; faculty of, 86–88; foreign partnerships and, 85–88; research funding and, 87; talent race and, 26, 31; women and, 86–88; as world-class university, 84–88

Klor de Alva, Jorge, 164

Knight, Jane, 28

knowledge-based economies, 33, 173, 189; branch campuses and, 62; for-profit institutions and, 142–52, 163–66; importance of, 5–8, 194–97; online courses and, 151–52; rankings and, 101, 136; world class universities and, 70–75, 78–82, 97 Korea Advanced Institute of Science and Technology (KAIST), 9, 26, 80–81

Korea Science and Engineering Foundation, 81

KPMG, 154

Laboratoria de Cybermetrics, 127
Lane, Jason, 160
Langenbach, Jeff, 157
Latin language, 35–36
Latombe, Jean-Claude, 35–36, 86–87
Laureate Education, 11, 142, 144,
   146–50, 156–62, 164–65
league tables, 11, 109, 110
Lemann, Nicholas, 173
Leninism, 163
Levin, Richard, 1, 32–35, 64, 190–91
Levy, Daniel, 148–49, 159, 161, 164
liberalization: Education City and, 53–60;
   NYU Abu Dhabi partnership and,
   43–53
Li Ka Shing, 72
Limkokwing University of Creative Tech-
   nology, 68–69
Lin Jianhua, 74–75
Litan, Robert, 186, 191
Liu, Nian Cai, 112–14, 116
London School of Economics (LSE),
   92–95
Los Angeles Times, 88
Lovejoy's guide, 108
Lumina Foundation, 133

Maclean, Alick, 102
Macleans magazine, 109, 138
Made in America provision, 184
Malaysia, 6, 122; affirmative action and,
   195; branch campuses and, 61; competition and, 23–24; for-profit institutions
   and, 68–69, 146, 160; global financial
   crisis and, 40; protectionism and, 6;
   rankings and, 118
Mao Zedong, 71
MARA Institute of Technology, 127
Marburger, John, 182
Marginson, Simon, 35, 117–18, 135
markets: benefits of academic trade and,
   188–93; branding and, 32 (see also

branding); Buy American rules and, 183–
   84; competition and, 22–36 (see also
   competition); for-profit institutions and,
   141–66; free trade and, 5–13, 167–93;
   future policy for, 194–98; General Agreement on Trade in Services (GATS) and,
   193; ICE assets and, 45; immigrants
   and, 185–87; Incheon Free Economic
   Zone and, 68, 80; "international" term
   and, 32; Made in America provision
   and, 184; MBA, 120–21; mercantilism
   and, 197; meritocracy and, 171–72 (see
   also meritocracy); protectionism and,
   6, 12, 175–93, 197–98; rankings and,
   120–21 (see also rankings); superclass
   and, 168–69; tuition and, 9, 14, 23–24,
   38–39 (see also tuition)
Marxism, 163
Massachusetts Institute of Technology
   (MIT), 45, 133; CREATE and, 82;
   Indian Institutes of Technology (IITs)
   partnership and, 76; Open Courseware
   program and, 34–35, 152; ranking of,
   114, 118; talent race and, 20, 26, 34
mathematics, 1–2, 16, 31, 85–86, 90, 96,
   113, 153, 174
Mauritius, 178
Max Planck Institute for Chemical Ecology, 180
McBurnie, Grant, 60–61
McGill University, 26–27
McKinsey & Company, 1, 30, 76, 172
Medill School of Journalism (Northwest-
   ern University), 53, 56, 58
Mehta, Pratap Bhanu, 177
mercantilism, 197
Merisotis, Jamie, 97, 133–34
meritocracy, 5, 12, 19, 169; China and,
   170–75; entrance exams and, 172–74;
   France and, 170–71; future policies
   and, 195–96; Harvard and, 172–73;
   Indian Institutes of Technology (IITs)
   and, 171–72; Ivy League and, 170; prep

schools and, 170; protectionism and, 175–93; rankings and, 103; world-class universities and, 79

Merten, Alan, 67

Mexico, 109, 146–47, 152, 158, 162

Microsoft, 185

Middle East, 4; competition and, 24; Education City and, 53–60; free speech and, 64–65; future policy for, 198; human rights and, 64–65; Israelis and, 53; non-U.S. branch campuses and, 60–69; NYU Abu Dhabi partnership and, 43–53; regional students and, 42; segregation and, 59; U.S. branch campuses and, 43–60. *See also* specific country

Mines Paris Tech, 126

Ministry of Higher Education, 6

Minkel, C. W., 183

Misra, Ashok, 177

Mitchell, W.J.T., 108

mobility, 3–4, 194; academic influx to Germany and, 19–20; academic influx to U.S. and, 3–4, 15–16, 19–22; *authentica Habita* and, 18; benefits of, 12–13; Bing Overseas Studies programs and, 31; Bologna Process and, 38; brain drain and, 8, 18, 25–28, 72, 176, 184; branch campuses and, 9, 42–69; cheaper transportation and, 5; Erasmus program and, 18; faculty and, 26, 28–31, 35; for-profit institutions and, 154, 158; Fulbright Program and, 21; future issues for, 36–41; global network universities and, 4; Great Dispersion and, 18; historical perspective on, 17–22; IDP Education and, 16; increased, 15; market issues and, 169, 175–77, 182, 186, 191; metaphorical view of, 29–36; new free trade and, 5–13; Observatory on Borderless Higher Education (OBHE) and, 15, 35; Open Courseware and, 34–35, 152; passports and, 17, 53; political instability and, 38–39; protectionism and,

175–93; rankings and, 101, 115; rapid growth of, 9, 37; redefinition of, 40–41; regional globalism and, 38; reverse commutes and, 27; September 11 attacks and, 6, 38, 180–81; talent race and, 15–20, 26–41; traditional patterns of, 7–8; world-class universities and, 93, 96

Monash University, 61

Monde, Le, 92

Mongolia, 121

Mroz, Ann, 116–18

multiculturalism, 14, 54

Mumford, David, 1

Murray, Walter, 86

Murthy, Narayana, 75–76

Nanjing University, 33–34, 62, 72

Nanyang Technological University, 83

National Academies, 187

National Academy of Sciences, 182

National Assessment and Accreditation Council (NAAC), 109

National Association of Independent Colleges and Universities, 108

National Board of Accreditation (NBA), 109

National Health Service (NHS), 179

National Knowledge Commission, 77

National Opinion Research Center, 106–7

National Research Council, 127

National Research Foundation, 82

National Science Foundation (NSF), 21–22

National Survey of Student Engagement (NSSE), 108–9, 137–38

National University of Mexico, 117

National University of Singapore, 2, 26–27, 83, 85, 117, 195–96

Nature, 113

NCAA Selection Show, 67

Nehru, Jawaharlal, 76–77

Netherlands, 128, 146

New Oriental, 174

Newsweek, 190

New York magazine, 51

New York Times, 20–21, 74–75, 103

New York Times Selective Guide to College, The (Fiske), 103

New York University (NYU), 3, 6, 27; Abu Dhabi partnership and, 43–53, 85; academic freedom and, 52; Bloom and, 46; faculty and, 46–47; financial incentives and, 47; idea capitals and, 44–45; portal campuses and, 4; quality issues and, 46–47, 52–53; Ross and, 51; Sexton and, 43–53, 67; Steinhardt School of Culture, Education, and Human Development and, 53

New Zealand, 24, 28, 109, 143, 147, 178

Nigeria, 146, 168

Nijsure, Sandeep, 184–85

Ningbo, 61, 187

Nobel laureates, 4, 113, 128, 190

No Child Left Behind Act, 137

Normans, 17

North Carolina State University, 68, 80

North Dakota State, 62

Northeastern University, 145

Northern Kentucky University, 83

Northwestern University, 9, 53, 72

Nottingham University, 187

Nyenrode Business Universiteit, 146

NYU Abu Dhabi Institute, 48

Oates, Mary-Louise, 48

Obama, Barack, 188

Observatory on Borderless Higher Education (OBHE) and, 15, 35, 38, 61, 66

Offshoring Higher Education (McBurnie and Ziguras), 60–61

Olcott, Don, 35, 38, 66

Olds, Kris, 66

O'Leary, John, 114–15

O'Neill, Theodore "Ted," 108

one-two-one program, 68

online learning, 4–5, 11, 29, 61; delivery modes and, 154; e-mail and, 152–53; faculty and, 53, 152–53; flexibility of, 153–54; for-profit institutions and, 142, 144–45, 150–59, 165; increased enrollment in, 151; networking and, 154; Open Courseware and, 34–35, 152; private sector and, 152; quality issues and, 155–57

Open Courseware program, 34–35, 152

Open University, 160

Organisation for Economic Co-operation and Development (OECD), 11, 147; AHELO and, 128–39; PISA and, 131–33; rankings and, 115, 118, 128–39; talent race and, 15, 22, 28

Osmania University, 39

Oxford University, 2, 44; academic influx of, 3; loss of prestige of, 97; ranking of, 114–15, 118–19, 123; talent race and, 20, 26–27

Oxford Union, 58

Pakistan, 180–81

Panama, 152–53

Paraguay, 146

party schools, 108, 135

passports, 17, 53

pathway programs, 144–45

Pécresse, Valérie, 92, 126

Peking University, 16, 34, 71–72, 112, 174

Peña, Jhon Harold, 152

People's Daily (Chinese newspaper), 71

Perkinson, Ron, 35, 143, 147, 151

Perry, Rick, 137

Persian Gulf, 6, 38; Education City and, 53–60; NYU Abu Dhabi partnership and, 43–53

Peru, 10

Peterson's guide, 108

Philippine Accrediting Association of Schools, Colleges and Universities (PAASCU), 109

Philippines, 40, 109, 122

physics, 16

Piatt, Wendy, 123

Picards, 17

Pitman, Isaac, 154

Pitroda, Sam, 77

Poland, 16, 17, 91

policy: affirmative action and, 16, 77, 93, 195; Bologna Process and, 38; Centre for Policy Research and, 177; Educational Policy Institute and, 133; First Amendment and, 47–50; Fulbright Program and, 21; future, 194–98; General Agreement on Trade in Services (GATS) and, 193; Institute for Higher Education Policy and, 133; mercantilism and, 197; meritocracy and, 5, 12, 19, 79, 169–72, 175, 192, 195–96; natural experiment for, 195; No Child Left Behind Act and, 137; one-two-one program and, 68; protectionism and, 6, 12, 175–93, 197–98; talent race and, 30–35; use of rankings and, 110; U.S. Supreme Court nominations and, 49; zero-sum games and, 7

portal campuses, 4

prep schools, 46, 103, 170, 173

Princeton Review, 108, 135

Princeton University, 43, 73, 114–15

Program for International Student Assessment (PISA), 131–33, 138

Project 211, 71

protectionism, 12, 197–98; academic, 175–88; affirmative action and, 195; benefits of academic trade and, 188–93; Buy American rules and, 183–84; China and, 6, 190; Communists and, 177; economic, 175–76; engineering and,

181–88; General Agreement on Trade in Services (GATS) and, 193; Germany and, 180; immigrants and, 185–87; India and, 6, 176–78, 194; Made in America provision and, 184; Malaysia and, 6; medical education and, 178–80; national security and, 180–81; native jobs and, 6–7; quality issues and, 180; quotas and, 176; talent and, 6–7; United Kingdom and, 182; United States and, 6–7, 180–93; visas and, 6–7, 17, 27, 31, 38, 63, 121, 180–86, 191–93

Prussia, 19

Qatar, 3, 9, 178; Cornell and, 157–58; Education City and, 53–60, 68; gas reserves of, 54–55; human capital strategy and, 55; media improvements in, 58–59; royal family of, 54

Qatar Foundation for Education, Science and Community Development, 54–60

Quacquarelli and Symonds, 115, 118

quality issues, 6, 9, 11–12, 147; American research university model and, 70; branch campuses and, 46–47, 53–57, 62–66; China and, 10, 71–75; Education City and, 55–58; Excellence Initiative and, 89–90; for-profit institutions and, 155–66; France and, 91–95; free trade in minds and, 171, 176–80, 185, 189, 191; Germany and, 89–91; India and, 62–63, 75–79; Italy and, 96; NYU and, 46–47, 52–53; online learning and, 155–57; protectionism and, 177, 180; rankings and, 102; regulation of, 159–66; Singapore and, 82–84; South Korea and, 79–82; Spellings Commission and, 137–38; talent race and, 29, 32, 35–37; United States and, 21, 137–40; world-class universities and, 70–99

Quan Yingyi, 72–73

Queen Margaret University, 61
quotas, 56, 163, 172–79, 183

Rabinovich, Itamar, 53
Race between Education and Technology, The (Goldin and Katz), 197
Raffles Education, 146
RAND Corporation, 7, 54, 129, 190
rankings, 5, 14, 194; accountability systems and, 137; AHELO and, 127–39; better information for, 127–40; bias and, 113–14, 118, 120, 126; birth of, 101–9; Carnegie Classifications and, 104–6; categorical approach and, 104; Center for Higher Education Development (CHE) and, 127–28, 136; citations and, 113, 115–16; Collegiate Learning Assessment (CLA) and, 129–30, 132; commercial guides and, 109–10; as consumer information tool, 104, 110; criticism of, 100–7, 113–14, 119; Educational Policy Institute and, 133; employer review and, 116; enrollment management and, 108; European Union and, 126–27; faculty quality and, 105, 116; for-profit institutions and, 147; France and, 100, 110, 125–27; gamesmanship and, 106; global, 109–27; individual disciplines approach and, 124; institutional resources and, 105; league tables and, 11, 109–10; MBA market and, 120–21; methodologies for, 100, 113–14; narrative style and, 103; National Opinion Research Center and, 106–7; niche-oriented, 108; opposition to, 104–5; outcomes-oriented approach and, 102; quality of life and, 103; reputation and, 104–6, 122; research universities and, 106, 114, 123; retention data and, 105; selectivity measures and, 105; self-perception and, 118–19; Shanghai Jiao Tong University and, 11, 100–1, 110,

112, 129, 135–36; sources for, 109–10; strategic planning and, 112–13; student reporters and, 103; student surveys and, 127–28; students' use of, 101; survey-based approach and, 102; test scores and, 120, 129; *Times Higher Education* and, 11, 115–19, 122–23, 126, 129, 135–36, 195; top party schools and, 108, 135; of top ten universities, 114; transparency and, 112–13; United Kingdom and, 114–19; United States and, 101–9; *U.S. News & World Report* and, 4, 10–11, 101–17, 124, 126, 138, 147; Voluntary System of Accountability (VSA) and, 138; yield factor and, 107–8
Ras al Khaimah, 67
Re$earch Infosource Inc., 110
Reader's Digest, 147
Reardon-Anderson, James, 55, 57, 60
recruitment, 4, 86, 120, 161, 164; Australia and, 23–24; China and, 72–73; competition over, 22–36 (*see also* competition); Education City and, 56–57; English language and, 24–25; graduate students and, 24–25; IDP Education and, 16; metaphorical view of, 29–36; non-English-speaking countries and, 24; researchers and, 28–29; reverse commutes and, 27; sex and, 24; Singapore and, 83; South Korea and, 81; talent and, 1, 5, 7, 12, 14–42 (*see also* talent); University of Warwick and, 14–15
Reforma, 109
regional globalism, 38
"Relationship of Government and Religion, The" (Sexton seminar), 48–50
religion, 48–50, 54, 86
Repubblica, La, 109
research, 194; benefits of academic trade and, 188–93; branch campuses and, 61; China and, 73, 188; CREATE and, 82; faculty incentives and, 21–22, 26; foreign coauthored papers and, 29; France

and, 92–95; future policy for, 195–98; government funding and, 187–91; KAUST and, 87; national security and, 181–82; Operation Campus and, 91–92; protectionism and, 188–93; rankings and, 106, 114, 123; Yale and, 33–35

Richards, Alison, 26

"Rising Above the Gathering Storm" (National Academies report), 187

RMIT International University, 61

Romania, 111

Rosberg, Gerald, 156, 164–65

Ross, Andrew, 51

Ross University, 145

Roth, Richard, 56, 58

Rothkopf, David, 168–70

Royal Melbourne Institute of Technology, 61

Rubin, Ron, 53

Russell Group, 123

Russia, 16, 22, 76, 91, 119, 151, 197

Saadiyat Island, 45

Sadlak, Jan, 95, 98

St. Petersburg State University, 197

Salmi, Jamil, 70, 98, 109, 122, 195

Sanders, Bernard, 184

Sanoff, Alvin, 103–5

Saoud, Fathy, 57–58

Sarkozy, Nicolas, 91–92, 125–26

satellite campuses. *See* branch campuses

SAT scores, 105, 129, 172–73

Saudi Arabia, 4; Abdullah endowment and, 84–85; Aramco and, 85; authoritarian regime of, 87–88; foreign partnerships and, 85–88; gays and, 87; KAUST and, 1–2, 10, 26, 84–88, 97–98; quality issues and, 84–88; treatment of Israelis and, 87; women and, 86–88; world-class universities and, 97

Sauvons la Recherche, 92

Saxenian, AnnaLee, 186

Scandinavia, 17, 36

Schleicher, Andreas, 133

School of International and Public Affairs (Columbia University), 92–93

school prayer, 49

Schramm, Carl, 191

Science Citation Index Expanded (SCIE), 113

Science magazine, 113

Sciences Po, 92–95

Scopus, 116

Scotland, 61

Securities Institute of Australia, 154

segregation, 59, 181

Selective Guide to Colleges, The (Fiske), 103

Seoul National University, 97

September 11 terrorist attacks, 6, 38, 180–81

sex, 24, 59

Sexton, John, 54, 67; admissions standards and, 46; NYU Abu Dhabi partnership and, 43–53; politics and, 51–52; quality issues and, 46–47; Shrum and, 48; teaching abilities of, 47–50

Shanghai, 34, 44

Shanghai Jiao Tong University, 3, 11, 95; Institute of Higher Education and, 112; Project 985 and, 72; rankings and, 11, 100–1, 110, 112, 129, 135–36; University of Michigan partnership and, 34

Shapiro, Harold, 145

Sheetz, Steven, 63

Sheffield University, 145

Sheikh Mohamed Scholars Program, 50

Sheil, Tony, 124

Sheraton Abu Dhabi, 48

Shih, Choon Fong, 25–26, 85

Shi Yigong, 72–73

Shrum, Bob, 48

Siang, Lim Kit, 122

Sibal, Kapil, 177

Silicon Valley, 185

Singapore, 2, 51, 195; branch campuses and, 61, 65; branding and, 84; competition and, 24–26; foreign partnerships and, 83–84; for-profit institutions and, 146, 151; graduate fellowships and, 83; human rights and, 84; INSEAD and, 2–3; online learning and, 155; research and, 188; setbacks in, 83–84; world-class universities and, 70, 82–84

Singapore International Graduate Award (SINGAS), 83

Singh, Manmohan, 77

Slate magazine, 172–73

Slovakia, 10

Social Science Citation Index (SSCI), 113

Sorbonne, 45, 61, 133

South Africa, 14, 40, 61, 168

Southern Cross University, 155

South Korea, 16, 23; branch campuses and, 4; economic growth of, 79–80; engineering and, 81; English and, 80–81; foreign partnerships and, 81; free trade and, 167; global financial crisis and, 39–40; higher education spending in, 80; Incheon Free Economic Zone and, 68, 80; quality issues and, 79–82; student losses of, 80; University Policy Division and, 80; world-class universities and, 79–82, 97

Spain, 17, 109, 127, 142, 156, 158

Spellings Commission, 137–38

Spiegel, Der, 109

S. P. Jain Institute of Management and Research, 62–63

Sputnik (Soviet satellite), 22

Sri Ramchandra Medical College and Research Institute, 178

Stanford University, 6, 27, 65; free trade in minds and, 174, 187; global policy of, 30–32; Katz review and, 30–32; KAUST and, 86–87; ranking of, 114, 117; superclass and, 168–69

Starbucks, 54

State University of New York (SUNY), 62, 80, 148

student nations, 17

students, 194; admittance rates of, 1–2; attention to rankings by, 101; brain drain and, 8, 18, 25–28, 72, 176, 184; coaching centers and, 2; entrance exams and, 2, 12, 74, 76, 120, 171–74; future policy for, 195–98; gauging demand of, 65; graduate, 24–25; human capital and, 8, 10, 149, 158–59, 166, 197; meritocracy and, 5, 12, 19, 79, 169–72, 175, 192, 195–96; mobility and, 3–9, 5, 12, 15–20, 26–41, 93, 96 (*see also* mobility); new free trade and, 5–13; Open Courseware and, 34–35, 152; as prized commodities, 1–2; protest issues and, 6; quotas and, 56, 163, 172–79, 183; recruitment of, 4, 23, 42, 86, 120, 161, 164; talent and, 1, 5, 7, 12, 14–42, 44–46 (*see also* talent); tuition and, 9, 14, 23–24, 38–39, 47, 60, 63, 74, 85, 93, 144, 147, 155, 158, 165, 177, 196; visas and, 6–7, 17, 27, 31, 38, 63, 121, 180–86, 191–93

subordination principle, 43

Subway, 54

Suh, Nam Pyo, 80–81

Sunday Times, 109

Sun Microsystems, 1

Superclass: The Global Power Elite and the World They Are Making (Rothkopf), 168–69

Swarthmore College, 46

Sweden, 147

Swiss Centre for Science and Technology Studies, 111

Switzerland, 18, 28, 111, 128, 158, 172

Sylvan Learning Systems, 11, 141–42

tailasan, 48

Taiwan, 16, 110

talent, 1; affirmative action and, 195; brain drain and, 8, 18, 25–28, 72, 176, 184; branch campuses and, 44–46, 55; competition for, 14–41; faculty and, 22–36; free trade in, 5–13, 170–71, 177, 183–88, 191–93; Fulbright Program and, 21; future policy for, 195–98; historical perspective on mobility and, 17–22; human capital and, 8, 10, 149, 158–59, 166, 197; idea capitals and, 44–45; meritocracy and, 5, 12, 19, 79, 169–72, 175, 192, 195–96; world-class universities and, 75, 82–84

Tamkang University, 110

Tata Institute of Social Sciences, 75

technology: benefits of academic trade and, 188–93; H-1B visas and, 184–86; human capital and, 197; immigrants and, 185–87; online learning and, 151–59; Silicon Valley and, 185

Tecnológico de Monterrey, 152

Temple University, 65

terrorism, 180–81

tertiary education, 19, 37, 70, 109, 132

Texas, 137

Texas A&M University, 3, 9; Aggies and, 54; College Station campus of, 57; Education City and, 53–60

Thailand, 122

THE-QS World University Rankings, 115

Thompson, Mary Kathryn, 26, 81

Thrift, Nigel, 15, 29, 42–43, 69

Tierney, William, 152

Times Good University Guide, The, 114–15

Times Higher Education, 11, 115–19, 122–23, 126, 129, 135, 136, 195

Times Higher Education Supplement, 114–15, 122

traveling scholars, 17–19

Tsinghua University, 16, 27, 72–73, 173–74

TÜBITAK (The Scientific and Technological Research Council of Turkey), 109

tuition, 9, 177, 196; branch campuses and, 47, 60, 63–64; China and, 74; Education City and, 60; for-profit institutions and, 144, 147, 155, 158, 165; Fulbright Program and, 21; full pay status and, 14; global financial crisis and, 39; KAUST and, 85; talent race and, 23–24, 38–39; world-class universities and, 74, 85, 93

Turkey, 16, 109

Twenty-first Century Managerial University, 144

twinning arrangements, 62

Umar, Ibrahim, 168

UNIACC, 145

United Arab Emirates (UAE), 3, 67; Abu Dhabi NYU partnership and, 43–53; censorship and, 51

United Kingdom, 28, 96, 167, 195–96; academic influx to, 20; Blair program and, 23; branch campuses and, 61; foreign student demographics of, 16, 28; global financial crisis and, 40; Indian Institutes of Technology (IITs) partnership and, 76; Observatory on Borderless Higher Education (OBHE) and, 15, 35; Office of Science and Innovation and, 29; online learning and, 155; PhD goals and, 25; protectionism and, 179, 182; rankings and, 109, 114–19; regional globalism and, 38

United Nations Educational, Scientific, and Cultural Organization (UNESCO), 15, 95, 159

United States, 2, 167; 198, academic influx to, 3–4, 15–16, 19–22; accountability systems and, 137; branch campuses and, 4, 61; branding and, 40; Buy American rules and, 183–84; consumer movement and, 104; declining research in, 73; Education City and, 53–60; falling global share of doctorates

United States (*cont.*)
in, 187; falling student market share
of, 22–23; First Amendment and, 3,
47–50; foreign student demographics
and, 16, 20–21; Fulbright Program
and, 21; future issues for, 36–37, 198;
German university model and, 20;
global financial crisis and, 39; Higher
Education Act and, 137; imitation of
universities of, 70; immigrants and,
185–87; increased competition and,
4 (*see also* competition); increased
university spending and, 21; international partnerships and, 6; locational
advantages of, 96; long-term prospects
of, 22–23; Made in America provision
and, 184; No Child Left Behind Act
and, 137; one-two-one program and,
68; protectionism and, 6–7, 180–93;
quality issues and, 21, 137–40; rankings
and, 101–9; regional globalism and, 38;
research universities of, 3–4; security issues and, 6, 38, 180–81; September 11
attacks and, 6, 38; students abroad of,
19–20
Universidad del Valle de México (UVM),
146–47
Universidad Europea de Madrid, 142
Universidad Virtual, 152
universities: admittance rates of, 1–2; alliance forging and, 2; branch campuses
and, 3–4, 42–69; branding and, 32, 40,
55–56; coaching centers and, 2; enrollment management and, 108; entrance
exams and, 2, 12, 74, 76, 120, 171–74;
first Western, 17; funding of, 3, 21;
future policy for, 195–98; gamesmanship and, 106; German model of, 20;
global network, 44; historical perspective on, 17–22; multiculturalism and,
14; new free trade and, 5–13; Open
Courseware and, 34–35, 152; partnerships and, 33–34; porous boundaries of,
2–3; protectionism and, 6, 12, 175–93;

197–98; quotas and, 56, 163, 172–79,
183; rankings and, 14 (*see also* rankings); recruitment and, 1–4, 23, 42, 86,
120, 161, 164; research, 3–4, 19, 20,
41, 43; as scholastic guilds, 17; sender
countries and, 15; tuition and, 9, 14,
23–24, 38–39 (*see also* tuition); world-
class, 10, 70–99
Universities UK, 28, 160
Universiti Sains Malaysia, 122
University and College Union, 161
University College, London, 118
University for the 21st Century, A (Duder-
stadt), 3
University Grants Commission, 126
University of Adelaide, 145
University of Albany (SUNY), 148,
159–60, 162
University of Auckland, 26
University of Bologna, 17, 20
University of California, Berkeley, 2, 6,
65, 72, 76, 85–87, 101–2, 114, 176,
186
University of Cambridge, 18, 20, 26, 44,
85, 97, 114–15, 118, 123, 168
University of Chicago, 20, 65, 108, 114,
118, 168–69
University of Colorado, 185
University of Delaware, 68
University of Göttingen, 20
University of Hong Kong, 27
University of Karlsruhe, 90
University of Liverpool, 43
University of Maastricht, 114
University of Malaya, 122
University of Malaysia, 195
University of Maryland, 17, 89, 171
University of Massachusetts, 157
University of Melbourne, 35, 117, 123–24
University of Michigan, 3, 34
University of Montana, 65
University of Munich, 36
University of New South Wales, 65,
83–84

University of North Texas, 185
University of Nottingham, 43, 61
University of Oregon, 114
University of Paris, 17–18, 20, 125
University of Pennsylvania, 73
University of Phoenix, 11, 144–45, 150–51, 157
University of Prague, 19
University of Stuttgart, 114
University of Sunderland, 155
University of Tennessee, 183
University of Texas at Austin, 85
University of Toronto, 28
University of Virginia, 20
University of Warwick, 14–15, 28–29, 42, 64, 69, 83, 168
University of Wisconsin, 66
University of Witwatersrand, 14
University Scholars Program, 48
University World News, 119, 126
Upadhyay, Vivek, 171–72, 177–78
U.S. Department of Defense, 181, 190
U.S. Department of Education, 23
Usher, Alex, 133
U.S. National Academy of Engineering, 81
U.S. News & World Report: influential Americans surveys and, 103–4; National Opinion Research Center and, 106–7; opposition to, 104–5; rankings by, 4, 10–11, 101–17, 124, 126, 138, 147; reputation and, 104–5, 106; yield factor and, 107–8
U.S. State Department, 181–82
U.S. Supreme Court, 49
Uvalic-Trumbic, Stamenka, 154, 159, 161, 163

Van Dyke, Nina, 123–24
Van Vught, Franz, 125
Venturesome Economy, The (Bhidé), 189–90
Vérillaud, Francis, 94
Vietnam, 155, 163

Viñoly, Rafael, 45
Virginia Commonwealth University, 53–54
Virginia Tech, 62–63
visas, 63, 121, 192–93; H-1B, 184–86, 191; security issues and, 6–7, 180–86; talent race and, 17, 27, 31, 38; U.S. Department of Defense and, 181; U.S. State Department and, 181–82
Voluntary System of Accountability (VSA), 138
von Humboldt, Wilhelm, 19

Wadhwa, Vivek, 184–86
Walden University, 142
Wall Street Journal, 121
Warner, Mark, 188
Washington Post Company, 144, 184
Washington Square, 43–47, 50
Webometrics Rankings of World Universities, 127
Weichold, Mark H., 57, 60
Weill Medical College (Cornell University), 53, 56
Westermann, Mariët, 47, 52–53
Western Michigan University, 62
"West Need Not Panic, The" (Levin), 190–91
Wharton School, 73
What Do Pictures Want? (Mitchell), 108
Where We Get Our Best Men (Maclean), 102
Whitney International University, 35, 143–44, 152–53
Wieruszowski, Helene, 19
Williams, Ross, 123–24
Williams College, 20
"Without Investment Our Top Universities Will Fall Behind Global Competition" (Piatt), 123
women, 6; *abayas* and, 3, 48, 52; Abu Dhabi and, 51–52; Education City and, 56, 59; for-profit institutions and, 148; KAUST and, 85–88; Saudi Arabia and,

women (*cont.*)
  86–88; segregation and, 59; sexual harassment and, 59
Woo Hyun Cho, 81
World Bank, 35, 70, 97–98, 109, 122,
  143, 164, 185, 195
world-class universities: American research
  university model and, 70; China and,
  70–75, 83–84, 91, 94–95, 97; English
  and, 93–94, 97; France and, 91–95, 98;
  Germany and, 89–91, 98; India and,
  70–71, 75–79, 84, 90, 94–95, 97–98;
  Kazakhstan and, 98; keeping students
  at home and, 70; limited number of,
  98–99; location and, 97–98; Project
  211 and, 71; Project 985 and, 71–72;
  risk in attempting to create, 95–99;
  role of geography and, 96; Saudi Arabia
  and, 84–88, 97; Singapore and, 82–84;
  South Korea and, 79–82, 97; status and,
  70; Western Europe and, 88–95
World Is Flat, The (Friedman), 3
World University Rankings, 115–16
World War II era, 3, 15, 20–21, 170, 198

Yale, 1, 26, 43, 101; Abu Dhabi and, 64;
  distinguished alumni of, 33; free trade in
  minds and, 168, 190–91; global policy
  of, 32–35; internationalization agenda
  of, 33–35; Joint Center for Biomedical
  Research and, 34; Joint Center for Plant
  Molecular Genetics and Agrobiotechnology and, 34; Levin and, 32–35; open
  courseware and, 152; ranking of, 118;
  research and, 33–35
Yau, Shing-Tung, 174
Yi, Pilnam, 80
yield factor, 107–8
Yi Rao, 72
Yonsei University, 80
Yu, Diane, 47
Yu, Michael, 174

Zayed University, 50–51
Zeit, Die, 127
zero-sum game, 7, 125, 192
Ziguras, Christopher, 60–61
Zoninsein, Manuela, 173–74